PERFORMING RESTORATION SHAKESPEARE

Performing Restoration Shakespeare embraces the performative and musical qualities of Restoration Shakespeare (1660–1714), drawing on the expertise of theatre historians, musicologists, literary critics, and – importantly – theatre and music practitioners. The volume advances methodological debates in theatre studies and musicology by advocating an alternative to performance practices aimed at reviving 'original' styles or conventions, adopting a dialectical process that situates past performances within their historical and aesthetic contexts, and then using that understanding to transform them into new performances for new audiences. By deploying these methodologies, the volume invites scholars from different disciplines to understand Restoration Shakespeare on its own terms, discarding inhibiting preconceptions that Restoration Shakespeare debased Shakespeare's precursor texts. It also equips scholars and practitioners in theatre and music with new – and much needed – methods for studying and reviving past performances of any kind, not just Shakespearean ones.

AMANDA EUBANKS WINKLER, Professor of Music History and Cultures at Syracuse University, is a cultural historian and musicologist specializing in British music and drama. She was the Co-Investigator for the AHRC research project 'Performing Restoration Shakespeare'. Her most recent book is *Music, Dance, and Drama in Early Modern English Schools* (Cambridge University Press, 2020).

CLAUDE FRETZ is Associate Professor of Shakespeare and Early Modern English Literature at Sun Yat-sen University (China). He is also Fellow of the research centre 'European Dream-Cultures' at Saarland University (Germany). He is the author of *Dreams, Sleep, and Shakespeare's Genres* (2020), and he has published various journal articles and book chapters on Shakespeare, early modern literature, representations of dreams and sleep in the Renaissance, modern theatre practice, and Restoration drama.

RICHARD SCHOCH is Professor of Drama at Queen's University Belfast, where he was Principal Investigator for the research project 'Performing Restoration Shakespeare'. His most recent books are *A Short History of Shakespeare in Performance* (2021) and *Writing the History of the British Stage* (2016), both published by Cambridge University Press.

PERFORMING RESTORATION SHAKESPEARE

EDITED BY

AMANDA EUBANKS WINKLER
Syracuse University

CLAUDE FRETZ
Sun Yat-sen University

RICHARD SCHOCH
Queen's University Belfast

Shaftesbury Road, Cambridge CB2 8EA, United Kingdom

One Liberty Plaza, 20th Floor, New York, NY 10006, USA

477 Williamstown Road, Port Melbourne, VIC 3207, Australia

314–321, 3rd Floor, Plot 3, Splendor Forum, Jasola District Centre, New Delhi – 110025, India

103 Penang Road, #05–06/07, Visioncrest Commercial, Singapore 238467

Cambridge University Press is part of Cambridge University Press & Assessment, a department of the University of Cambridge.

We share the University's mission to contribute to society through the pursuit of education, learning and research at the highest international levels of excellence.

www.cambridge.org
Information on this title: www.cambridge.org/9781009241199

DOI: 10.1017/9781009241212

© Cambridge University Press & Assessment 2023

This publication is in copyright. Subject to statutory exception and to the provisions of relevant collective licensing agreements, no reproduction of any part may take place without the written permission of Cambridge University Press & Assessment.

First published 2023
First paperback edition 2025

A catalogue record for this publication is available from the British Library

ISBN 978-1-009-24120-5 Hardback
ISBN 978-1-009-24119-9 Paperback

Cambridge University Press & Assessment has no responsibility for the persistence or accuracy of URLs for external or third-party internet websites referred to in this publication and does not guarantee that any content on such websites is, or will remain, accurate or appropriate.

Contents

List of Figures		*page* vii
List of Tables		ix
List of Music Examples		x
Notes on Contributors		xi
Foreword		xvii
Joseph Roach		
Acknowledgements		xxi
List of Abbreviations		xxiii

    Introduction: New Shakespeare for a New Era   1
    Amanda Eubanks Winkler, Claude Fretz, and Richard Schoch

1   From Boards to Books: The Circulation of Shakespearean Songs in Manuscript and Print during the Interregnum   15
    Sarah Ledwidge

2   Heroic Shakespeare at Lincoln's Inn Fields   38
    Stephen Watkins

3   More than a Song and Dance? Identifying Matthew Locke's Incidental Music for *Macbeth*   61
    Silas Wollston

4   Cross-Dressing in Restoration Shakespeare: *Twelfth Night* and *The Tempest*   79
    Fiona Ritchie

5   Performing Restoration Shakespeare in the Eighteenth Century   97
    James Harriman-Smith

6	An Actor's Perspective on Restoration Shakespeare *Louis Butelli*	118
7	Staging Restoration Shakespeare with Restoration Music *Robert Eisenstein*	132
8	Davenant's Lady Macduff and the Subversion of Normative Femininity in Twenty-First-Century Performance *Sara Reimers*	142
9	Facts as Ideas: The Theatricalisation of Scholarship *Kate Eastwood Norris*	163
10	Syncopated Time: Staging the Restoration *Tempest* *Amanda Eubanks Winkler and Richard Schoch*	180

Bibliography   199
Index   211

Figures

0.1 Sir William Davenant (1606–1668) by William Faithorne, after John Greenhill, published 1672. Reproduced courtesy of the Folger Shakespeare Library, Washington, DC, under a Creative Commons Attribution-ShareAlike 4.0 International License. *page 3*

0.2 William Dolle, engraving of scenes at Dorset Garden Theatre, in Elkanah Settle's *The Empress of Morocco* (1673). Reproduced courtesy of the Folger Shakespeare Library, Washington, DC, under a Creative Commons Attribution-ShareAlike 4.0 International License. 6

5.1 *The History of King Lear, A Tragedy: As it is now acted at the King's Theatres. Revived, with Alterations, by N. Tate* (London: Hitch et al., 1756), 29. Reproduced courtesy of the British Library Board. 98

5.2 *The History of King Lear: As it is performed at The Theatre Royal in Covent Garden* (London: R. Baldwin and T. Becket, 1768), 34. Reproduced courtesy of the Folger Shakespeare Library, Washington, DC, under a Creative Commons Attribution-ShareAlike 4.0 International License. 106

6.1 The witches (Emily Noël, Rachael Montgomery, Ethan Watermeier) and Duncan (Louis Butelli) in the Folger Theatre's 2018 production of Sir William Davenant's *Macbeth*. Reproduced courtesy of the Folger Theatre and the research project 'Performing Restoration Shakespeare', led by Queen's University Belfast and funded by the Arts and Humanities Research Council (AHRC) in the United Kingdom. 119

6.2 Duncan's murder in the Folger Theatre's 2018 production of Sir William Davenant's *Macbeth*. Reproduced courtesy of the Folger Theatre and the research project 'Performing Restoration Shakespeare', led by Queen's University Belfast and funded by the Arts and Humanities Research Council (AHRC) in the United Kingdom. 128

6.3 Ian Merrill Peakes as Macbeth in the Folger Theatre's 2018 production of Sir William Davenant's *Macbeth*. Reproduced courtesy of Folger Theatre and the research project 'Performing Restoration Shakespeare', led by Queen's University Belfast and funded by the Arts and Humanities Research Council (AHRC) in the United Kingdom. 129

7.1 The witches (Emily Noël, Rachael Montgomery, Ethan Watermeier) in the Folger Theatre's 2018 production of Sir William Davenant's *Macbeth*. Reproduced courtesy of Folger Theatre and the research project 'Performing Restoration Shakespeare', led by Queen's University Belfast and funded by the Arts and Humanities Research Council (AHRC) in the United Kingdom. 138

8.1 Karen Peakes as Lady Macduff and Owen Peakes as Fleance in the Folger Theatre's 2018 production of Sir William Davenant's *Macbeth*. Reproduced courtesy of Folger Theatre and the research project 'Performing Restoration Shakespeare', led by Queen's University Belfast and funded by the Arts and Humanities Research Council (AHRC) in the United Kingdom. 148

9.1 Kate Eastwood Norris as Lady Macbeth in Folger Theatre's 2018 production of Sir William Davenant's *Macbeth*. Reproduced courtesy of the Folger Theatre and the research project 'Performing Restoration Shakespeare', led by Queen's University Belfast and funded by the Arts and Humanities Research Council (AHRC) in the United Kingdom. 165

Tables

1.1	Shakespeare song sources, 1630–1660	*page* 17
3.1	Locke's violin-band music	64

Music Examples

1.1 Fourth phrase of 'What shall he have that killed the deer' — page 36

3.1 'Low' writing for the second part in Locke's Curtain Tune 'The Fantastick', US-NYp Drexel MS 3976, 4–6 — 71

3.2 'High' writing for the second part in Locke's Sarabrand used in *The Tempest* (1674), published in *The English Opera, or, the Vocal Musick in Psyche* (London, 1675), 65–6 — 74

Notes on Contributors

AMANDA EUBANKS WINKLER (CO-EDITOR) is Professor of Music History and Cultures at Syracuse University. Her publications include the book *O Let Us Howle Some Heavy Note: Music for Witches, the Melancholic, and the Mad on the Seventeenth-Century English Stage* (Indiana University Press, 2006); two editions of Restoration-era theatre music; and, with Linda Austern and Candace Bailey, an essay collection *Beyond Boundaries: Rethinking Music Circulation in Early Modern England* (Indiana University Press, 2017), and *Music, Dance, and Drama in Early Modern English Schools* (Cambridge University Press, 2020). Other recent work has engaged with practice-based research, including workshops that staged excerpts of Davenant's *Macbeth* and Gildon's *Measure for Measure* (Folger Theatre) and Middleton's *The Witch* (Blackfriars Conference). From 2017 to 2020 she was Co-Investigator on 'Performing Restoration Shakespeare', a research project funded by the AHRC (UK). As part of that project, she served as music director for a workshop of the Restoration-era *Tempest* (Shakespeare's Globe) and co-led a workshop for scholars and served as a consultant for a full professional production of Davenant's *Macbeth* (Folger Theatre). Her most recent book, co-authored with Richard Schoch, is *Shakespeare in the Theatre: Sir William Davenant and the Duke's Company* (Arden Bloomsbury, 2021).

CLAUDE FRETZ (CO-EDITOR) is Associate Professor of Shakespeare and Early Modern English Literature at Sun Yat-sen University (China). He is also a Fellow of the DFG-funded research centre 'European Dream-Cultures' at Saarland University (Germany). His PhD is from the Shakespeare Institute, University of Birmingham (UK). Fretz's primary research interest lies with the dramatic works of Shakespeare in their early modern (Elizabethan and Jacobean) contexts. He is also interested in appropriations and adaptations of Shakespeare, and is actively involved in interdisciplinary research projects related to dream cultures.

His research has attracted funding in China, the UK, Germany, and Luxembourg. Fretz is the author of *Dreams, Sleep, and Shakespeare's Genres* (Palgrave Macmillan, 2020), which explores how Shakespeare uses images of dreams and sleep to define his dramatic worlds. He has also published various journal articles and book chapters on Shakespeare, on early modern literature, on representations of dreams and sleep in the Renaissance, on modern theatre practice, and on Restoration drama. His work has appeared in journals including *Shakespeare, Concentric: Literary and Cultural Studies, Restoration: Studies in English Literary Culture 1660–1700, Cahiers Élisabéthains: A Journal of English Renaissance Studies, Etudes Epistémè, Shakespeare Jahrbuch*, and others. He formerly worked as Research Fellow on the AHRC-funded project 'Performing Restoration Shakespeare'.

RICHARD SCHOCH (CO-EDITOR) is Professor of Drama at Queen's University Belfast, where he was Principal Investigator for 'Performing Restoration Shakespeare' (2017–2020), an international research project funded by the AHRC. He is the author of *A Short History of Shakespeare in Performance, Writing the History of the British Stage: 1660–1900, Not Shakespeare*, and *Shakespeare's Victorian Stage*, all published by Cambridge University Press. His most recent book, co-authored with Amanda Eubanks Winkler, is *Shakespeare in the Theatre: Sir William Davenant and the Duke's Company* (Arden Bloomsbury, 2021). Schoch has served on the editorial boards of *Shakespeare Quarterly* and *Shakespeare Bulletin*, and has received fellowships from the Leverhulme Trust, the Folger Shakespeare Library, Stanford Humanities Center, and the Harry Ransom Center.

LOUIS BUTELLI has worked for the past twenty-five years as an actor, director, teacher, and writer. As an actor, he has appeared Off-Broadway in Punchdrunk's *Sleep No More* – a noir immersive version of *Macbeth* – and performed Shakespeare in all fifty American states and across Europe. He is proud to be associated with Folger Theatre, in Washington, DC, where he has appeared in twelve productions, including his solo show *Gravedigger's Tale*, which toured the United States with the Folger's First Folio exhibition in 2016. As a director, he co-created *Cyclops: A Rock Opera*, based on Euripides, which was jury nominated for the Pulitzer Prize in Drama, and a musical version of *Romeo and Juliet* commissioned by Lincoln Center Education. He is the recipient of a Helen Hayes Award for Outstanding Supporting Actor and New York Musical Festival Award for Best Actor.

KATE EASTWOOD NORRIS is a theatre maker with over thirty years of experience on the American stage. She is also an educator, director, and guest artist for multiple universities, including Mary Baldwin University's Shakespeare and Performance programme, from which she received her MFA, Pacifica Graduate Institute, from which she earned an MA in Engaged Humanities and Creativity, and Georgetown University. Kate received two Helen Hayes Awards for Outstanding Performance, and a Barrymore Award for the same. She is a member of Actor's Equity Association, the Jungian Society for Scholarly Studies, and a company member of Woolly Mammoth Theatre, in Washington, DC.

ROBERT EISENSTEIN is a founding member of the Folger Consort and has been Program Director since 1977. Recent projects include a programme featuring dramatic readings from *Merchant of Venice* with actors including Sir Derek Jacobi and Richard Clifford. In addition to the US performances, the programme was presented at the Sam Wanamaker Playhouse at Shakespeare's Globe in London. In 2018, Eisenstein served as musical director for a production of Davenant's *Macbeth* at Folger Theatre, part of the 'Performing Restoration Shakespeare' research project. He delivers public lectures related to each Folger Consort programme and frequently participates in conferences and workshops at the Folger Shakespeare Library. In addition to his work with the Consort, he is the Director Emeritus of the Five College Early Music Program, in western Massachusetts, where he taught music history and coordinated and directed student performances of medieval, Renaissance, and baroque music. He performs regularly on viola da gamba, violin, and medieval fiddle, often with the Massachusetts viol consort Arcadia Viols. He is a recent recipient of the Thomas Binkley Award (Early Music America) for outstanding achievement in performance and scholarship by the director of a college early music ensemble.

JAMES HARRIMAN-SMITH is a lecturer in Restoration and eighteenth-century literature at the University of Newcastle, UK, and a trustee of the British Society of Eighteenth-Century Studies. He is the author of *Criticism, Performance and Passions in the Eighteenth Century* (Cambridge University Press, 2021) and various chapters and articles on literature and theatre in French and English from the seventeenth to the nineteenth century. His next book will examine how past performance practice might inform the work of contemporary theatre professionals.

SARAH LEDWIDGE received her PhD in musicology from Trinity College Dublin, where she received the Home Hewson Bursary. Her area of research is the origin, circulation, and cultural significance of Shakespearean theatre music. In 2017–2018 she took part in the project 'Performing Restoration Shakespeare' in conjunction with Shakespeare's Globe and the Folger Shakespeare Library. Sarah has recently delivered papers at the following conferences: British Shakespeare Association (2018), Society for Musicology in Ireland (2017), and Cultures of Mortality, at Shakespeare's Globe (2016). Sarah trained as an undergraduate singer at Birmingham Conservatoire, following this with an MMus in vocal performance from Guildhall School of Music and Drama, London. She has sung with many leading opera companies and orchestras, and her interest in Shakespeare's songs was kindled by three seasons as a vocalist with the Royal Shakespeare Company.

SARA REIMERS is Lecturer in the Department of Theatre at the University of Bristol. She studied for her AHRC-funded PhD in the Department of Drama, Theatre and Dance at Royal Holloway, University of London, where she wrote her thesis on casting and the construction of gender in contemporary stagings of Shakespeare's plays. Following the award of her PhD she continued working at Royal Holloway as a Senior Teaching Fellow and subsequently as an AHRC Creative Economy Engagement Fellow, leading the 'Making an Appearance' research project. Sara is also a director and dramaturg and frequently uses practice-as-research methods to explore classical texts through performance.

FIONA RITCHIE is Associate Professor of Drama and Theatre in the Department of English at McGill University and a member of the editorial board for *Shakespeare Quarterly*. She is the author of *Women and Shakespeare in the Eighteenth Century* (2014) and the co-editor (with Peter Sabor) of *Shakespeare in the Eighteenth Century* (2012), both published by Cambridge University Press. Her volume on Sarah Siddons and John Philip Kemble is forthcoming in Arden's Shakespeare in the Theatre series. She is currently working on a project that explores women and regional theatre in the long eighteenth century funded by the Social Sciences and Humanities Research Council of Canada.

JOSEPH ROACH is Sterling Professor Emeritus of Theater and Professor Emeritus of English at Yale University. He has chaired the Department of Performing Arts at Washington University in St. Louis, the Interdisciplinary PhD in Theatre at Northwestern University, and the

Department of Performance Studies at New York University (NYU). His books include *It* (University of Michigan Press, 2007), which is a study of charismatic celebrity, *Cities of the Dead: Circum-Atlantic Performance* (Columbia University Press, 1996), which won the James Russell Lowell Prize from the Modern Language Association and the Calloway Prize from NYU, and *The Player's Passion: Studies in the Science of Acting* (University of Michigan Press, 1993), which won the Barnard Hewitt Award in Theatre History. Roach has also published essays in *Theatre Journal, Theatre Survey, The Drama Review, Theatre History Studies, Discourse, Theater, Text and Performance Quarterly*, and others. He has served as Director of Graduate Studies in English and Chair of the Theater Studies Advisory Committee at Yale.

STEPHEN WATKINS is Lecturer in English Literature at the University of Derby, where he researches seventeenth-century literature, theatre history, and performance. He currently serves as Chair of the Premodern Performance Cultures Network, an international forum for scholars, students, and practitioners interested in pre-1800 performance, and is Visiting Fellow of the Centre for Medieval and Renaissance Culture at the University of Southampton. His articles and reviews have appeared in *Shakespeare Bulletin, Huntington Library Quarterly, Renaissance Studies, The Seventeenth-Century Journal, The London Journal*, and *Restoration*, and he is currently writing a short book on *Acting Shakespeare in the Restoration*.

SILAS WOLLSTON has combined scholarship and performance in a varied career, working between 2013 and 2017 as an Affiliated Lecturer in Music at the University of Cambridge. His research initially grew from questions raised by the performance of music by Matthew Locke, and he is the co-editor (with John Cunningham) of a volume of Locke's violin band music for the Musica Britannica series. As a council member of the Handel Institute, he is editing Handel's *Hercules* (HWV60) for the Hallische Händel-Ausgabe and he has published research into Handel's compositional method and borrowing practice.

Foreword

Joseph Roach

Alone in a wash of cruel fluorescent light, a self-absorbed woman is gesticulating. She jerks her limbs away from her torso, raising them sideways in opposition, one hand open, the other a clenched fist. Then, hissing out an imprecation, she quickly reverses her hand positions with remarkable precision for one so agitated. Addressing a phantom interlocutor as busy people pass by without taking notice of her, she repeats herself with intensity that anywhere else but here would mark her as eccentric, if not mad. Between spasms, she mutters. Between mutters, she starts over again. But, in this special case, her behaviour is not diagnosable by reference to the tic disorders in the DSM-5. She is the award-winning actress Kate Eastwood Norris rehearsing the role of Lady Macbeth in William Davenant's musical version of Shakespeare's play at Folger Theatre.

The show is less than two weeks away from previews, and I am in the room as an invited guest-observer at one full day of rehearsal, a rare privilege – and responsibility. At this stage in the rehearsal process, any ensemble could be at its most vulnerable as well as its most creative juncture, particularly when the professional stakes are high and the artistic risk is a big one. As Norris tries out different gestures for new readings of her lines – lines that have not been heard from a stage in centuries – a long-lost Lady Macbeth, one of 'undaunted temper' (not 'mettle', as Shakespeare would have it), begins to emerge from her struggle. Part of that struggle is learning to let go of so many famous words and substitute others alien to the tongue and heart of an actress who has played the role in Shakespeare's version. Not the First Folio's 'But screw your courage to the sticking place / And we'll not fail', for instance, but rather, 'Bring your courage to the fatal place', as the more delicately abstracted Davenant version would have her phrase it. So grammatically similar, yet so different poetically, making the privileged witnessing of an exceptionally gifted actress running her lines such a compelling study in the fierce concentration needed to re-memorise and re-embody them as something – or, if she succeeds, someone – new.

Meanwhile, all around Lady Macbeth, stage crew work cheek by jowl with the devilishly singing Witches, who match pitches (or not) with members of the Folger Consort marking the score in the improvised musicians' loft above. Startlingly – for anyone accustomed to the norm of a more unitary authority in the conduct of rehearsals – specialist theatre historians and musicologists consult with cast members one-on-one or in small breakout groups in the nooks and crannies of the venerable 'Elizabethan-replica' Folger stage and its 250-seat house. As he re-works the Witches' physical business in the caldron scene, veteran stage director Robert Richmond, with only three weeks rehearsal time allotted to the show instead of the usual four, cannot be faulted if he is worrying that too many cooks might spoil the broth. At the same time, he has on his own authority introduced another layer of complication to an already complex challenge by creating a framing device and wrapping it around the story told by Shakespeare and Davenant. The performers of every role except one in this *Macbeth* represent the neurologically diverse inmates of Bedlam, the notorious London snake pit. So, in addition to personating one of the characters in Davenant's adaptation, each actor I'm watching is also trying to create an identity for the asylum inmate who is playing that character. Let out of iron grates on the sides of the stage and temporarily freed of their chains, they are all putting on a musical in which they seize the occasion to replace blunted stage props with real knives so that they can murder their Warden, who has drawn the short straw and is condemned to play King Duncan. But unlike the similarly double-cast inmates of the Asylum of Charenton who assassinate Jean-Paul Marat under the direction of the Marquis de Sade, the demented artists-in-residence at Bedlam Rep are not rid of Warden Duncan yet, because he is going to reappear twice as his Ghost.

To one who has directed many plays himself, including a number by Shakespeare and several from the long eighteenth century, seeing this boldly innovative approach to the neglected repertoire of Restoration Shakespeare is thrilling – and scary. Both John Downes, the veteran prompter for the Duke's Company, which originated Davenant's *Macbeth* in 1664, and Samuel Pepys, the veteran playgoer of the age, refer to the Duke's hit production as an 'Opera'. They are arguably almost half right, certainly in terms of added difficulty points. Three weeks flash by quickly enough when one is staging Henry Purcell and Nahum Tate's *Dido and Aeneas* (c. 1688) with orchestral rehearsals and incidental choreography for another coven of mischief-making Witches, as I have done, or a straight version of the dreaded 'Scottish Play', which I have more than once thought of doing but each time settled on a less intimidating choice. Stage violence, for instance, to cite but one of the challenges, can take up much more rehearsal time than expected and still inspire worry that it hasn't been enough. Now I am spending a day with the members of a company doing both a baroque opera and the legendarily accident-prone early modern tragedy in the same place at the same time. They are also reviving a play never seen by living theatregoers, most of whom think they already know it well. Producers and audiences alike must adjust their expectations to a cast with four leads, because Davenant bookends the Macbeths with the Macduffs, a virtuous couple whose expanded roles counterbalance the evil one with neoclassical symmetry.

Yet even these risks, I'm thinking, are still not the most daring. As part of an experimental process of putting scholars and artists to work together in pursuit of new discoveries in the performing arts, past and present, everybody at this rehearsal has had to give up something. That something entails some part of his, her, or their customary professional or professorial authority in the ego circus that any theatrical production or collective scholarly research project in the humanities can so easily become. But everybody I see here, like the laser-focused Lady Macbeth working up her part in preparation for her entrance, clearly has something urgently collaborative to do, even if at this stage there may not be in every case complete agreement about what that is.

'Everybody' in this project begins with Amanda Eubanks Winkler, Claude Fretz, and Richard Schoch, this volume's editors. They comprise the leadership team of 'Performing Restoration Shakespeare', the UK's AHRC-funded international and multi-disciplinary investigation of hands-on revivals of seventeenth-century works for modern audiences. I call them 'the Davenauts' for short. They have already produced a public showing of extended musical scenes from Davenant and John Dryden's adaptation of *The Tempest, or The Enchanted Island* (1667) in the Sam Wanamaker Playhouse adjacent to Shakespeare's Globe on London's Bankside. Now they are bringing in six additional scholars to join cast and crew in the rehearsal process for *Macbeth* as a fully staged Equity production at the Folger.

Moved by the academic expertise and professional skill deployed around me in the foyer, house, and stage, I am excited to see the meaning of the words *rehearsal* and *research* overlapping in the work unfolding before my eyes. Nevertheless, cautionary cognates in two foreign words for rehearsal complicate my witness: the French say *la répétition*; Germans, *die Probe*. Clearly, the number of repetitions necessary to get this beast of a show ready for an audience limits the extent of the probing required by collaborative research on site. Grateful for a further privileged invitation, I join a small breakout coaching session with actors not immediately called for a scene. Three exquisitely physicalised gestures graphically depicted in Franciscus Lang's *Dissertatio de actione scenica* (1727) – 'issuing a command', 'delivering a message', and 'expressing emotions in silence' – pique their curiosity in the playable possibilities of using period gestures not as artificially appliquéd attitudes but as naturally embodied actions that feel right with the language and costumes. When we return to the general rehearsal, however, the director announces that henceforth period gestures will not be used in the show. If performing Restoration Shakespeare in a modern repertory company were easy, someone would have done it before.

So, the act curtain in my mind rises, and the essential purpose of the project takes centre stage. While respectful of the findings of the original practices movement in the study of early modern production (e.g., 'Shakespeare in parts'), the Davenauts are not seeking to replicate rehearsal practices or to reconstruct the physical staging of the period with overriding fidelity to antiquarian detail. This is not a bird they want to catch, nor is it their net. That is true for many reasons, not the least of which is that the elaborate moveable scenery of the Restoration proscenium stage developed by Davenant won't fit on the Wanamaker or Folger stages. What will fit on any stage managed by receptive producers is the practical and theoretical knowledge aggregated by the editors and contributors to this volume. These leading scholars and performing artists want the following chapters to make the magic of late seventeenth-century multi-mediated stagecraft live in the imaginations of readers and theatregoers today – live in the way that Shakespeare's plays do, not as bugs in amber but as birds on the wing. *Performing Restoration Shakespeare* would seem to mark the culmination of the eye-opening research that they have conducted together up until the end of the three-year term of the AHRC grant. Or might it mark just the beginning?

Acknowledgements

Our principal thanks are due to the Arts and Humanities Research Council (AHRC) in the United Kingdom for generously funding the research project 'Performing Restoration Shakespeare' (2017–2020), from which this edited volume has arisen. We warmly thank our project partners – the Folger Shakespeare Library and Shakespeare's Globe – without whose collaboration our practice-based research and public engagement would not have been possible. We especially thank Kathleen Lynch, Janet Alexander Griffin, Owen Williams, Garland Scott, and Peter Eramo at the Folger and Will Tosh at the Globe for their unflagging commitment to our project over several years. Walter Rissmeyer and Joe Bruncsak at Blue Land Media did an outstanding job in producing our six documentary videos on Restoration Shakespeare.

All the chapters in this volume are written by members of the project's research teams, and so reflect their contributions to our collaborative work. We also wish to acknowledge the additional contributions made by research team members whose work does not appear in this volume: Emily Baines, Michael Cordner, Lisa A. Freeman, Trevor Griffiths, Tim Keenan, Katherina Lindekens, Elaine McGirr, Deborah Payne, Ted Tregear, and Andrew R. Walkling. Among the artists involved in our staging of *Macbeth* and *The Tempest*, we are especially grateful for the involvement and expertise of Emily Barber, Philip Bird, Dominic Brewer, Chris Genebach, Emily Noël, Ian Merrill Peakes, and Karen Peakes. We thank the project's advisory board – Michael Burden, Rebecca Herissone, Peter Holland (chair), and Tiffany Stern – for their wise counsel and advice.

At Syracuse University, Amanda would like to thank the College of Arts and Sciences for providing teaching release and research funding. Her colleagues in the Department of Art and Music Histories have been unfailingly supportive – Sarah Fuchs and Romita Ray even attended the 2019 Restoration Shakespeare showcase at the Globe. She would also like to thank Sally Smith at Queen's University Belfast for her advice on the

AHRC grant submission. At Sun Yat-sen University, Claude would like to thank Xu Dejin and the School of Foreign Languages for providing encouragement, time, and funding to work on his projects, including this and other publications on Restoration Shakespeare. At Queen's University Belfast, Claude's thanks go to Liz Fawcett for sharing her expertise on research impact and to colleagues in the School of Arts, English, and Languages for support and encouragement, especially Chen-En Ho, Ramona Wray, and Mark Thornton Burnett. Also at Queen's University Belfast, Richard would like to thank Sally Smith, Peter Stephenson, and James Dillon in the Research and Enterprise Directorate for their support and guidance, and Zara McBrearty in the Media Relations office for helping us to engage a wider audience with our research.

Emily Hockley at Cambridge University Press has been a patient and supportive editor. We thank the three anonymous peer reviewers for their helpful comments, Samantha Bassler for preparing the index, and Ranjith Kumar and his colleagues at Lumina Datamatics for overseeing the production process.

Abbreviations

EBBA	English Broadside Ballad Archive (ed. Patricia Fumerton) (https://ebba.english.ucsb.edu/)
STC	Short Title Catalogue number (Alfred W. Pollard and Gilbert R. Redgrave (eds.), *A Short-Title Catalogue of Books Printed in England, Scotland, & Ireland and of English Books Printed Abroad 1475–1640*, 2nd ed., ed. William A. Jackson, Frederick S. Ferguson, and Katherine F. Pantzer, 3 vols. (London: Bibliographical Society, 1976–1991)
Thomason	G. K. Fortescue, *The Catalogue of the Pamphlets, Books, Newspapers, and Manuscripts Relating to the Civil War, the Commonwealth, and Restoration, Collected by George Thomason, 1640–1661*, 2 vols. (London: by order of the Trustees of the British Museum, 1908)
Wing	Donald Wing, *Short-title catalogue of books printed in England, Scotland, Ireland, Wales, and British America, and of English books printed in other countries, 1641–1700*, 3 vols. (New York: Columbia University Press, 1945–1951)

Library Sigla

F-Pc	Paris, Conservatoire
GB-Bc	Birmingham Central Library
GB-En	Edinburgh, National Library of Scotland
GB-Eu	Edinburgh University Library
GB-Ge	Glasgow University, Euing Music Library
GB-Lbl	London, British Library
GB-Lna	London, The National Archives
GB-Lpro	London, Public Record Office
GB-Ob	Oxford, Bodleian Library

GB-Och	Oxford, Christ Church Library
US-NH	New Haven (CT), Yale University, Irving S. Gilmore Music Library
US-NHub	New Haven (CT), Yale University, Beinecke Rare Book and Manuscript Library
US-NYp	New York Public Library
US-Ws	Washington, DC, Folger Shakespeare Library

Introduction: New Shakespeare for a New Era
Amanda Eubanks Winkler, Claude Fretz, and Richard Schoch

When the English Civil War began in 1642, London playhouses were closed down. A temporary parliamentary edict issued on 2 September 1642 proclaimed that 'Publike Stage-playes' were unbecoming in 'the Seasons of Humiliation … too commonly expressing lascivious Mirth'.[1] By 1647, the ban on theatrical performance had become permanent. Yet this interdiction did not result in total suppression of dramatic activity during the Interregnum. Private performances, whether in houses or schools, continued to take place. More publicly, William Beeston tried but failed to re-establish Beeston's Boys (a popular troupe consisting mainly of boy actors that performed from 1637 to 1642) at the Cockpit, but he succeeded in being granted title to what remained of the Salisbury Court Theatre in 1652. Meanwhile, playwrights such as Sir William Davenant circumvented the ban on stage plays by producing dramatic spectacles generically designated as 'operas' because they consisted of singing, declamation, and changeable scenery.[2] Indeed, Davenant gained approval from Oliver Cromwell's government in the 1650s to produce 'Heroick Representations' – the most famous of which was *The Siege of Rhodes* (1656) – initially at his own residence Rutland House and later in the Cockpit theatre in Drury Lane.[3] Yet the formal ban on dramatic entertainment did mean that London's public theatres could not officially reopen until 1660, when Charles II returned from his European exile and the monarchy was restored.

---

[1] Cited in Leslie Hotson, *The Commonwealth and Restoration Stage* (New York: Russell & Russell, 1962), 36.
[2] Scenic effect was a crucial feature of early English opera, as Davenant advertised on the title pages of *The Siege of Rhodes* (1656), *The Cruelty of the Spaniards in Peru* (1658), and *The History of Sir Frances Drake* (1659). See Andrew Walkling's *Masque and Opera in England, 1656–1668* (Abingdon: Routledge, 2017).
[3] William Davenant uses the term 'Heroick Representations' in *A Proposition for the Advancement of Moralitie by a New Way of Entertainment of the People* (London, 1654 [/3]), 2.

Shortly after assuming the throne, Charles II granted exclusive theatrical patents to his courtiers Thomas Killigrew and Sir William Davenant, establishing the theatrical duopoly controlled by the King's Company (led by Killigrew) and the Duke's Company (led by Davenant). The rival companies continued until 1682, when they were merged and became known as the United Company. Because theatres had been suppressed for eighteen years, few new plays were available to perform when commercial theatrical activity resumed in 1660. Necessity alone compelled the new patentees to stage the old stock drama from before the Civil War: principally, the works of Ben Jonson, William Shakespeare, and Francis Beaumont and John Fletcher.

Comprised largely of veteran actors from before the closure of the theatres, the King's Company regarded itself as the authentic successor to the pre-1642 King's Men, the company in which Shakespeare had been sharer, playwright, and actor. On the basis of their claim for continuity in the theatrical profession, Killigrew's company secured (or possessed by default) the rights to most of the plays earlier performed by the King's Men, including twenty-two of Shakespeare's plays deemed to be the most popular. The Duke's Company, however, was made up of younger actors, including Thomas Betterton, destined to become the most important tragedian of his time. After petitioning Charles II for the right to reform or rework earlier plays, Davenant was granted rights to perform eleven plays, including nine by Shakespeare: *Hamlet, Henry VIII, King Lear, Macbeth, Measure for Measure, Much Ado About Nothing, Romeo and Juliet, The Tempest,* and *Twelfth Night*.[4]

Initially, the two companies staged Shakespeare's plays mostly unaltered. *Othello, Henry IV, The Merry Wives of Windsor,* and *Hamlet* were successful, but problems with other plays – especially the comedies – soon became apparent. Samuel Pepys, whose famous diary offers more eyewitness accounts of Restoration Shakespeare than any other source, noted on 1 March 1662 that *Romeo and Juliet* was 'the play of itself the worst that ever I heard in my life'.[5] He was even more critical of an unrevised *A Midsummer Night's Dream* which he saw on 29 September 1662: 'I sent for some dinner ... and then to the King's Theatre, where we saw *Midsummer's*

---

[4] For a discussion of how pre-1642 plays were divided between the King's Company and the Duke's Company, see Amanda Eubanks Winkler and Richard Schoch, *Shakespeare in the Theatre: Sir William Davenant and the Duke's Company* (London: Arden Bloomsbury, 2021), 33–9.

[5] Robert Latham and William Matthews, eds., *The Diary of Samuel Pepys: A New and Complete Transcription*, 11 vols. (Berkeley: University of California Press, 1971), vol. III, 39.

Figure 0.1   Sir William Davenant (1606–1668) by William Faithorne, after John Greenhill, published 1672

Night's Dream, which I had never seen before, nor shall ever again, for it is the most insipid ridiculous play that ever I saw in my life.'[6]

It did not take long for Davenant, whose portrait is shown in Figure 0.1, to realise that he could make a name for himself and his company by staging revised versions of Shakespeare. Under his bold and imaginative leadership, the Duke's Company gained a reputation for staging Shakespeare's plays with pioneering theatrical innovations. Davenant's adaptations arose partly from necessity, because the plays given to the Duke's Company were comparatively few in number and written in a manner deemed unsuited for the tastes of Restoration audiences. Davenant's first adaptation, performed in 1662, was *The Law against Lovers*, based on *Measure for Measure* and *Much Ado About Nothing*.

---

[6] Latham and Matthews, eds., *Diary of Samuel Pepys*, vol. III, 208.

When Pepys saw *The Law against Lovers* on 18 February 1662, he commented: 'I went to the Opera [i.e., Davenant's theatre in Lincoln's Inn Fields], and saw *The Law against Lovers*, a good play and well performed, especially the Little Girle's (whom I never saw act before) dancing and singing.'[7] One of the 'Little Girle's' whose performance Pepys so admired was Mary ('Moll') Davis, a member of the Duke's Company throughout the 1660s and known particularly for her skill as a singer and dancer. Mary Davis was not the first woman that Pepys saw on the stage, because actresses were part of Restoration theatre right from the start. Indeed, the appearance of professional actresses in England is one of the defining features of the Restoration stage. For the first time, Lady Macbeth, Juliet, Ophelia, Beatrice, and Isabella were played not by boys, but by women. Nor would there be any return to past theatrical conventions, because in 1662 Charles II had issued a royal patent banning boy actors from being cast in female roles. And so, the Restoration theatre produced the first generation of professional English actresses. In addition to Mary Davis, that inaugural generation also included Nell Gwynn (who became mistress to Charles II) and Mary Saunderson (who married Thomas Betterton). The novelty of women appearing on the London stage, along with its unembarrassed potential for erotic allure, helps to explain in part how Shakespeare was adapted in the Restoration. In revising *Macbeth*, for example, Davenant substantially expanded the role of Lady Macduff, partly to create a virtuous counterpoint to the villainous Lady Macbeth and partly to provide good roles for the women in the Duke's Company. Davenant's and Dryden's adaptation of *The Tempest* created more roles for actresses – Sycorax, Caliban's sister; Dorinda, Miranda's sister; and Milcha, Ariel's companion – while the new character Hippolito was performed as a 'breeches role', a male character played by an actress and usually in costume that explicitly displayed her figure.

As implied by Davenant's expansion and invention of dramatic characters, Restoration versions of Shakespeare often entailed strong rewritings of the original text, frequently with a new emphasis on the mixed genre of tragicomedy and musical and scenic divertissements. Some adaptations explicitly responded to the new political reality – a once deposed but now restored monarchy – by affirming royal power and denouncing regicide and rebellion in ways that sometimes effaced the moral ambiguities of Shakespeare's precursor texts. Thus, most of Shakespeare's history plays and Roman tragedies were converted into political commentaries. Given

---

[7] Latham and Matthews, eds., *Diary of Samuel Pepys*, vol. III, 32.

the close personal and legal connections between the stage and the crown, we cannot be surprised that the English Restoration theatre effectively operated as an extension of the court.

Other alterations to Shakespeare's texts were dictated by changing literary and poetic style. Restoration dramatists and their audiences valued direct, unadorned language much more than figurative speech. Davenant's *Macbeth* refers literally to the 'last minute of recorded time' rather than metaphorically to the 'last syllable'. Symmetry in dramatic structure was prized more highly than the messy subplots found in many Shakespeare plays. Thus, Davenant and Dryden created the role of Hippolito (a man who had never seen a woman) in their version of *The Tempest* as a counterpart to Miranda (a woman who had never seen a man). Meanwhile, Nahum Tate endorsed the royalist ethos of the Restoration stage by ensuring that both a chastened Lear and his virtuous daughter Cordelia survive in his 'happy ending' version of *King Lear*.

In terms of the two most fundamental aspects of Shakespeare in performance – the acting and the text – the Restoration theatre did not perform Shakespeare's plays the same way that Shakespeare's own company had performed them only decades earlier. Restoration theatre artists did not view Shakespeare's works as immutable dramatic masterpieces but believed that they needed to be reshaped and refined before they could be properly presented on the stage. Dryden's prologue to his version of *The Tempest* lauds Shakespeare as the venerable 'Root' out of which the Restoration stage has freshly emerged: 'As when a Tree's cut down, the secret Root / Lives under ground, and thence new branches shoot; / So, from old Shakespeare's honour'd dust, this day / Springs up and buds a new reviving Play.'[8]

Changing theatrical tastes also meant changes in theatrical production. Because plays were now performed exclusively indoors (initially, in converted tennis courts) and because Charles II and his courtiers had grown accustomed during their exile on the continent to seeing elaborate movable scenery used in theatrical productions, the Restoration theatre was poised to make its mark through spectacle and scenic effects. Benefiting from Davenant's work with Inigo Jones and his assistant John Webb on the final Stuart court masques performed at the Banqueting House, the Duke's Company in the 1660s and 1670s exploited the theatre's full

---

[8] Thomas Shadwell, William Davenant, and John Dryden, *The Tempest, or the Enchanted Island: A Comedy* (1674), in *Five Restoration Adaptations of Shakespeare*, ed. Christopher Spencer (Urbana: University of Illinois Press, 1965), 'Prologue', lines 1–4.

Figure 0.2   William Dolle, engraving of scenes at Dorset Garden Theatre, in Elkanah Settle's *The Empress of Morocco* (1673)

potential for spectacular *mise en scène*, including movable painted scenery (see Figure 0.2). After the company's move to the larger Dorset Garden Theatre in 1671, elaborate new machines enabled both people and objects to fly across the stage. The integration of music and dance with scenic and machine-based spectacle, practised previously only in court masques, was brought to the Restoration public stage with renewed vigour.

Although the King's Company eventually copied the elaborate staging introduced by their rivals, the Duke's Company always remained more innovative. The eyewitness testimony of the spectator Samuel Pepys and the prompter John Downes offers a case in point. On 7 January 1667 Pepys saw a performance of Davenant's adaptation of *Macbeth*, which expanded the roles of Macduff and Lady Macduff, introduced the new role of Duncan's ghost, and ramped up the entertainment value with additional singing and dancing. Pepys praised Davenant's version of Shakespeare's tragedy as 'a most excellent play in all respects, but especially in divertisement, though it be a deep tragedy; which is a strange perfection in a tragedy, it being most proper here and suitable'.⁹ According to Pepys, the play's divertissements – such as the witches' comical and operatic performances – did not diminish the tragedy, but rather complemented it. Indeed, the spectacle was itself the 'perfection' of the tragedy, the culmination of its theatrical potential. John Downes, the long-serving prompter for the Duke's Company, extolled the combination of visual spectacle with singing and dancing in his description of the lucrative revival of Davenant's *Macbeth* (1673) at the new Dorset Garden Theatre:

> [B]eing drest in all it's Finery, as new Cloath's, new Scenes, Machines, as flyings for the Witches; and with all the Singing and Dancing in it ... it being all Excellently perform'd, being in the nature of an Opera, it Recompenc'd double the Expence; it proves still a lasting play.¹⁰

Downes also served as prompter for Thomas Shadwell's 1674 operatic version of Davenant and Dryden's *The Tempest*, the most lavish and commercially successful production of Restoration Shakespeare. The opening stage direction, which seeks to represent the storm conjured up by Prospero, sets a high bar for multimedia performance spectacle: to the sound of a sizeable orchestral ensemble, 'Several Spirits in horrid shapes fl[y] down amongst the Sailors, then rising and crossing in the Air.'¹¹ As with *Macbeth*, stage spectacle and box office income went hand in hand for this much revived and 'all New' version of *The Tempest*: 'having all New in it; as Scenes, Machines ... all things perform'd in it so Admirably well, that not any succeeding Opera got more Money'.¹² As musicologist Michael Burden rightly concludes, 'scenes and machines were an intrinsic part of the nascent genre of dramatick opera', a genre that includes some of the most vibrant, successful, and long-lived Restoration adaptations of Shakespeare.¹³

Understanding Restoration Shakespeare

F. J. Furnivall's 1892 variorum edition of *The Tempest* included in its appendix the full text of Shadwell's 1674 revision of the Dryden–Davenant adaptation of Shakespeare's play. As might be expected of the man who founded The New Shakspere Society, Furnivall included the famous

---

⁹ Latham and Matthews, eds., *Diary of Samuel Pepys*, vol. VIII, 7.
¹⁰ John Downes, *Roscius Anglicanus, or an Historical Review of the Stage* (London: Printed and sold by H. Playford, 1708), 33.
¹¹ Shadwell, Davenant, and Dryden, *The Tempest, or the Enchanted Island*, 117.
¹² Downes, *Roscius Anglicanus*, 34.
¹³ Michael Burden, 'Shakespeare and Opera', in *Eighteenth-Century Shakespeare*, ed. Peter Sabor and Fiona Ritchie (Cambridge: Cambridge University Press, 2012), 204–24 (209).

Restoration version of *The Tempest* in his scholarly edition so that it might be despised all the more easily: 'unless we read it, no imagination, derived from a mere description, can adequately depict its monstrosity'.[14] In so doing, he set the precedent for a century's worth of literary scholarship that has felt free to dismiss Restoration Shakespeare as parasitic deformations of the superior original plays.

Furnivall's condemnation also set narrow terms for future critical enquiry, defining Restoration Shakespeare as a purely literary object, more or less ignoring its life on the stage. As evident in G. C. D. Odell's *Shakespeare from Betterton to Irving* (1920) and Montagu Summers's *Shakespeare Adaptations* (1922), the result of this constrained perception was that scholars focused overwhelmingly on textual adaptation, explaining how Restoration versions deviated from their Shakespearean originals (e.g., in plot, structure, character, and imagery) and how those deviations could often be read as veiled pro-royalist commentary. Literary bias still operates in recent – and valuable – scholarship, including Sandra Clark's 1997 edition of Restoration Shakespeare and Barbara Murray's meticulous play-by-play analysis in *Restoration Shakespeare: Viewing the Voice* (2001).[15] While there have been important studies of the general performance aspects of Restoration drama, especially Peter Holland's *The Ornament of Action* (1979), Jocelyn Powell's *Restoration Theatre Production* (1984), and Timothy Keenan's *Restoration Staging, 1660–74* (2017), the core performance aspects of Restoration adaptations of Shakespeare have been systematically overlooked ever since scholars such as Judith Milhous documented their synthesis of script, song, and music.[16]

Accordingly, a principal historiographical aim of this volume is to rebalance scholarship by interrogating how Restoration Shakespeare operated as a complex theatrical experience and not merely as a dramatic text, let alone a dramatic text presumed inferior to its precursor. Overturning the longstanding literary emphasis in scholarship, this volume constitutes the

---

[14] F. J. Furnivall, ed., *A New Variorum of Shakespeare*, vol. 9 (Philadelphia: J. B. Lippincott Co., 1892), viii.
[15] Sandra Clark, ed., *Shakespeare Made Fit: Restoration Adaptations of Shakespeare* (London: Everyman, 1997); Barbara A. Murray, *Restoration Shakespeare: Viewing the Voice* (Madison, NJ: Fairleigh Dickinson University Press, 2001).
[16] Peter Holland, *The Ornament of Action: Text and Performance in Restoration Comedy* (Cambridge: Cambridge University Press, 1979); Jocelyn Powell, *Restoration Theatre Production* (London: Routledge & Kegan Paul, 1984); Timothy Keenan, *Restoration Staging, 1660–74* (Abingdon: Routledge, 2017); Judith Milhous, 'The Multimedia Spectacular on the Restoration Stage', in *British Theatre and Other Arts, 1660–1800*, ed. Shirley Strum Kenny (Washington, DC: Folger Books, 1984), 41–66.

first edited collection that investigates Restoration Shakespeare from multiple material, critical, and performative perspectives. As such, it promises to increase our understanding of Restoration Shakespeare by investigating how the plays were – and continue to be – the basis for performances that integrate acting, singing, music, and dance within an overall dramatic narrative. The present volume does not seek to replicate previous studies of Restoration Shakespeare from the perspectives of textual revision, political context, or original staging conditions (including scenery).[17] Instead, all the contributors to this volume share a commitment to studying Restoration adaptations of Shakespeare not as relics of a theatrical past but as vehicles for performance that can transcend their printed texts and their original political and material staging conditions.

Performance as Research

The inspiration for this volume arises from the international research project 'Performing Restoration Shakespeare' – generously funded by the Arts and Humanities Research Council in the United Kingdom between 2017 and 2020 – for which the editors of this volume were Principal Investigator (Schoch), Co-Investigator (Eubanks Winkler), and Research Fellow (Fretz). In partnership with the Folger Shakespeare Library and in collaboration with Shakespeare's Globe, the project brought together scholars and practitioners in theatre and music to investigate how and why Restoration adaptations of Shakespeare's plays succeeded in performance in their own time and how and why they can succeed in performance today.

This volume's contributors are drawn from the research teams assembled for the project's various scholarly and performance events, with each contributor having participated in at least one of the project's core activities. The project's first event was an open workshop on Shadwell's operatic version of *The Tempest* (1674) held in the Sam Wanamaker Playhouse at Shakespeare's Globe (London, July 2017).[18] Throughout the week-long workshop, a research community of academics and artists reflected on and performed three scenes from the play that richly blend drama and music: the frightening 'Masque of Devils' (2.4), the charming duet 'Go thy way' between Ferdinand and Ariel (3.4), and the stately 'Masque of Neptune' (5.2). We learned a great deal in that inaugural workshop, not just about

---

[17] For an overview of scenic practice in Restoration playhouses, see Holland, *Ornament of Action*, 19–54.
[18] An archival recording of the event is available for study purposes at Shakespeare's Globe.

the performance aspects of Restoration Shakespeare but also, and equally importantly, about how to find a common language for scholars and artists in the rehearsal room.[19]

Profiting from that initial experience, we then undertook a more ambitious task by partnering with the Folger Shakespeare Library, Folger Theatre, and the early modern music ensemble Folger Consort to mount a full professional production of Davenant's *Macbeth* (c. 1664), with participating scholars actively contributing to the creative process throughout rehearsals. Directed by Robert Richmond, the production of Restoration *Macbeth* ran at the Folger Theatre in Washington, DC, from 6 to 23 September 2018.[20] Adopting a play-within-a-play concept, the production was set in St Mary Bethlehem Hospital ('Bedlam') in London, two weeks after the Great Fire of London in September 1666. Recalling Peter Weiss's *Marat/Sade*, the Bedlam inmates perform Davenant's *Macbeth* and use the performance to murder the hospital's warden (cast as Duncan in the play) and then to take over the institution where they had been held as virtual prisoners. Yet this framing device did not prevent the production from actively embracing the distinctive aspects of Davenant's *Macbeth*, most especially the musical set pieces sung by the three witches, for which we used Amanda Eubanks Winkler's edition of John Eccles's late seventeenth-century score.[21] Reflecting the appeal that Restoration Shakespeare can have for audiences today, the entire run was sold out before the first preview performance.[22]

Our project's final public event took us back to the Sam Wanamaker Playhouse, where we held a Restoration Shakespeare showcase in July 2019 for a mixed audience of the general public, theatre and music professionals, and scholars in Shakespeare studies, theatre history, and musicology. The showcase included reprised performances of the duet 'Go thy way' from the Dryden-Davenant version of *The Tempest* and two scenes from

---

[19] See Claude Fretz, '"marvellous and surprizing conduct": The "Masque of Devils" and Dramatic Genre in Thomas Shadwell's *The Tempest*', *Restoration: Studies in English Literary Culture, 1660–1700*, 43.2 (Fall 2019): 3–28.

[20] A full video recording of the production is available for study purposes at the Folger Shakespeare Library.

[21] Amanda Eubanks Winkler, ed., *Music for Macbeth* (Middleton, WI: A-R Editions, 2004).

[22] For discussions of the revival of Davenant's *Macbeth* at the Folger Theatre in 2018, and for its implications for modern theatre practice, see Claude Fretz, 'Performing Restoration Shakespeare "Then" and "Now": A Case Study of Davenant's *Macbeth*', *Concentric: Literary and Cultural Studies*, 48.1 (March 2022): 27–56; Sara Reimers and Richard Schoch, 'Performing Restoration Shakespeare Today: Staging Davenant's *Macbeth*', *Shakespeare Bulletin*, 37.4 (Winter 2019): 467–89; and Deborah C. Payne, '"Damn you, Davenant!": The Perils and Possibilities of Restoration Shakespeare', *Restoration and Eighteenth-Century Theatre Research*, 32.1 (Summer 2017): 21–40.

Davenant's *Macbeth*, with Kate Eastwood Norris recreating her performance as Lady Macbeth from the 2018 Folger Theatre production. The afternoon concluded with a roundtable discussion on the challenges and rewards of performing Restoration Shakespeare today with Will Tosh from Shakespeare's Globe and Robert Richmond and Robert Eisenstein, who were, respectively, stage director and music director for our production of Restoration *Macbeth*. Norris and Eisenstein are both contributors to this volume.

'Performing Restoration Shakespeare' is hardly the first research project that brings together academics and artists to study historical performance. In recent decades, scholars in Shakespeare studies and musicology have repeatedly collaborated with artists to recreate as best they can original performance styles or playing conditions. Within Shakespeare studies, such approaches – sometimes referred to as 'Original Practices' – are prominent in practice-based research and published scholarship that creates and reflects upon productions at Shakespeare's Globe (including the Sam Wanamaker Playhouse) and the reconstructed Blackfriars Playhouse at the American Shakespeare Center. Many valuable insights have been gained from those pioneering efforts. Yet the historical authenticity paradigm underpinning such research has itself been challenged on historicist grounds: contemporary performance practice cannot forsake its own here-and-now reality to retrieve past experiences; the impulse to recover 'original' styles arises from modernist values about purity of artistic form; and original early modern performances were created through improvisations that by definition cannot be precisely recovered or even fully known.[23] Others argue that the claim of 'restorative' artistic practice to approximate composer or authorial intention is itself anti-theatrical, precisely because it denies performance its own hermeneutic agency, reducing it to a messenger on its creator's behalf.[24]

Mindful of these critiques, 'Performing Restoration Shakespeare' explicitly did not adopt the paradigm of 'Original Practices', nor did it make any claims whatsoever to historical authenticity. The very nature of Restoration

---

[23] See, inter alia, Peter Kivy, *Authenticities: Philosophical Reflections on Musical Performance* (Ithaca, NY: Cornell University Press, 1995); Alan Dessen, '"Original Practices" at the Globe', in *Shakespeare's Globe: A Theatrical Experiment*, ed. Christie Carson and Farah Karim-Cooper (Cambridge: Cambridge University Press, 2008), 45–54; Richard Taruskin, *Text and Act: Essays on Music and Performance* (Oxford: Oxford University Press, 1995); and Bruce Haynes, *The End of Early Music* (Oxford: Oxford University Press, 2007).

[24] Cary Mazer, 'Historicizing Spontaneity', in *Shakespeare's Sense of Character*, ed. Yu Jin Ko and Michael Shurgot (Burlington, VT: Ashgate, 2012), 85–98.

Shakespeare reminds us that the vitality of theatre lies in innovation, not replication. Instead of reinstating what it presumed to be an authentic or authoritative version of Shakespeare's plays, the English Restoration theatre – the first generation to do Shakespeare 'after' Shakespeare – changed absolutely everything: the script, the performers, the music, the *mise en scène*, the location and layout of the theatres, and the composition of the audience. And so our project, in its public performances of scenes from *The Tempest* and in its full production of *Macbeth*, has sought to turn the insights of performance studies back onto performance itself, enacting the principle that historical performance genres are intelligible only in a dialectical sense: that is, historical sources and scholarly expertise are not abandoned but *transformed* into new events for new audiences, with the past and present existing in creative tension.

This volume reflects two of the core principles of our research project on Restoration Shakespeare: first, that published scholarship and research-led theatre and music practice are complementary activities, each enriching the other; and second, that Restoration Shakespeare is best understood as a performance event that embraces and integrates drama, music, dance, and scenic spectacle, rather than simply as a dramatic text. Accordingly, the contributions to this volume take a multidisciplinary and a multi-modal approach, with contributions from theatre historians, musicologists and literary critics, as well as leading theatre and music practitioners. Far from reducing Restoration adaptations of Shakespeare to simply being topical versions of the original plays, the ten chapters in this volume attempt to do full justice to this distinctive but under-studied historical performance genre.

Collection Overview

Reflecting its interdisciplinary approach to studying Restoration Shakespeare, this volume is organised by methodology and materiality rather than by chronology, dramatic genre, or elements of performance practice. The first three chapters investigate some of the archival sources, intellectual contexts, and processes of revision that together reveal the distinctiveness of Restoration Shakespeare. Examining the transmission of Shakespeare's songs into the Restoration period, Sarah Ledwidge argues that the popularity of music in Restoration Shakespeare can be partly explained by the hitherto unacknowledged circulation of Shakespeare's songs in print and manuscript during the Interregnum. Situating Davenant's adaptation of *Macbeth* within the broader context of his playmaking career, Stephen Watkins highlights the connections and discrepancies between *Macbeth* and the heroic operas and plays that Davenant himself wrote and produced in the 1650s and 1660s. In so doing, Watkins demonstrates how the dramaturgical alterations made to *Macbeth* conform to Davenant's particular authorial style. Finally, Silas Wollston examines 'The Rare Theatrical' compositions of Matthew Locke, showing that many of them date from the same time as the *Macbeth* productions mounted by the Duke's Company in 1664 and 1667. Wollston further contends that these compositions enable us to reconstruct Locke's instrumental music for *Macbeth*, which encompassed the first and second music performed before the play commenced, a curtain tune, and act tunes.

Chapters 4 to 7 outline the enduring theatrical life of Restoration Shakespeare, beginning in the 1660s but extending (for some plays) into the nineteenth century. They also consider some of the performances created in recent years by the research project 'Performing Restoration Shakespeare' in partnership with the Folger Shakespeare Library. Fiona Ritchie explores how the Restoration convention of the 'breeches role' – a male character played by a female actor dressed in male attire – was influenced by the first appearances of professional women actors on the English stage in the early 1660s. Investigating the appeal of Restoration Shakespeare for later generations of actor-managers, James Harriman-Smith discusses how David Garrick used Nahum Tate's *King Lear* – more than half a century after it was written – as an intermediary between himself and Shakespeare's original play. Harriman-Smith's chapter is followed by structured interviews with two performing artists, both of whom were involved in the 2018 Folger Theatre production of Davenant's *Macbeth*. Louis Butelli, who played Duncan, reflects on the complexity of finding the right acting style for a contemporary performance of Restoration Shakespeare, the challenges posed to an actor by Davenant's language, and the benefits of having scholars and artists working side by side. Robert Eisenstein draws on his experience as musical director for the Folger Consort to articulate the creative tension between musicians who are committed to historically informed practice and stage directors who are less motivated by historicist concerns. Reflecting on the challenges of staging historical performance genres today, he proposes a range of solutions to satisfy musicians, actors, directors, and audiences alike.

Following on from Eisenstein's account of contemporary music and theatre performances, Chapters 8–10 reflect on how the scholar-artist collaborations in the research project 'Performing Restoration Shakespeare' can articulate a new model for the practice-based study of historical performance. In so doing, these concluding chapters seek to advance methodological debates in theatre studies and musicology by advocating an alternative to performance practices aimed at reviving 'original' styles or conventions. Collectively, they articulate a dialectical process that understands historical performances on their own artistic and contextual terms, but then uses that understanding to reanimate them for audiences today. Drawing on her observation of rehearsals for *Macbeth* at the Folger in 2018 and also on her later experience of devising scholar-artist workshops with actors from Lazarus Theatre in London, Sara Reimers explores the underappreciated radical potential of Davenant's Lady Macduff. Kate Eastwood Norris, who played Lady Macbeth in the Folger production, explains the logistical and creative parameters of her undertaking, details how she collaborated with the production's scholarly team, and argues that the essential creativity of both scholarship and performance can help academics and artists to forge a productive alliance. In the final chapter, Amanda Eubanks Winkler and Richard Schoch offer a first-hand account of how scenes from the Shadwell-Dryden-Davenant adaptation of *The Tempest* were developed through scholar-artist collaboration and performed in the Sam Wanamaker Playhouse in 2017. This practice-based experiment reveals how the present necessarily reconfigures the past, such that the performance of any historical work is inevitably shaped by present-day actualities, whether the bodies of the actors, the performance space itself, or the expectations of both artists and audiences.

As revealed by the content and focus of its various chapters, this volume has two main goals, one about scholarly substance and one about scholarly method. With respect to the substance of scholarship, we hope that this volume, the first devoted to Restoration Shakespeare in performance, will encourage scholars from multiple disciplines to discard any notion they might have that Restoration Shakespeare is at best an inferior form of dramatic poetry or at worst a deformation of Shakespeare's theatrical genius. With respect to the methods of scholarship, we hope that our collective experience of working in a fully sustained way with actors and musicians on Restoration versions of *The Tempest* and *Macbeth* will encourage other scholars and other performing artists to take up this neglected but theatrically compelling repertoire to create yet further performances nourished by a dialogue between the archive and the rehearsal room, enriched by the union of scholarly creativity and artistic imagination.

CHAPTER 1

From Boards to Books: The Circulation of Shakespearean Songs in Manuscript and Print during the Interregnum

Sarah Ledwidge

This chapter considers the impact of musical practices during the Interregnum on the Restoration performances of Shakespeare that followed. Understanding the circulation and performance of Shakespearean song during the years when England's theatres were closed (1642–1660) is key to explaining how and why Shakespeare's works came to be adapted and 'musicked' by Restoration dramatists and composers. The manuscript and printed sources which have survived from this period indicate that certain theatrical and musical practices survived the suppression of public performances and that dramatic song remained popular, though it may have found alternative contexts for performance. Musical sources that were created and used during the Interregnum bridge the gap between pre- and post-Restoration musical style and help map the development of dramatic song in England.

Recent valuable studies have focused on the circulation of Shakespeare's plays, music-making in general, and the circulation of dramatic music during the Interregnum.[1] While the cultural restrictions of the Civil War and Commonwealth inevitably impeded new theatrical works, those surveys of the period's literature confirm a continued interest in drama and dramatic song. Emma Depledge has exposed as myth, furthermore, the notion that Shakespeare experienced a lull in popularity during the period, tracing the continued publication of his plays in such modified forms as drolls,

---

[1] See Emma Depledge, *Shakespeare's Rise to Cultural Prominence: Politics, Print and Alteration* (Cambridge: Cambridge University Press, 2018), 13–38; Candace Bailey, 'The Challenge of Domesticity in Men's Manuscripts in Restoration England', in *Beyond Boundaries: Rethinking Music Circulation in Early Modern England*, ed. Linda Phyllis Austern, Candace Bailey, and Amanda Eubanks Winkler (Bloomington and Indianapolis: Indiana University Press, 2017), 114–26; Katherine R. Larson, *The Matter of Song in Early Modern England: Texts in and of the Air* (Oxford: Oxford University Press, 2019), 96–109; Mary Chan, 'Drolls, Drolleries and Mid-Seventeenth-Century Dramatic Music in England', *Royal Musical Association Research Chronicle*, 15 (1979): 117–73.

play ballads and dramatic extracts.[2] The present study proposes that the continued circulation of Shakespearean song – here defined as any song performed in part or in full in a Shakespeare play – together with the reading and perhaps performance of those redacted and modified play texts, enabled Shakespeare's plays to remain fresh in public memory throughout the years of theatrical curtailment.

Setting the Musical Scene: A Blurring of Boundaries

When considering the various ways in which Shakespearean song circulated during the Interregnum, it is important to recognise that boundaries of time, professionalism, place, media and genre were less distinct than is sometimes supposed. Dale Randall has warned against the dangers of omitting the period 1642–1660 from studies of seventeenth-century drama, arguing that the stylistic differences between pre-war and Restoration works cannot possibly be understood without taking into consideration material produced in the intervening years.[3] By the same token, new musical practices did not spring up suddenly in 1642 nor end abruptly in 1660. It is therefore important to acknowledge material produced and performed in the years leading up to and directly following the closure of the theatres in order to establish a clear picture of England's musical scene at that time. Accordingly, Table 1.1 lists manuscripts and prints dating from the 1630s to the 1660s.

A particularly blurry boundary existed at this time between the activities of occupational and recreational musicians.[4] Some musical sources for Shakespearean song which have survived were certainly used within private musical circles where occupational and recreational musicians performed side by side. The experiences of composers during this unique period of music-making undoubtedly shaped the music of Restoration Shakespeare. While Charles I was still alive, there appear to have been sporadic employment opportunities for royal musicians: in 1642, for instance, the Cavaliers at Oxford sent for 'Musick, Players and Ladies to entertain the time with', and in October 1643 Prince Rupert and his men 'danced through the

---

[2] Depledge, *Shakespeare's Rise to Cultural Prominence*, 9–10, 13–38. Depledge challenges Gary Taylor's assertion that the late Interregnum was the lowest point in Shakespeare's reception history (Gary Taylor, *Reinventing Shakespeare: A Cultural History from the Restoration to the Present* (New York: Weidenfeld & Nicolson, 1987), 11.

[3] Dale Randall, *Winter Fruit: English Drama 1642–60* (Kentucky: University Press of Kentucky, 1995), 8.

[4] See Bailey, 'The Challenge of Domesticity in Men's Manuscripts', 116–17.

Table 1.1 *Shakespeare song sources, 1630–1660*

Song	Source	Source Type	Text	Music	Tune Direction
AS YOU LIKE IT					
O Sweet Oliver	US-NYp Drexel 5612 (keyboard anthology), c. 1620–1660, ff. 11v–14r	SIA		✓	
	John Playford, *Musicks recreation on the viol, lyra-way* (London: W. G., 1661; Wing P2495), p. 95	MIM		✓	
Under the Greenwood Tree	Philomusus, *The marrow of complements* (London: for Humphrey Moseley, 1654; Wing M719), pp. 153–4	VPA	✓		
What Shall He Have That Killed the Deer?	John Hilton, *Catch that Catch can* (London: for John Benson and John Playford, 1652; Wing H2036), p. 30	SA	✓	✓	
CYMBELINE					
Hark, Hark the Lark	GB-Ob Don.c.57, 1640s–1660s, f. 40v	SA	✓	✓	
HAMLET					
Bonny Sweet Robin/The Tyrant/Fair Angel of England'	US-NYp Drexel 5612, ff. 96v–97r	SIA		✓	
	Loves Return, Or, The Maydens Joy … Tune, Now the Tyrant, or, the Maydens sigh (London: for F. Grove, 1623–1661; EBBA 36485)	B			✓
	The Sea-mans Compass … To the Tune of, The Tyrant hath stoln (London: for F. G., 1623–1661; EBBA 31900)	B			✓
	Good and true, fresh and new Christmas carols (London: E. P. for Francis Coles, 1642; Wing G1036), sig. A5r	SBA			✓
	Loves fierce desire, and hopes of Recovery … To an excellent new Tune, or, Fair Angel of England (London: for T. Vere, 1644–1680; EBBA 30440)	B			✓
	Loves fierce desire, and hopes of Recovery … To a delicate new Tune, or, Fair Angel of England (London: for Tho. Vere, 1644–1682; EBBA 31930)	B			✓

Table 1.1 (cont.)

Song	Source	Source Type	Text	Music	Tune Direction
	Englands Monethly Observations and Predictions, for the Yeare of our Blessed Saviour, 1653 … The Tune is, Faire-Angel of England (London; for W. Gilbertson 1647–1665; EBBA 30880)	B			✓
	The two Jeering Lovers … To a dainty new tune, called, Now the tyrant hath stolen, &c (London: for William Gilbertson, 1647–1665; EBBA 36423)	B			✓
	The Young-womans Complaint … The Tune is, What should a young woman do with an old man, &c. Or, The Tyrant (London: for W. Gilbertson, 1647–1665; EBBA 32045)	B			✓
	Englands Monthly Predictions for this present year 1649 (1648–1649; EBBA 36091)	B			✓
	F-Pc Rés. 1185 (Bull/Cosyn keyboard MS), c. 1652, pp. 268–71	SIA		✓	
	A Courtly new ballad of the Princely wooing of the fair Maid of London by King Edward (for F. Coles, T. Vere and William Gilbertson, 1658–1664; EBBA 31712)	B			✓
	R. Johnson, *The croun garland of golden roses* (London: for W. Gilbertson, 1659; Wing J791), sig. F5v	VA			
In Youth When I Did Love	Francis Kirkman, *The Wits, or, Sport upon sport* (London: for Henry Marsh, 1662; Wing W3218), p. 58	VPA	✓		
How Should I Your True Love Know Walsingham	US-Ws v.a.399 (Charles Shuttleworth's book), c. 1600–c. 1725, f. 16v	VA	✓		
	Bernard Fonteyn, *Monsieur Sullemans soete vryagi* (Amsterdam: Paulus Matthijsz, 1643), sig. A3v	MA		✓	
	D. R. Camphuysen, *Stichtelyche Rymen* (Amsterdam, 1647), p. 100	MA		✓	

	GB-Lbl Add. MS 27879 (Bishop Percy's Manuscript), mid-seventeenth century, f. 47	SBA	✓	
	F-Pc Rés. 1185, no. 58	SIA		✓
HENRY IV, PART 2				
And Robin Hood, Scarlet and John	GB-Lbl Add. MS 27879, f. 8r	SBA	✓	
	The jolly pinder of Wakefield (London: for F. Coles, T. Vere and W. Gilberson, 1658–1664; Wing J895A)	B	✓	
Do Me Right and Dub Me Knight	GB-Ob Mus. F17–19 (Hammond Partbooks), 1655–1666, Altus vol. 3, ff. 50v–51r Tenor vol. 4, ff. 21v–22r; Bassus vol. 5, ff. 50v–51r	Vo	✓	
When Arthur First in Court Began	GB-Lbl Add. MS 27879, f. 16v	SBA	✓	
	Robert Pollard, *Choyce drollery, songs & sonnets* (London: J. G., 1656; Wing C3916), pp. 70–2	VA	✓	
KING LEAR				
Come O'er the Broom Bessie	*M. William Shakespeare, his true chronicle history of the life and death of King Lear* (London: Jane Bell, 1655; Wing S2957), sig. G2r	Dr	✓	
He That Has and a Little Tiny Wit	*M. William Shakespeare, his true chronicle history of the life and death of King Lear*, sigs F2v–F3r	Dr	✓	
MEASURE FOR MEASURE				
Take, O Take those Lips Away	GB-Ob Ashmole 47, c. 1630s–1640s, f. 130v	VPA	✓	
	US-NYp Drexel 4257 (*John Gamble's Commonplace Book*), 1630s–1650s, no. 16	SA	✓	✓
	John Fletcher, *The bloody brother* (London: R. Bishop, 1639; STC 11064), pp. 65–6	Dr	✓	
	John Fletcher, *The tragoedy [sic] of Rollo Duke of Normandy* (London: Leonard Lichfield, 1640; STC 11065), pp. 65–6	Dr	✓	
	US-NYp Drexel 4041 (songs, duets and trios for voice and continuo), c. 1640s, f. 34r	SA	✓	✓
	GB-Och MS Mus. 434 (bass part book containing solo songs by John Wilson), 1650–1675, ff. 1r–2v	SA	✓	✓

Table 1.1 (cont.)

Song	Source	Source Type	Text	Music	Tune Direction
	John Playford, *Select musicall ayres and dialogues for one and two voyces to sing to the theorbo lute or basse violl composed by John Wilson* (London: for John Playford, 1652; Wing P2502), p. 2	MA		✓	
	Musophilus, *The Card of courtship* (London: J. C., 1653; Wing C489), p. 93	VPA	✓		
	GB-Ob Mus.b.1 (songs by John Wilson), c. 1656, f. 19v	SA	✓	✓	
	GB-Lbl Add. MS 11608 (*John Hilton's Manuscript*), 1656–1659, f. 56r	SA	✓	✓	
	John Wilson, *Select ayres and dialogues* (London: W. Godbid, 1659; Wing W2909), p. 1	MA	✓	✓	
THE MERCHANT OF VENICE					
Tell Me Where is Fancy Bred	William Shakespeare, *The most excellent historie of the merchant of Venice* (London: for William Leake, 1652; Wing S2938), sig. E3v	Dr	✓		
THE MERRY WIVES OF WINDSOR					
Come Live With Me and Be My Love	GB-Ob Ashmole 47, f. 100v	VPA	✓		
	GB-Ob Eng. poet. e. 97, c. 1630s–1640s, p. 183	VA	✓		
	US-W's v.a.96 (4), c. 1640, ff. 39v–40v	VA	✓		
	US-NHub Osborn MS b. 150, c. 1644, p. 195	VPA	✓		
	The dying teares of a true Lover forsaken, made upon his Death-bed the houre before his Death (London: for E. Wright, 1648; EBBA 36063)	B			
	GB-Ob Rawl. poet. 117 (the Wase MS), mid-seventeenth century, f. 204 rev.	VA	✓		
	Izaak Walton, *The compleat angler* (London: T. Maxey, 1653; Wing W661), pp. 184–6	VPA	✓		
Fie on Sinful Fantasy	Philomusus, *The marrow of complements*, pp. 151–2	VPA	✓		

Play / Song			Type	Source
A MIDSUMMER NIGHT'S DREAM				
You Spotted Snakes		✓	Dr	*The merry conceited humors of Bottom the weaver* (London: for F. Kirkman and H. Marsh, 1661; Wing S2937), sig. A3
MUCH ADO ABOUT NOTHING				
Sigh No More Ladies	✓	✓	Vo	GB-Och MSS Mus. 736–8, early to mid-seventeenth century vols. 1 and 2, ff. 3r–4r vol. 3, f. 3
		✓	VPA	Philomusus, *The marrow of complements*, p. 152
OTHELLO				
And Let Me the Cannikin Clink		✓	Dr	William Shakespeare, *The tragoedy of Othello, the Moore of Venice* (London: for William Leak, 1655; Wing S2939), p. 31
King Stephen was and a Worthy Peer		✓	SBA	GB-Lbl Add. MS 27879, ff. 291v–292r
		✓	Dr	William Shakespeare, *The tragoedy of Othello, the Moore of Venice*, p. 31
The Willow Song		✓	Dr	William Shakespeare, *The tragoedy of Othello, the Moore of Venice*, p. 77
THE TAMING OF THE SHREW				
It Was the Friar of Orders Grey		✓	MA	John Playford, *The English dancing master* (London: Thomas Harper, 1651; Wing P2477), p. 84
THE TEMPEST				
Full Fathom Five		✓	SA	US-NYp Drexel 4041, ff. 67v–68r
		✓	Vo	US-NH Misc. MS 170. Filmer 4 (partbooks containing John Wilson's vocal trios), mid-seventeenth century
				Cantus primus, 4a, f. 20v
				Cantus secundus, 4b, f. 14v
				Cantus bassus, 4c, f. 20r
	✓		Vo	US-Ws v.a.411 (leaves excised from John Playford's partbooks, GB-Ge MSS Euing R.d.58-61), 1650–1667
				Cantus primus f. 3r
				Cantus secundus f. 4v
				Cantus bassus f. 2r
				Basso continuo f. 1v

Table 1.1 (cont.)

Song	Source	Source Type	Text	Music	Tune Direction
	John Wilson, *Cheerfull ayres or ballads* (London: W. Hall, 1659; Wing W2908) Cantus primus pp. 6–7 Cantus secundus p. 5 Cantus bassus p. 5	SA/Vo	✓	✓	
	GB-Bc Acc. No. 57316, Location No. S747.01 (missing leaves from GB-Eu Dc.1.69), 1660s, p. 87	Vo	✓	✓	
	GB-Ob Mus.d.238 (secundus to the primus GB-Eu DC.1.69), 1660s, f. 48r	Vo	✓	✓	
Where the Bee Sucks	GB-Ob Don.c.57, f. 75r	SA	✓	✓	
	US-NH Misc. MS 170. Filmer 4 Cantus primus, 4a, f. 21r Cantus secundus, 4b, f. 15r Cantus bassus, 4c, f. 20v	Vo	✓	✓	
	US-Ws v.a.411 Cantus primus, f. 3v Cantus secundus, f. 5v Cantus bassus, f. 2v Basso continuo, f. 1v	Vo	✓	✓	
	John Wilson, *Cheerfull ayres or ballads* Cantus primus pp. 8–9 Cantus secundus p. 6 Cantus bassus p. 6	SA/Vo	✓	✓	
	GB-Bc Acc. No. 57316, Location No. S747.01, p. 88 and unnumbered leaf	Vo	✓	✓	
	GB-Ob Mus.d.238, f. 48v	Vo	✓	✓	
	John Hilton, *Catch that catch can* (London: W. Godbid for J. Playford, 1667; Wing H2039), pp. 126–7	SA	✓	✓	
TWELFTH NIGHT					
Come Away Death	Philomusus, *The marrow of complements*, p. 155	VPA	✓		
	US-NYp Drexel 4257, no. 118	SA	✓		
O Mistress Mine	Philomusus, *The marrow of complements*, pp. 154–5	VPA	✓	✓	

Title	Source	Type	✓
O' the Twelfth Day of December	GB-Lbl Add. MS 27879, f. 25v	SBA	✓
	Robert Pollard, *Choyce drollery, songs & sonnets*, pp. 78–80	VA	✓
There Dwelt a Man in Babylon	*An excellent Ballad Intituled, The Constancy of Susanna* (London: for John Wright, 1602–1658; EBBA 30043)	B	✓
THE TWO NOBLE KINSMEN			
The George Alow	*The Sailors onely Delight Shewing the brave Fight between the George-Aloe, the Sweep-stake, and certain Frenchmen at Sea* (London: for F. Coles, 1655–1658; EBBA 30851)	B	✓
THE WINTER'S TALE			
Get You Hence	US-NYp Drexel 4041, ff. 131v–132r	SA	✓
Jog On	John Playford, *The English dancing master*, p. 53	MA	✓✓
	An antidote against melancholy made up in pills (London: Mer. Melancholicus, 1661; Wing D66A), pp. 73–4	VA	✓
Lawn as White as Driven Snow	John Wilson, *Cheerfull ayres or ballads* Cantus primus pp. 64–5 Cantus secundus pp. 46–7 Cantus bassus pp. 46–7	SA	✓
	GB-Ob Mus.d.238, ff. 62v	Vo	✓

* On *Bonny Sweet Robin*'s complex tune associations see Claude M. Simpson, *The British Broadside Ballad and Its Music* (New Brunswick and New Jersey: Rutgers University Press, 1966), 61–4.

Source Type Abbreviations
B   Broadside
Dr Drama
MA Music anthology
MIM Music instruction manual
SA Song anthology (with music)
SBA Song and ballad anthology (text only)
SIA Solo instrumental anthology
VA Verse anthology
Vo Vocal partbook
VPA Verse and prose anthology

streetes openly with musick before them, to one of the Colleges, where after they had stayed about halfe a houre, they returned back againe dancing with the same musick before them'.[5] Leslie Hotson has found evidence that Prince Rupert's men heard a play during that half hour, in which the same group of musicians might conceivably have participated.[6] Once the King fled into exile, however, some of England's leading musical figures – Matthew Locke (b. 1621–1623, d. 1677) and Nicholas Lanier (1588–1666), for instance – also left the country. Lanier seemingly spent his time in the Low Countries feeling 'old, unhappye in a manner in exile, plundered not only of his fortune, but of all his musicall papers, nay, almost of his witts and vertue'.[7] Both composers returned to England prior to the Restoration, during which time Locke composed a substantial body of domestic consort music (transmitted in GB-Lbl Add. MS 17108),[8] and Lanier his Italianate *Hero and Leander* recitative 'Nor com'st thou yet', arguably 'the first use of true recitative in English music'.[9] Yet both also made music with recreational musicians such as Samuel Pepys before and after the Restoration:

> Here I met with Mr. Lock and Pursell, Maisters of Musique; and with them to the Coffee-house into a room next the Water by ourselfs. Here we had a variety of brave Italian and Spanish songs and a Canon for 8 Voc:, which Mr. Lock had newly made on these words: *Domine salvum fac Regem*, an admirable thing.
>
> So home, and find all my good company I had bespoke, as, Coleman and his wife and Laneare [Lanier], Knipp and her surly husband. and good music we had, and among other things, Mrs. Coleman sang my words I set of *Beauty retire*, and I think it is a good song and they praise it mightily.[10]

So music written during the Interregnum for private or domestic performance by mixed groups of occupational and recreational musicians undoubtedly paved the way for the Restoration Shakespeare scores that

---

[5] *England's Memorable Accidents, From the 19th of Decemb. to the 26th of the same, 1642* (London: for Stephen Bowtell, 1642; Thomason E.244[26]), 127; William Ingler, *Certaine informations from severall parts of the kingdome, 30 October–6 November 1643* (London: for Henry Overton, 1643–1644; Thomason E.75[3]), 319.

[6] Leslie Hotson, *The Commonwealth and Restoration Stage* (Cambridge, MA: Harvard University Press, 1928), 9.

[7] Letter from Lanier to Constantijn Huygens describing himself in the third person; quoted in Michael I. Wilson, *Nicholas Lanier: Master of the King's Musick* (London and New York: Routledge, 1994), 202.

[8] Peter Holman, 'Matthew Locke', *Grove Music Online*, http://oxfordmusiconline.com.

[9] Ian Spink, 'Nicholas Lanier (ii)', in 'Lanier family', *Grove Music Online*, http://oxfordmusiconline.com.

[10] *The Diary of Samuel Pepys: A Selection*, ed. Robert Latham (London: Penguin Books, 1985), diary entries 21 February 1660 and 3 January 1666.

followed. Matthew Locke, for instance, went on to contribute music to Restoration adaptations of *The Tempest*, *Henry VIII*, and possibly *Macbeth*.

While the closure of the theatres ruled out large-scale dramatic performances in those venues, organised musical gatherings and performances in private houses blurred the boundary between public and domestic performance space. This is illustrated by the activities of former court musicians Henry Lawes (1596–1662) and John Wilson (1595–1674), who remained in England and found employment as music tutors. Lawes held musical evenings at his house where his friends and students would perform alongside him.[11] Not only did such gatherings dissolve boundaries of musical professionalism, but they also illustrate the point that the terms 'public' and 'domestic' are not mutually exclusive where mid-seventeenth-century performance spaces are concerned. Other similar musical circles around the country, including those attended by Wilson, are well documented, and as we shall see, it was amongst those musical circles that many of our primary sources were used.[12] Since dramatic performances during the period were necessarily clandestine, and since the convention of the public concert grew out of less formal seventeenth-century musical meetings, performances could be both public and domestic, and feature music written and performed by both occupational and recreational musicians.[13]

Owing to further bans on public musical performance, song and ballad repertoire became essentially confined to domestic spaces, a fact which is reflected in the types of Commonwealth sources for Shakespearean songs which have survived. Source types which are present in large numbers in Table 1.1 include song anthologies, broadsides and vocal partbooks, all of which lend themselves superbly to at-home performance, and some of which bear sure sign of it (for instance GB-Lbl Add. MS 11608, discussed later in this section). While previously respected court composers such as Lawes and Wilson may have found ways to survive the Interregnum, life was made more difficult for performing musicians, who were ostracised in the same way as actors. Ballad singers, for instance, were equated with rogues in a ban of 1649:

> Ballad singers, wheresoever they are or may be apprehended, shall forfeit all Books, Pamphlets, Ballads and Papers by them exposed to sale, and shall,

[11] Ian Spink, 'Henry Lawes', *Grove Music Online*, http://oxfordmusiconline.com.
[12] See Alan Howard, 'A Midcentury Musical Friendship: Silas Taylor and Matthew Locke', in *Beyond Boundaries*, ed. Austern, Bailey, and Eubanks Winkler, 127–49, and Bruce Bellingham, 'The Musical Circle of Anthony Wood in Oxford during the Commonwealth and Restoration', *Journal of the Viola da Gamba Musical Society of America*, 19 (1982): 6–70.
[13] The Editors of *Encyclopædia Britannica*, 'Concert', www.britannica.com/art/concert.

> by such as shall by vertue of this Act seize upon them, be conveyed and carryed to the House of Correction, there to be whipt as common Rogues, and then dismissed.[14]

That act could be viewed as an attack on the politically explosive material contained in some mid-century ballads rather than on singing as a profession. An act against vagrants which came into effect in 1657, though, leaves no doubt about the lowly status of musical performers and the impossibility of earning a living that way:

> And be it further Enacted ... That if any person or persons commonly called Fidlers or Minstrels, shall at any time after the said First day of July, be taken playing, fidling and making musick in any Inn, Ale-house or Tavern, or shall be taken proffering themselves, or desiring, or intreating any person or persons to hear them play ... That every such person and persons so taken shall be adjudged ... and declared to be Rogues, Vagabonds and Sturdy Beggers, and shall be proceeded against and punished ...[15]

The picture that emerges, then, is of a society where musical performance – particularly performance of song repertoire – could thrive only in clandestine or private circumstances.

Another blurry boundary prevailed between the two systems of literary transmission that Arthur F. Marotti claims competed and co-existed in England from the sixteenth to the eighteenth century – manuscript and print.[16] While print became increasingly popular for transmission of the song lyric it did not quickly overtake manuscript culture, and manuscript certainly remained the preferred medium for musical notation until after the Restoration.[17] Indeed, the close relationships between certain manuscript and printed collections hint at scribal copying; Table 1.1's GB-Eu Dc.1.69, for instance, bears close enough resemblance to John Wilson's printed *Cheerfull ayres* to suggest filiation.[18] Twenty-three of the fifty-six sources listed in Table 1.1 transmit music: of those twenty-three, fourteen are manuscripts and nine are prints. In the case of purely textual sources,

---

[14] *Acts and Ordinances of the Interregnum, 1642–1660*, 3 vols., ed. C. H. Firth and R. S. Rait (Ontario: Tannritchie Publishing, 2005), vol. II, 252.

[15] *An act against vagrants, and wandring, idle, dissolute persons. At the Parliament begun at Westminster the 17th day of September, an. Dom. 1656* (London: Hen. Hills and John Field, 1657; Wing E972), 2–3.

[16] Arthur F. Marotti, *Manuscript, Print and the English Renaissance Lyric* (Ithaca, NY, and London: Cornell University Press, 1995), 1.

[17] Rebecca Herissone, *Musical Creativity in Restoration England* (Cambridge and New York: Cambridge University Press, 2013), 61.

[18] See John P. Cutts, 'Seventeenth-Century Songs and Lyrics in Edinburgh University Library Music MS DC.1.69', *Musica Disciplina*, 13 (1959): 169–94 (170).

however, only seven are manuscripts while fifteen are prints.[19] Where the transmission of Shakespearean song during the Interregnum is concerned, those figures certainly reflect a preference of manuscript for music and print for the song lyric.

If publication is defined as the communication of a work to others, then manuscripts and prints may both be classed as publications.[20] Harold Love emphasises the importance of differentiating between 'an initiatory act and a replicatory act', and it is the initiatory act of publication which this study measures; in other words, a manuscript and a print transmission of a song both have a value of one.[21] It is true that early modern manuscripts were not usually reproduced (though sometimes they were bought and sold), and yet multiple copies of one book were produced during a print run. The actual dissemination and readership of prints and manuscripts, however, is impossible to measure and must therefore remain unquantifiable. The concept of manuscripts as scribal publications has been developed by Love and A. I. Doyle.[22] Scribal publication can be described as the production of a manuscript for the purpose of dissemination, a description to which many of the sources collated in Table 1.1 answer. GB-Lbl Add. 11608, for example, was probably copied for immediate use by John Hilton's (1599–1657) circle, and US-Ws v.a.411 was amongst loose papers assembled by John Playford (1623–1687) for use by the Old Jewry Music Society (see the section 'The Transmission of Shakespearean Song during the Interregnum').[23]

New kinds of drama emerged during the Interregnum, and the fluidity of the boundaries between those various genres enabled the continued circulation and performance (albeit surreptitious or domestic) of Shakespeare's plays and songs. This increase in the variety of dramatic forms was perhaps partly due to efforts to circumvent the 1642 ban on stage plays. Drolls and drolleries, for instance, were distinct from plays, and some Commonwealth Shakespeare abridgements, which are discussed

---

[19] The remaining sources transmit neither music nor Shakespearean text; only their tune directions connect them with Shakespeare.
[20] A. I. Doyle, 'Publication by Members of the Religious Orders', in *Book Production and Publishing in Britain, 1375–1475*, ed. Jeremy Griffiths and Derek Pearsall (Cambridge: Cambridge University Press, 1989), 109–23 (110).
[21] Harold Love, *Scribal Publication in Seventeenth-Century England* (Oxford: Clarendon Press, 1993), 44.
[22] Doyle, 'Publication by Members of the Religious Orders'; Love, *Scribal Publication in Seventeenth-Century England*.
[23] Mary Chan, 'John Hilton's Manuscript British Library Add. MS 11608', *Music & Letters*, 60.4 (1979): 440–9 (444); Richard Charteris, *An Annotated Catalogue of the Music Manuscripts in the Folger Shakespeare Library, Washington, D.C.* (New York: Pendragon Press, 2005), 226.

in more detail later, fall within this category and transmit Shakespearean song.[24] If they were performed during the Interregnum, such adaptations not only prolonged previous theatrical and musical practice, but also paved the way for Shakespearean adaptation after the Restoration.

In music too, indistinct boundaries between genres facilitated performance possibilities, while the intersection of drama and music during the period crucially prefigured the structure of Restoration Shakespeare. The pre-Restoration musical productions of William Davenant were ambiguously titled *The First Days Entertainment at Rutland-House, By Declamations and Musick*, and *The Siege of Rhodes Made a Representation by the Art of Prospective in Scenes, And the Story sung in Recitative Musick*; the latter was in fact registered with the Stationers' Company as a 'maske'.[25] Masques survived the 1650s by setting aside their traditional courtly rhetoric, and became instead musical dramas which were no doubt influential on the types of Restoration productions that emerged.[26] The earlier court masques, though, were not forgotten: the subject matter of Thomas Jordan's *Cupid His Coronation* (1654), for instance, clearly displays nostalgia for lost courtly traditions.[27] John Playford's *English dancing master* (1651), furthermore, ostensibly preserves old English 'country' dances, and yet that material was sourced from theatrical works, particularly the antimasque and revels sections of Ben Jonson's court masques. Under the pretence, then, of publishing an anthology which harked back to simpler pre-war times and folk customs, Playford (a known royalist) used those popular, rustic tunes to remind England of her lost courtly traditions and ensure the survival of those musical forms.[28]

Though the activities of occupational ballad singers were curtailed during the Interregnum, the music and words of pre-Civil War ballads, including those appropriated by Shakespeare, continued in circulation and performance. There appears to have arisen, though, a boundary of performance practice between those ballads and modern vocal music, as

---

[24] See Chan, 'Drolls, Drolleries and Mid-Seventeenth-Century Dramatic Music'.
[25] *A Transcript of the Registers of the Worshipful Company of Stationers, from 1640–1708, A.D.*, 3 vols. (London: privately printed, 1913), vol. II, 81.
[26] See Andrew Walkling, *Masque and Opera in England, 1656–1688* (Abingdon: Routledge, 2017), 5–19, and Susan Wiseman, *Drama and Politics in the English Civil War* (Cambridge: Cambridge University Press, 1998), 126–9.
[27] See Amanda Eubanks Winkler, *Music, Dance, and Drama in Early Modern English Schools* (Cambridge: Cambridge University Press, 2020), 92, 98–9.
[28] John Playford, *The English dancing master: or, Plaine and easie rules for the dancing of country dances* (London: Thomas Harper, 1651; Thomason E.626[7]). On Playford's political intentions, see Keith Whitlock, 'John Playford's *The English Dancing Master* 1650/51 as Cultural Politics', *Folk Music Journal*, 7.5 (1999): 548–78, and Peter Lindenbaum, 'John Playford: Music and Politics in the Interregnum', *Huntington Library Quarterly*, 64.1–2 (2001): 124–38.

Margaret Cavendish, a writer and music enthusiast, was at pains to point out to the 'Harmonious Voice[d]' Eleonora Duarti:

> for the Vulgar and Plainer a Voice is, the Better it is for an old Ballad … neither should Old Ballads be Sung so much in a Tune as in a Tone, which Tone is betwixt Speaking and Singing … and Ballads are only Proper to be Sung by Spinsters, and that only in Cold Winter Nights, when a Company of Good Huswifes are Drawing a Thread of Flax …[29]

It is unclear whether those so-called 'old ballads' were considered musically distinct from the modern, oftentimes royalist ballads which were banned in 1649 (see earlier in this section). Table 1.1 demonstrates that early ballads such as 'Walsingham', 'Bonny Sweet Robin' and 'O Sweet Oliver' – which certainly pre-dated their use by Shakespeare – continued to circulate during the Interregnum, and that ballads printed during the period continued to be sung to older tunes. It is perhaps to this repertoire that Cavendish referred.

The Transmission of Shakespearean Song during the Interregnum

Table 1.1 lists sources of Shakespearean song created around the time of the closure of the theatres. Of course, many manuscripts and broadsides are at best only vaguely dateable. It must be assumed, furthermore, that sources created prior to the period in question continued to be used and shared. The table confirms, nonetheless, that Shakespearean songs remained in vogue and were still copied out, printed, sung and read though performance of their respective plays was banned. My basis for the inclusion of songs in Table 1.1 was to confine the enquiry to those which were likely sung – either in full or in part – in Shakespeare's plays, thereby excluding spoken references to pre-existing songs. Ross Duffin has thoroughly covered all musical references in the Shakespearean canon;[30] the present study is rather an examination of the circulation of songs *performed* during the plays. It is true that a certain amount of conjecture is necessary to determine whether short snippets of song text were spoken or sung, stage directions for singing being sparse and inconsistent in the First Folio. We cannot know, moreover, whether popular songs which pre-dated their use by Shakespeare

---

[29] *Sociable Letters: Margaret Cavendish*, ed. James Fitzmaurice (Ontario: Broadview Press, 2004), letter 202.
[30] Ross W. Duffin, *Shakespeare's Songbook* (New York and London: W. W. Norton & Company, 2004).

were certainly sung to the tunes which have survived. Nonetheless, for the purposes of developing the argument it is necessary to postulate on a case-by-case basis which songs were sung and to what tunes. Only first editions of printed anthologies are listed, except where later editions transmit new material, John Hilton's *Catch that Catch can* (1667) being a case in point.

Table 1.1's dramatic sources (Dr) point to a desire to continue theatrical practices, at least in print, while the theatres were closed. Those sources may have been privately read or used in the types of at-home performances described in 'Setting the Musical Scene' and thus they played a vital role in keeping Shakespeare's plays and songs current despite the ban on playing. Three of Shakespeare's plays were printed in quarto during the 1650s, complete with their songs: *The Merchant of Venice* (1652), *King Lear* (1655) and *Othello* (1655). Two Shakespearean drolls also maintained a degree of original musical content: *The merry conceited humors of Bottom the weaver* (1661), and 'The Grave-makers, out of *Hamlet* Prince of Denmark' in *The Wits, or, Sport upon sport* (1662). Francis Kirkman's preface to *The Wits* suggests that the drolls contained in that volume were privately acted when the theatres were closed.[31] Meanwhile, Shakespearean songs continued to circulate independently of their dramatic associations in song and ballad anthologies, vocal partbooks, solo keyboard anthologies, verse and prose anthologies, and broadsides. All told, I have traced thirty-two Shakespearean songs in sources created during the period. Since those transmissions are too numerous to consider in detail, the present chapter will proceed by examining the contribution of three important musicians – John Wilson, John Playford and John Hilton – through the lens of those songs which circulated most widely.

Six of the thirty-two songs occur more frequently than others: 'Take, o take those lips away' (*Measure for Measure*), 'Come live with me and be my love' (*The Merry Wives of Windsor*), 'Bonny sweet Robin' and 'Walsingham' (*Hamlet*), and 'Full fathom five' and 'Where the bee sucks' (*The Tempest*). The *Tempest* songs were retained in Restoration adaptations of the play, though set to new music at various points, proving that their continued circulation during the Interregnum ensured their viability for Restoration audiences. 'Come live with me' and the two *Hamlet* songs certainly predated their use by Shakespeare, and it is probable that those snippets were still sung to their original tunes in Restoration performances.[32]

---

[31] Francis Kirkman, *The Wits, or, Sport upon sport* (London: for Henry Marsh, 1662; Wing W3218), 16.
[32] See F. W. Sternfeld, *Music in Shakespearean Tragedy*, 2nd ed. (London: Routledge and Kegan Paul, 1967), 68–78, 59–61; and Duffin, *Shakespeare's Songbook*, 103–4, 72–4, 422–4.

In the case of pre-existing songs, it is impossible to determine whether they continued to circulate because of their general popularity or because of their association with Shakespeare. Indeed, the fact that only fragments of those songs were sung in the plays perhaps weakens the Shakespearean argument. The songs which likely originated with their plays, however, surely retained their Shakespearean associations when copied into anthologies. It is significant that those highly popular songs 'Take, o take those lips away', 'Full fathom five' and 'Where the bee sucks' all circulated during the Interregnum in musical settings by the composer John Wilson. Wilson was connected with the King's Men from 1614 to 1629 and became a prominent musical figure in Oxford during the Interregnum. The evidence suggests that Wilson's music, ideal as it was for private performance, served as a bridge between pre- and post-Restoration Shakespeare, keeping dramatic songs alive and relevant while England's theatres remained dark.

Of the songs that make up this study, the most widely transmitted during the Interregnum was 'Take, o take those lips away', used by Shakespeare in *Measure for Measure* and later set to music by Wilson.[33] The song's evident popularity may attest to a protracted enthusiasm for the play, given that William Davenant's *Law against Lovers* – an amalgamation of *Measure for Measure* and *Much Ado About Nothing* – was the first Shakespearean adaptation to be staged after theatres reopened.[34] Intriguingly though, Davenant chose to replace 'Take, o take those lips away' with new songs. Charles Gildon reinstated 'Take, o take' in his own, later adaptation of the play, *Measure for Measure, Or Beauty the Best Advocate* (1700), though it was likely set to new music, possibly by John Weldon.[35] Following Davenant's revival, Wilson's music was reprinted in one new anthology compiled by John Playford (*The treasury of musick*, 1669), and that print was identical to Playford's previous prints of the song.[36] It seems, then, that Wilson's song's evident popularity rests mainly in the Caroline era and Interregnum, while Davenant's omission and Gildon/Weldon's presumed modernisation serve as examples of the wider desire to update Shakespeare for Restoration audiences.

---

[33] It is generally agreed that Wilson's musical setting – the earliest setting which has survived – must post-date *Measure for Measure*'s first performance since Wilson would have been too young to have composed it in 1604.

[34] Davenant's *Law against Lovers* was performed in 1662, though not printed until 1673.

[35] Roger Fiske, *English Theatre Music in the Eighteenth Century* (London: Oxford University Press, 1973), 14.

[36] See Gary Taylor and Andrew J. Sabol, 'Middleton, Music, and Dance', in *Thomas Middleton and Early Modern Textual Culture: A Companion to the Collected Works*, ed. Gary Taylor and John Lavagnino (Oxford: Clarendon Press, 2007), 119–81 (167).

The song's intertheatricality may have been another reason behind its protracted popularity, given its secondary use in the collaboratively written *Bloody Brother* or *Rollo Duke of Normandy*, performed by Shakespeare's company around 1616 and published in 1639 and 1640. In *Rollo* – allegedly co-written by John Fletcher, Ben Jonson, George Chapman and Philip Massinger – the song acquired a supplementary, somewhat lewd second verse which is stylistically incongruous with the first.[37] Scholars have long disagreed on the song's provenance: while some argue that verse one is the work of Shakespeare and verse two the creation of the authors of *Rollo*, others conclude that the song originated in *Rollo* and was a late interpolation for a Jacobean revival, possibly an adaptation by Thomas Middleton (1580–1627), of *Measure for Measure*.[38] All sources with the exception of *Measure for Measure* transmit the second verse. Wherever and however the song originated, the existence of a second verse would certainly have rendered it apt for abstract performance at pre-Restoration musical gatherings.

Wilson's music for 'Take, o take' circulated in manuscript and in anthologies printed by John Playford. One manuscript in particular, GB-Lbl Add. MS 11608, shows distinct signs of domestic consumption and aural transmission, and was likely used within its author John Hilton's own musical circle.[39] Such gatherings enabled Shakespearean song to survive the Interregnum's theatrical and musical drought, thus reinforcing Shakespeare's suitability for performance and adaptation when theatres reopened. Hilton's and two other unidentified hands are present in the manuscript, and while it is true that 'Take, o take' was copied by another scribe than Hilton, Mary Chan has shown that all three scribes were involved in the compilation of the volume from its inception.[40] The volume as a whole was clearly used for performance and shows signs of aural transmission: on folio 63v, for instance, 'The treble I tooke & prickt / downe as mr Thorpe sung it'. The version of 'Take o take' transmitted

---

[37] On *The Bloody Brother*'s authorship, see Dinah Birch, ed., 'Bloody Brother, The, or Rollo, Duke of Normandy', in *Oxford Companion to English Literature*, ed. Dinah Birch, online ed. (Oxford University Press, 2009), http://www-oxfordreference-com.

[38] On arguments for Shakespearean authorship of verse one, see John H. Long, *Shakespeare's Use of Music: The Final Comedies* (Gainesville: University of Florida Press, 1961), 23; Frederick W. Sternfeld, 'Appendix II: *Take, O Take Those Lips Away*', in *Measure for Measure*, ed. J. W. Lever (London: Methuen & Co., 1965), 201. For the Jacobean interpolation theory, see E. K. Chambers, *William Shakespeare: A Study of Facts and Problems*, 2 vols. (Oxford: Clarendon Press, 1930), vol. I, 455; Taylor and Sabol, 'Middleton, Music, and Dance', 167–8. For postulation of an anonymous archetypal song anterior to both plays, see Peter J. Seng, *The Vocal Songs in the Plays of Shakespeare* (Cambridge, MA: Harvard University Press, 1967), 183.

[39] Chan, 'John Hilton's Manuscript', 444–5.

[40] Chan, 'John Hilton's Manuscript', 443.

in GB-Lbl Add. MS 11608 differs notably from the song's other sources by way of its highly ornamented melody line.[41] The ornamentation itself bears further testament to aural transmission, since the in-score ornaments appear to have been added by the scribe around his initial transcription,[42] while the elaborate figures at the foot of the page seem typical of the Italianate performance style in vogue during the latter half of the century.[43]

Wilson's three-voice arrangements of Robert Johnson's Jacobean settings of 'Full fathom five' and 'Where the bee sucks' also belong to an era when staged performances of *The Tempest* were a distant memory and dramatic song was performed in non-theatrical settings.[44] Wilson's rearrangement of Johnson's solo songs as part songs perhaps represents an early effort to update Shakespeare for a new cultural landscape, namely for private musical meetings. Wilson's *Cheerfull ayres* (1659) preserved Johnson's solo songs with their basso continuo parts alongside Wilson's own settings, thus providing a variety of performance possibilities for recreational music makers. *The Tempest* was revived and rewritten as *The Enchanted Island* for the Restoration stage in 1667, and it is likely that new music was composed by John Banister (1624/5–1679) for that production.[45] That being so, as with his adaptation of *Measure for Measure*, Davenant chose to update *The Tempest*'s music despite the survival and circulation of Wilson's songs past the Restoration. If Wilson's settings were as popular during the Interregnum as the quantity of surviving sources suggests, it is not surprising that Davenant would want to replace music associated with the period of theatrical curtailment with music that more closely reflected the excitingly new musical and dramatic styles of Restoration theatre.

Of the sources for the *Tempest* songs collated in Table 1.1, GB-Ob Don.c.57 alone transmits Johnson's solo version rather than Wilson's later arrangements; that version of 'Where the bee sucks' is nonetheless attributed to Wilson, implying that Wilson's Commonwealth-era settings

---

[41] For a discussion of variants between sources, see Taylor and Sabol, 'Middleton, Music, and Dance', 167.
[42] Taylor and Sabol, 'Middleton, Music, and Dance', 167.
[43] For a discussion of aural transmission and Italian vocal style, see Rebecca Herissone, 'Daniel Henstridge and the Aural Transmission of Music in Restoration England', in *Beyond Boundaries*, ed. Austern, Bailey, and Eubanks Winkler, 165–86 (171–7).
[44] John P. Cutts's view that the *Tempest* songs printed by Wilson were his arrangements of Johnson's originals is here accepted: 'Robert Johnson: King's Musician in His Majesty's Public Entertainment', *Music & Letters*, 36.2 (1955): 110–25 (111).
[45] See Matthew Locke, *Dramatic Music*, ed. Michael Tilmouth, Musica Britannica, 51 (London: Stainer and Bell, 1986), xviii, and Amanda Eubanks Winkler, 'A Thousand Voices: Performing Ariel', in *A Feminist Companion to Shakespeare*, 2nd ed., ed. Dympna Callaghan (Chichester: Wiley Blackwell, 2016), 520–39 (529).

replaced Johnson's original to the degree that Wilson was often mistakenly credited as the composer. All other sources for the two songs – with the exception of US-NYp Drexel 4041 which transmits only the text – are vocal partbooks, ideal volumes for use at informal musical gatherings. One set of partbooks in particular was unquestionably used in this context: GB-Bc Acc. No. 57316 constitutes leaves removed from GB-Eu Dc.1.69, a manuscript which transmits the cantus primus of many items from *Cheerfull ayres*; the corresponding cantus secundus partbook is held at the Bodleian Library (GB-Ob Mus, d. 238), and the whereabouts of the bassus book is unknown.[46] Copied by Edward Lowe (*c.* 1610–1682) – an Oxford-based organist and music tutor – those partbooks were certainly connected with the mid-century musical circle in Oxford of which Wilson was himself a member, and would therefore have been used by local musicians and students.[47] The version of 'Where the bee sucks' transmitted in the Edinburgh/Birmingham manuscript provides three additional and unique verses, allegedly 'made by Mr Smith secretary to the Archbishop of Canterbury' and circulated to Lowe by 'Madame Trumbull'. The fact that Smith, Trumbull and Lowe were near neighbours is further testament to the manuscript's use by local performers.[48] The additional verses recast the protagonist – Shakespeare's Ariel – as Cupid, thus substituting the song's theatrical context for a more commonplace mythological theme appropriate to Interregnum performance settings.

Two further sets of partbooks transmitting Wilson's *Tempest* songs confirm the songs' popularity in locations outside of Wilson's immediate sphere, and one set in particular displays signs of use into the Restoration. US-NH Misc. MS 170 Filmer 4 belonged within a Kent-based musical circle, possibly associated with the recreational musician Edward Filmer (d. 1650), and transmits early Restoration works such as John Banister's music for *The Indian Queen* (first performed 1664) alongside pre-publication versions of Wilson's songs and music from earlier periods.[49] The presence of those later pieces, copied onto blank pages left between earlier transcriptions of Jacobean and Caroline music, gestures to the co-existence of old and new musical styles and repertoire during the early Restoration.

---

[46] *Edinburgh University Library Manuscript Ms, Dc. 169*, ed. Elise Bickford Jorgens, English Song 1600–1675, vol. 8 (New York and London: Garland Publishing, 1987), v.

[47] See Bellingham, '"The Musical Circle of Anthony Wood', 33–4; Cutts, 'Seventeenth-Century Songs and Lyrics', 170; Eubanks Winkler, 'A Thousand Voices', 531.

[48] See Cutts, 'Seventeenth-Century Songs and Lyrics', 172; Eubanks Winkler, 'A Thousand Voices', 531–3.

[49] Robert Ford, 'The Filmer Manuscripts: A Handlist', *Notes*, 34.4 (1978): 814–25 (817).

US-Ws v.a.411 comprises leaves removed from a set of partbooks (GB-Ge MSS Euing R.d.58–61) for the purpose of performance. The leaves in question, copied by Playford, were originally among loose papers compiled for use by the Old Jewry Music Society. They transmit Wilson's versions of the two *Tempest* songs, along with three other Wilson songs.[50] Playford published 'Where the bee sucks' and other songs from those papers in his 1667 print of John Hilton's collection *Catch that Catch can*. In Playford's preface to that edition, his acknowledgement of his friends' 'Excellent Musical performances, when it was thrown before you in loose Papers' perhaps identifies the Folger leaves and their use by that particular musical circle.[51] If so, Playford's 1667 print serves as a link between Commonwealth musical performances and the Restoration.

A probable fourth Wilson setting of a Shakespearean song came into print during the Interregnum, though apparently it neither circulated as widely as his other offerings nor survived into the Restoration. 'Lawn as white as driven snow' from *The Winter's Tale* was printed in *Cheerfull ayres* and copied into GB-Ob Mus.d.238 (cantus secundus to the treble volume GB-Eu Dc.1.69, from whence the leaves containing 'Lawn as white' have been removed and lost).[52] Even pre-Civil War, the circulation of songs from *The Winter's Tale* was somewhat limited, indicating a less strong written and/or performance tradition than the *Tempest* songs. *The Winter's Tale*, unlike *The Tempest*, was certainly not revived for the Restoration stage, an indication that its popularity had waned.

The preponderance of publications by Playford listed in Table 1.1 is unsurprising since he dominated the music publishing scene from 1651 to 1684.[53] Crucially, while Playford emerged as something of a champion of John Wilson's music, printing more than fifty of Wilson's songs all told during his publishing career, he was also largely responsible for the continued print circulation of those pre-Shakespearean popular tunes which may well have been retained in performances of Restoration Shakespeare.[54] His *English Dancing Master* (1651) and *Music's Recreation on the Viol* (1661)

---

[50] Charteris, *An Annotated Catalogue*, 226.
[51] John Hilton, *Catch that Catch can* (London: W. Godbid for J. Playford, 1667; Wing H2039), i. See also Stacey Houck, 'John Playford and the English Musical Market', in *'Noyses, sounds and sweet aires': Music in Early Modern England*, ed. Jessie Ann Owens (Washington, DC: The Folger Shakespeare Library, 2006), 48–61 (50).
[52] Cutts, 'Seventeenth-Century Songs and Lyrics', 172.
[53] Margaret Dean-Smith, 'John Playford (i)', rev. Nicholas Temperley, *Grove Music Online* (2013), http://oxfordmusiconline.com.
[54] Vincent Duckles, 'The "Curious" Art of John Wilson (1595–1674): An Introduction to his Songs and Lute Music', *Journal of the American Musicological Society*, 7.2 (1954): 93–112 (94).

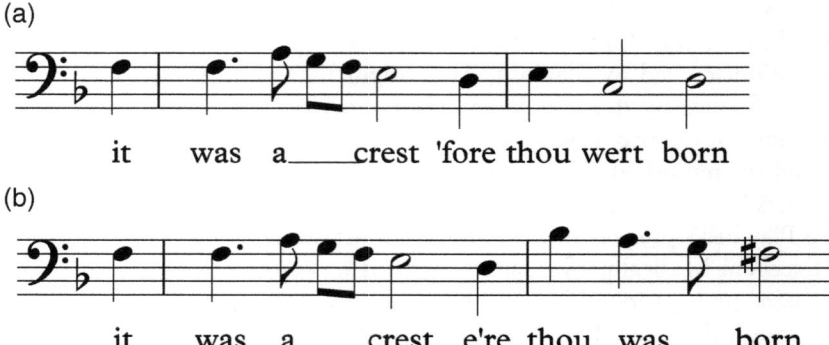

Music Example 1.1   Fourth phrase of 'What shall he have that killed the deer': (a) Us-Ws v.a.409, f. 17r and (b) *Catch that Catch can* (London, 1652), 30.

transmit the popular pre-Civil War tunes 'The friar and the nun' ('It was the friar of orders grey', *The Taming of the Shrew*), 'Jog on' (*The Winter's Tale*) and 'Hunts up' ('O sweet Oliver', *As You Like It*).[55] It was not unusual for pedagogical volumes to contain popular old tunes, which all three of those were by the mid-seventeenth century. The backward-looking, nostalgic undercurrent of *The English dancing master* has already been noted, and the fact that it ran to eighteen editions, the last dated 1721, is testament to the enduring appeal of that repertoire during the Interregnum and Restoration. Petruchio's snippet of 'It was the friar' was retained in John Lacey's Restoration adaptation *Sauny the Scot or The Taming of the Shrew* (performed in 1667 and printed in 1698), and was presumably still sung to its original tune, printed by Playford during the Interregnum.

Playford's print of Hilton's *Catch that Catch can* (1652) demonstrates the desire to update and refresh original Shakespearean song settings for Commonwealth consumers, a trend which would continue into the Restoration. *Catch that Catch can* transmits a musically up-to-date version of the Shakespeare song 'What shall he have that killed the deer?' (*As You Like It*). The song is also present in the pre-Civil War catch anthology US-Ws v.a.409, and that version seems to belong to an earlier musical era than the printed form. Music Example 1.1, for instance, shows the manuscript's simple, modal version of the fourth phrase of the song compared with Hilton's more elaborate and harmonically up-to-date cadential figure.

---

[55] See the relevant entries in Duffin, *Shakespeare's Songbook* for those songs' histories.

Though v.a. 409 is excluded from Table 1.1 on the grounds that it may have been compiled as early as 1625,[56] its importance must be acknowledged since the modernised version of its music transmitted in *Catch that Catch can* illustrates an effort — as do Wilson's *Tempest* trios — to update Shakespearean song for a unique musical era, a practice which continued in earnest when public playing resumed.

That Shakespeare's plays and their songs survived the closure and even demolition of England's theatres is borne out not only by the zeal of their Restoration adaptors, but also by their uninterrupted presence in manuscript and print through the Interregnum. Early modern anthologists played no small part in prolonging Shakespeare's popularity; dramatic songs were routinely treated as paratexts to be read and sung independently of their plays, and yet surely retained their dramatic associations for consumers. Musicians meanwhile circumnavigated the various restrictions placed upon musical performance, and their irrepressible enthusiasm for dramatic songs fuelled the phenomenon that would come to be known as Restoration Shakespeare.

---

[56] Ross W. Duffin, 'Catching the Burthen: A New Round of Shakespearean Musical Hunting', *Studies in Music from the University of Western Ontario*, 19–20 (2000): 1–15 (9–15). For an argument for the later date of *c.* 1650 for US-Ws v.a.409, see Laura Estill, *Dramatic Extracts in Seventeenth-Century English Manuscripts: Watching, Reading, Changing Plays* (Newark: University of Delaware Press, 2015), 154, n. 45.

CHAPTER 2

Heroic Shakespeare at Lincoln's Inn Fields

Stephen Watkins

MACDUFF   From *Duncan's* Grave, methinks, I hear a groan
That call's a loud for justice.
LADY MACDUFF   If the Throne
Was by *Macbeth* ill gain'd, Heavens Justice may,
Without your Sword, sufficient vengeance pay.
Usurpers lives have but a short extent,
Nothing lives long in a strange Element.
MACDUFF   My Countreys dangers call for my defence
Against the bloudy Tyrants violence.
LADY MACDUFF   I am afraid you have some other end,
Than meerly *Scotland's* freedom to defend.
You'd raise your self, whilst you wou'd him dethrone;
And shake his Greatness, to confirm your own.
That purpose will appear, when rightly scan'd,
But usurpation at the second hand.
Good Sir, recall your thoughts.
MACDUFF   What if I shou'd
Assume the Scepter for my Countrey's good?
Is that an usurpation? can it be
Ambition to procure the liberty
Of this sad Realm; which does by Treason bleed?
That which provokes, will justifie the deed.[1]

This fraught exchange between Lady Macduff and her husband, coming as it does midway through William Davenant's adaptation of *Macbeth* (1664), neatly combines the aesthetic and political impulses that drive the play to its highly charged but ultimately restorative conclusion. Macduff feels sure he must act to stop the tyrannical Macbeth, newly crowned as

---

I am grateful to Niall Allsopp, Amanda Eubanks Winkler, Richard Schoch, and Sarah Smyth for their comments on an earlier draft of this chapter.

[1] William Davenant, *Macbeth: A Tragedy*, in *Five Restoration Adaptations of Shakespeare*, ed. Christopher Spencer (Urbana: University of Illinois Press, 1965), 3.2.9–28.

King of Scotland, from wreaking havoc across the realm; he thus seeks to avenge the murdered Duncan and secure the long-term safety of the nation. Lady Macduff, however, questions her husband's motives for intervening in affairs of state that should not, by rights, concern him. She interrogates his planned course of action and openly challenges his personal motives for proposing it. Macduff, on the one hand, insists that if defending '*Scotland's* freedom' requires him to wrest the reins of power from a usurping monarch, then he is surely justified in doing so. His wife, on the other hand, sees nothing in his response to the crisis but hypocrisy and self-interest: such manoeuvring, to her eyes, would merely constitute 'usurpation at the second hand'.

Davenant adapted *Macbeth* sometime before November 1664, for the Duke of York's Company, his own patent theatre company housed at Lincoln's Inn Fields. The earliest performance we know of occurred on 5 November, when Samuel Pepys mentions seeing it for the first time.[2] Alongside its topical politics, which I will discuss in detail later, this new scene between the Macduffs flaunts another radical departure from its Jacobean parent text. Eschewing Shakespeare's blank verse in favour of the heroic couplet, a poetic form newly fashionable among Restoration playwrights, the Macduffs' dialogue generates a rhetorical energy that animates the ensuing debate about the limits of monarchical authority in ways its contemporary audiences could hardly fail to register. Davenant had been experimenting with the heroic couplet since at least 1656, when he wrote the libretto for his through-composed opera, *The Siege of Rhodes*, first produced privately at Rutland House and later publicly at the Cockpit theatre in Drury Lane.[3] Following the official reopening of London's theatres at the Restoration, Davenant expanded *Rhodes* into two parts, now presenting them as spoken plays rather than as operatic entertainments,

---

[2] William Van Lennep, Emmett L. Avery, Arthur H. Scouten, George Winchester Stone, Jr., and Charles Beecher Hogan, eds., *The London Stage, 1660–1800*, 5 parts in 11 vols. (Carbondale: Southern Illinois University Press, 1960–1968), vol. I, 85. Dating Davenant's adaptation remains problematic; see Arthur H. Scouten, 'The Premiere of Davenant's Adaptation of *Macbeth*', in *Shakespeare and the Dramatic Tradition: Essays in Honor of S. F. Johnson*, ed. W. R. Elton and William B. Long (Cranbury, NJ: Associated University Presses, 1989), 286–93. In what follows, I add weight to Christopher Spencer's argument for a date of late 1663 or early 1664, with the production Pepys saw in November 1664 essentially reflecting Davenant's text as we find it in both the 1674 printed quarto and the Yale manuscript copy. See Christopher Spencer, ed., *Davenant's Macbeth from the Yale Manuscript: An Edition, with a Discussion of the Relation of Davenant's Text to Shakespeare's* (New Haven, CT: Yale University Press, 1961), 15–16.

[3] See Andrew R. Walkling, *Masque and Opera in England, 1656–88* (Abington: Routledge, 2017), 143–92; Stephen Watkins, 'The Protectorate Playhouse: William Davenant's Cockpit in the 1650s', *Shakespeare Bulletin*, 37.1 (2019): 89–109.

albeit retaining significant amounts of music. Thereafter, the rhymed heroic play – typified by its idealised protagonists, supernatural spectacle and music, exotic settings, and themes of love, honour, sovereignty, and succession – quickly established itself as the dominant genre of the 1660s, pressing writers such as Roger Boyle, Earl of Orrery, Robert and Edward Howard, and John Dryden into its service.[4] When it came to adapting *Macbeth* in the winter of 1663/4, the heroic play must have seemed an appealing model for Davenant to follow.

By and large critics have proved reluctant to bring together these two strands of Davenant's Restoration playwriting career – his heroic plays and operas, as epitomised by *Rhodes*, and his Shakespeare adaptations.[5] As a result, I suggest we have failed to meet his *Macbeth* on its own generic terms. As the performance history of *Rhodes* makes clear, the development of Restoration heroic drama is intimately bound up with the development of seventeenth-century English opera, to the point where such clear distinctions between play and opera begin to hinder rather than help critical analysis. Following James A. Winn's call for a revised history of the Restoration stage that more flexibly accounts for the connections between dramatic and musical forms, in this chapter I read Davenant's changes to Shakespeare's text as an attempt to bring the play in line with the operatic heroic dramas produced alongside it in the 1660s at Lincoln's Inn Fields as well as at the rival playhouse, Thomas Killigrew's Theatre Royal in Bridges Street.[6] I show how *Macbeth* draws on the dramatic and musical conventions, generic structures, and thematic preoccupations articulated by *Rhodes* and subsequent heroic plays to reorient its own moral, political, and aesthetic topography on distinctively Carolean lines. In the final section of this chapter, I suggest that *Macbeth*, now understood as part of a wider fashion for heroic/operatic works at Lincoln's Inn Fields, reveals a subtle yet significant shift in Davenant's own dramaturgical praxis at a relatively late stage in his career, a shift previously unnoticed by theatre historians and literary critics alike. By placing the Restoration *Macbeth*

---

[4] Nancy Klein Maguire, *Regicide and Restoration: English Tragicomedy, 1660–1671* (Cambridge: Cambridge University Press, 1992).

[5] In addition to *Macbeth*, Davenant also wrote and produced *The Law Against Lovers* (1662; an adaptation of *Measure for Measure* and *Much Ado About Nothing*), *The Rivals* (1663; *The Two Noble Kinsman*), and, with John Dryden, *The Tempest, or the Enchanted Island* (1667; *The Tempest*).

[6] James A. Winn, 'Heroic Song: A Proposal for a Revised History of English Theatre and Opera, 1656–1711', *Eighteenth-Century Studies*, 30.2 (Winter, 1996/7): 113–37. More recently, Andrew R. Walkling has termed these hybrid performance texts 'spectacle-tragedies'; see his *English Dramatick Opera, 1661–1706* (Abingdon: Routledge, 2019), 82–116.

in dialogue with its surrounding repertory instead of reading it solely, and reductively, through Shakespeare's original text, a more nuanced and intriguing history of the stage in the mid-1660s begins to emerge.

Davenant and the Origins of the Heroic Play

According to Dryden, Davenant was the first exponent of the heroic play in England. In a prefatory essay attached to *The Conquest of Granada* (1672), Dryden traces the genre's origins back to Davenant's operatic experiments in the 1650s:

> For Heroick Plays, (in which onely I have us'd it without the mixture of Prose) the first light we had of them on the *English* Theatre was from the late Sir *William D'Avenant*: It being forbidden him in the Rebellious times to act Tragedies and Comedies, because they contain'd some matter of Scandal to those good people, who could more easily dispossess their lawful Sovereign than endure a wanton jeast; he was forc'd to turn his thoughts another way: and to introduce the examples of moral vertue, writ in verse, and perform'd in Recitative Musique.[7]

Here, Dryden presents the creation of the operatic heroic play as a fortuitous accident of history. Constrained by Puritan killjoys who wrested control of the country following the regicide of Charles I in 1649, Dryden argues that Davenant was forced to experiment with new performance styles to circumvent the prohibition on stage plays that remained in force until 1660. Musical performances were not subject to the same legal restrictions as mimetic drama in Protectorate England (Cromwell himself was an enthusiastic music aficionado), so the argument goes that Davenant compromised by reluctantly setting his dramatic scripts to music.[8] *Rhodes*, Dryden tells us, which introduced the English public to recitative singing and painted moveable scenery as well as to the first professional female performer to grace a public stage, took its cue from 'the *Italian* Opera's [*sic*]' (9) and French plays by the likes of Pierre Corneille. The formal shift from drama to music, from straight play to opera, was accompanied too by a change in dramatic content: these works no longer celebrated the indecorous and ethically dubious characters that so frequently populate pre-Civil War dramas, Dryden tells us, but instead presented audiences with 'examples of moral vertue' (9).

---

[7] John Dryden, 'Of Heroique Playes: An Essay', in *The Works of John Dryden*, ed. H. T. Swedenberg Jr. et al., 20 vols. (Berkeley and Los Angeles: University of California, 1956–2002), vol. IX, 8–18 (9).
[8] Patrick Little, 'Music at the Court of King Oliver', *The Court Historian*, 12 (2007): 173–91.

Dryden's account is broadly accurate in terms of the theatrical innovations Davenant oversaw in the Interregnum but entirely wrongheaded in identifying the elder playwright's motivations for them. His essay assumes that Davenant's experiments with opera during the 1650s was a purely pragmatic concern, a necessary evil thrust upon him by the draconian strictures of an anti-theatrical Puritanism. It was only after Charles II liberated Davenant from this oppressive regime, Dryden claims, that he finally 'review'd his *Siege of Rhodes*, and caus'd it to be acted as a just Drama' (9), that is, as the spoken play it was always intended to be. Dryden's dismissal of Davenant's musical experimentation, however, reflects his own deeply ambivalent feelings about the use of music in theatrical contexts.[9] In reality, Davenant had openly embraced musical drama some twenty years before staging *Rhodes*. During the 1630s, he collaborated with the designer Inigo Jones and composers such as Nicholas Lanier and Henry Lawes on a number of court masques for Charles I and his wife, Henrietta Maria – including the last masque produced before the outbreak of war, *Salmacida Spolia* (1640). Moreover, in 1639, Davenant was granted a licence to construct a new playhouse in which to stage spectacular 'Action[s], musical Presentments, Scenes, Dancing and the like' before a paying public.[10] This project was quickly abandoned, but Davenant's intentions to establish a scenic theatre at least seventeen years before his first Rutland House productions shows the disingenuity of Dryden's claim that his hand was forced into producing operatic entertainments during the Protectorate.[11]

It is clear from Davenant himself that *Rhodes* and its successors – *The Cruelty of the Spaniards in Peru* (1658) and *The History of Sir Francis Drake* (1659) – were conceived from the very beginning as operatic, or at least musical, entertainments, brilliantly exploiting continental developments in recitative, instrumental music, and perspective scenography.[12] In his treatise *A Proposition for Advancement of Moralitie, by a New Way of Entertainment of the People*, published anonymously in 1653, Davenant set out his vision for a morally and aesthetically reformed theatre that would

---

[9] James A. Winn, *'When Beauty Fires the Blood': Love and the Arts in the Age of Dryden* (Ann Arbor: University of Michigan Press, 1992), 162–231.
[10] Thomas Rymer, *Foedera* (London, 1735), xx, 377–8; quoted in Mary Edmond, *Rare Sir William Davenant: Poet Laureate, Playwright, Civil War General, Restoration Theatre Manager* (Manchester: Manchester University Press, 1987), 75.
[11] John Freehafer, 'Brome, Suckling, and Davenant's Theatre Project of 1639', *Texas Studies in Language and Literature*, 10 (1968): 367–83.
[12] While *The History of Sir Francis Drake* was, like *Rhodes*, likely through-sung, there is no evidence that this was the case for *The Cruelty of the Spaniards in Peru*; however, *Peru* does call for complex scenography, dance, and acrobatic episodes. See Walkling, *Masque and Opera*, 154–6.

engender positive relations with the Protectorate state. Submitted to the Council of State for review, the *Proposition* argues that the government should work to educate and 'civilise the people', thereby 'procuring much ease to themselves, and benefit to those that are govern'd'.[13] One way to achieve that agreeable outcome, Davenant insisted, would be through 'Heroick Representations at the publick charge' (2). Davenant sets out to show how these '*Heroicall Pictures*' would combine visual and musical spectacle – 'Musick and wholsome discourses' with 'ingenious *Mechanicks*, as *Motion* and *Transposition of Lights*' (14) – in order 'not onely [to] divert the people from disorder, but by degrees enamour them with consideration of the conveniences and protections of Government' (15). Thus, his state-sponsored theatre would serve as 'an *Academy* or *Schoole* of *Morality*' (20), presenting heroic narratives and exemplary characters through which audiences would learn the lessons and virtues required for the smooth running of society. Avoiding the 'softer arguments' of plays from the pre-1642 repertory, which would merely 'make the people effeminate', these heroic operas would instead take full advantage of the new technical possibilities available in England to 'warme and incite [spectators] to Heroicall Attempts, when the State shall command them; and bring into derision the present Vices and Luxury' (21–2).

The *Proposition* succinctly joins together the material and technical aspects of theatrical production that we eventually see in the Protectorate operas and Restoration heroic plays. To do so, it draws freely on what Colin Burrow and Brandon Chua term Davenant's 'heroic idiom'.[14] Embracing the theatre's full range of semiotic systems, Davenant's heroic idiom unites the verbal and thematic ('love and honour' plots) with the visual and musical technologies first developed at Rutland House and later honed at the Cockpit and Lincoln's Inn Fields (operatic spectacle).

While the *Proposition* describes the visual and musical elements used to express Davenant's heroic idiom, the thematic ideas are first articulated in his unfinished epic, *Gondibert: An Heroick Poem*, published in 1651. *Gondibert* follows the adventures of its eponymous hero, who proves his military capabilities against his rival, Prince Oswald, in single combat before retiring to convalesce at the house of the natural philosopher, Astragon.

---

[13] [William Davenant], *A Proposition for Advancement of Moralitie, by a New Way of Entertainment of the People* (London, 1654[/3]), 1.
[14] Colin Burrow, *Epic Romance from Homer to Milton* (Oxford: Clarendon Press, 1993), 240; Brandon Chua, *Ravishment of Reason: Governance and the Heroic Idioms of the Late Stuart Stage, 1660–1690* (Lanham, MD: Bucknell University Press, 2014).

Once there, he meets and immediately falls in love with Astragon's only daughter, Birtha. As they begin their courtship, news arrives from the court of King Aribert in Lombardy that Gondibert has been named his heir. The final cantos of the poem turn on the question of whether Gondibert will accept his public duty, which involves succeeding Aribert as king on the latter's death and marrying his daughter, Princess Rhodalind, or whether he will follow his heart and marry his true love, Birtha.

According to the lengthy preface published in 1650 in anticipation of the poem itself, Davenant insists that the characters in *Gondibert* are 'deriv'd from the distempers of Love, and Ambition: for Love and Ambition are too often the raging Feavers of great mindes'.[15] Thus, in Book 2, canto 8, for example, Gondibert privately reveals to Astragon his struggle to reconcile his love for Birtha with his sense of duty towards Aribert and Rhodalind:

> Think not Ambition can my duty sway;
> I look on *Rhodalind* with Subjects Eies,
> Whom he that conquers, must in right obey.
>
> And though I humanly have heretofore
> All beauty lik'd, I never lov'd till now;
> Nor think a Crown can raise his valew more,
> To whom already Heav'n does Love allow.   (2.8.26–7)

This kind of plot, in which an ideal protagonist is forced to choose between private love on the one hand and public honour, duty, and ambition on the other, becomes a staple of the Restoration heroic plays and operas that follow.[16] Indeed, Davenant's precedent for *Gondibert* itself seems to have been the fashionable 'love and honour' tragicomedies of the 1630s, to which he himself contributed plays such as *Love and Honour* (1634).[17] Davenant reveals in the *Preface* to *Gondibert* that he had such pre-war dramatic models in mind when composing his poem: 'I cannot discerne by any help from reading or learned men ... that any Nation hath in representment of great actions (either by *Heroicks* or *Dramaticks*) digested Story into so pleasant and instructive a method as the English by their *Drama*: and by that regular species (thought narratively and not in *Dialogue*) I have drawn the body of an Heroick Poem' (15–16). The relationship, then, between heroic drama, poetry, and opera is more symbiotic than standard accounts of this period have been prepared to concede.

---

[15] William Davenant, *Gondibert*, ed. David F. Gladish (Oxford: Clarendon Press, 1971), 13.
[16] See Winn, 'Heroic Song', 115.
[17] Martin Butler, *Theatre and Crisis, 1632–1642* (Cambridge: Cambridge University Press, 1984), 55–83; Kevin Sharpe, *Criticism and Compliment: The Politics of Literature in the England of Charles I* (Cambridge: Cambridge University Press, 1987), 54–108.

In the 1656 edition of *Rhodes*, Davenant stresses that the heroic action of the opera is similarly intended 'to advance the characters of virtue in the shapes of valor and conjugal love'.[18] The plot centres on the newly married Italians, Alphonso and Ianthe, who are visiting Rhodes, just as Solyman the Magnificent arrives with his formidable Ottoman armada to besiege the island. Driven by his desire to prove a worthy military hero, Alphonso chooses to stay and fight alongside his Christian hosts, despite their insistence that he should return with Ianthe to safety in Italy. Fearful for her husband's life, Ianthe eventually travels to Solyman's camp to implore him to call off his attack. Stunned by her beauty and virtue, Solyman grants Ianthe and her husband safe passage out of Rhodes, but demurs from calling off his offensive. On hearing of her interference and of Solyman's release of his female prisoner, who 'was his own by right of war' (3.196), Alphonso becomes suspicious of his wife's fidelity, and the opera ends on an ambiguous note as Solyman proves more magnanimous and chivalrous than the Christian Italian, who is left only too aware of how poorly he has treated his wife throughout the siege.

Rhodes was revived sometime between 1659 and 1661, and eventually published in two parts in 1663 with a dedicatory epistle to Davenant's friend, Edward Hyde, Earl of Clarendon, Lord Chancellor of England. This epistle reiterates many of the points set out in the earlier *Preface* and *Proposition* relating to heroic poetry and opera, most notably its intermingling of 'Martial encounters' with 'conjugal vertues' (A3ᵛ). The expanded scenes added to part 1 in 1663 introduce Solyman's own wife, Roxolana, as a counterpoint to the virtuous Ianthe. Along with *Gondibert*, *Rhodes* quickly established itself as a chief dramaturgical model for the heroic dramas that followed. Orrery's *The Generall* (c. 1661–3), Robert Howard and Dryden's *The Indian Queen* (1663) and Dryden's solo sequel *The Indian Emperour* (1665), Dryden's *The Conquest of Granada* (1672), and Edward Howard's *The Usurper* (1669) were all produced at Killigrew's Theatre Royal in the opening decades of the Restoration, while Orrery's *Henry the Fifth* (1664), *Mustapha* (1665), and *Tryphon* (1669) were staged by Davenant and the Duke's Company at Lincoln's Inn Fields. All are variations on the love and honour plots described, while many of them invest inordinate amounts of creative energy in musical and scenic spectacle to produce wonder and admiration in their audiences.

---

[18] William Davenant, *The Siege of Rhodes*, in *Drama of the English Republic, 1640–1660*, ed. Janet Clare (Manchester: Manchester University Press, 2002), 193–233 (195).

These heroic plays also share ideological as well as aesthetic commitments pertinent to their moment of production. As Richard Law has observed, the Restoration heroic play became an opportunity to celebrate 'the restoration of legitimate sovereignty in the state', while Maguire claims that, collectively, they 'betray an obsession with figures of monarchy, with usurpation and regicide, and with recuperation of royal power' that reflects contemporary political discourse.[19] All these heroic plays raise questions, to varying degrees, about the nature of sovereignty and political allegiance, questions that Davenant first explored in the 1650s, and which took on a renewed urgency in the wake of the return of the Stuart monarchy in May 1660. Frequently, they engage the psychological language of the philosopher Thomas Hobbes, albeit often without recourse to his controversial political ideas.[20] Time and again, the plays staged in the first years of Charles II's reign confront their audiences with unworthy, overambitious upstarts who are nevertheless ultimately ousted in favour of legitimate rulers. Davenant's *Macbeth* thus reflects the preoccupations of the broader repertory of plays of which it forms a crucial part. Like the 1663 edition of *Rhodes*, *Macbeth* centres on two opposing married couples – the Macduffs now serving as foils for the Macbeths – while characters meditate on how best to reconcile uxorious love with public duty and personal honour. Davenant's adaptation also concerns a corrupt usurper who is ultimately thwarted by the restoration of a rightful heir, in the vein of Orrery's *The Generall* or Howard's *The Usurper*. Finally, *Macbeth* uses the full range of scenic and musical technology available at Lincoln's Inn Fields to create its effects; although, as we shall see, it does so in markedly different ways to Davenant's earlier heroic productions.

Macbeth's Heroic Idiom

Returning to the dialogue between the Macduffs quoted at the beginning of this chapter, we can see that the scene contains all the aesthetic and ideological hallmarks that characterise the Restoration heroic play. As well as deploying the trademark couplet, its dissection of political and ideological

---

[19] Richard Law, 'The Heroic Ethos in John Dryden's Heroic Plays', *Studies in English Literature 1500–1900*, 23.3 (1983): 389–98 (394); Maguire, *Regicide and Restoration*, 5.
[20] Davenant had addressed the *Preface* to *Gondibert* to Hobbes in 1650. On his ambivalent engagement with Hobbes's political philosophy, see Niall Allsopp, *Poetry and Sovereignty in the English Revolution* (Oxford: Oxford University Press, 2020), 26–56, 139–65; James R. Jacob and Timothy Raylor, 'Opera and Obedience: Thomas Hobbes and *A Proposition for Advancement of Moralitie* by Sir William Davenant', *The Seventeenth Century*, 6.2 (1991): 205–50 (215–33).

perspectives on questions of legitimate power, monarchical authority, and tyranny is typical of the genre as we find it in the early 1660s. *Macbeth* displays both the obsession with usurpation and the anxiety around rightful restoration that Maguire and others ascribe to plays of contemporaries such as Orrery and Howard. It is abundantly clear from the text that Macbeth is an unlawful usurper of the Scottish throne, but what procedures should be undertaken to remove him, and who should replace him, prove much more insoluble questions. When Macduff offers to assume the burden of power himself, his wife suspects an ulterior motive. She worries that he seeks a crown to which he, like Macbeth, has no just claim. It is 'not by your Title due' (3.2.33), she says. To seize power in this way, even in the defence of his fellow subjects, would make Macduff 'at best *unjustly* Good' (3.2.36; my emphasis). Macduff might not yet be as bad as Macbeth; however, his wife worries that her husband is still being dangerously ambitious in his own way: 'You, by your Pitty which for us you plead, / Weave but Ambition of a finer thread' (3.2.37–9).

The word 'ambition' ricochets through *Macbeth* and serves as a key term in Davenant's wider heroic idiom.[21] We have seen how both *Gondibert* and *Rhodes* pit love against ambition in their plots. In his reply to the *Preface* to *Gondibert*, Hobbes observes that 'Ambition … has somewhat Heroique in it, and therefore must have place in an Heroique Poem.'[22] A prime indicator of the heroic, ambition nevertheless proves to be a rather protean term, adjusting its moral tenor as it crosses the 1660 divide. In the *Preface* itself, Davenant defines ambition benignly 'as no more then an extraordinary lifting of the feet in the rough ways of Honor, over the impediments of Fortune' (13). Gondibert is faced with a stark choice between love and ambition, but these are still both positive attributes, connoting commitment to one's true love and duty to one's nation, respectively. As is clear from Lady Macduff's speech in 3.2, however, 'ambition' takes on a much darker, malevolent flavour in *Macbeth*, being equated almost exclusively with tyranny and sin. 'Ambition', she declares 'urg'd [Macbeth] to that bloudy deed' – Duncan's murder – and she urges her husband 'never' to be led by 'Ambition' (3.2.4–5). No longer simply the propulsion required to overleap 'the impediments to Fortune', ambition now leads to the *neglect* of one's duty to one's country in favour of personal glory.

---

[21] Mongi Raddadi, *Davenant's Adaptations of Shakespeare* (Uppsala: Studia Anglistica Upsaliensis, 1979), 99.
[22] Thomas Hobbes, 'The Answer of Mr Hobbes to Sir Will. D'avenant's *Preface* before *Gondibert*', in Davenant, *Gondibert*, 45–55 (50).

We might reflect that *Macbeth*'s macabre fascination with 'ambition' parallels a general impulse by royalists at the Restoration to diagnose that passion as the overriding cause of the political upheavals of the 1640s and 1650s. For example, in *A Memento Directed to all Those that Truly Reverence the Memory of King Charles the Martyr* (1662), Roger L'Estrange emphasises that 'The true *Cause* of the late War, was *Ambition*', while Thomas Forde observes that 'Though *Charls* was innocent', for those opposing him, 'it was a crime enough that he was *King*, and stood in the place that ambition aimed at.'[23] On the stage, Samuel Tuke's immensely popular *The Adventures of Five Hours* (1663) similarly links rebellion with unchecked ambition. As Geraldo and Ernesto discuss the Dutch motivations for internecine struggle against their Spanish rulers, they hit upon its various causes: the Dutch populace at large are said to have been fomented by religious zealotry but their rulers in the nobility were prompted to the same end by that 'which made the Devil himself Rebel, / Ambition'.[24]

Unlike the *Preface*, then, where ambition is seen as a positive, even necessary, attribute for a public figure, Davenant's *Macbeth* exploits recent royalist assessments of the Civil War to inveigh against ambition as a futile and destructive force that erodes one's sense of honour, duty, and loyalty. Early in the play, for example, Lady Macbeth muses over her husband's letter in which he informs her of his sudden and unexpected elevation as Thane of Cawdor. She immediately looks to the ultimate prize but is concerned that her husband's moral rectitude will preclude him from attaining his true desire. It is not that Macbeth lacks 'ambition', she says,

> but the ill
> Which should attend it: what thou highly covet'st
> Thou covet'st holily! alas, thou art
> Loth to play false; and yet would'st wrongly win! (1.5.54–7)

The changes to Shakespeare's text here are highly significant. In the original, Lady Macbeth simply talks about what her husband *would* have: 'What thou wouldst highly, / That wouldst thou holily'.[25] In Davenant's version,

---

[23] Roger L'Estrange, *A Memento Directed to all Those that Truly Reverence the Memory of King Charles the Martyr* (London: Printed for Henry Brome, 1662), C1ᵛ; Thomas Forde, *Virtus Rediviva; Or, A Panegyrick On the Late K. Charls the I. Second Monarch of Great Britain* (London: Printed by R. and W. Leybourn, for William Grantham, 1660), B8ʳ.

[24] Samuel Tuke, *The Adventures of Five Hours* (London: Printed for Henry Herringman, 1663), 11. The opening scene of Roger Boyle's *Tryphon* similarly identifies ambition as the lead cause of turmoil in the state; see *The Dramatic Works of Roger Boyle, Earl of Orrery*, ed. William Smith Clark II, 2 vols. (Cambridge, MA: Harvard University Press, 1937), vol. I, 1.1.1–110.

[25] William Shakespeare, *Macbeth*, ed. Sandra Clarke and Pamela Mason (London: Bloomsbury, 2015), 1.5.20–1.

Macbeth *covets*. It would appear that here Lady Macbeth is invoking the psychological vocabulary of Thomas Hobbes. In chapter 6 of *Leviathan* (1651), Hobbes explicitly equates covetousness with ambition, writing that these two passions represent the very same 'appetite' merely applied to different objects: 'AMBITION' is the '*Desire* of Office, or precedence' while 'COVETOUSNESSE' is the '*Desire* of Riches'.[26] According to his wife, that Macbeth *covets* suggests that he desires both power and wealth even as he lacks the 'ill' necessary to achieve his aims. Davenant appears to be attracted to Hobbes's language of insatiable appetite here, as he foregrounds what Hobbes terms the 'generall inclination of all mankind', that is, 'a perpetuall and restlesse desire of Power after power, that ceaseth only in Death'.[27] Lady Macbeth signals that her husband is hungry for power, while failing to acknowledge his (and her) obligation in natural law not to resist the current sovereign, which forms the central tenet of Hobbes's political philosophy.[28]

This sense of restless agitation in opposition to obligation permeates the play throughout. Immediately before carrying out the murder, Macbeth briefly discusses the events of the last few days with Banquo. Duncan has shown himself to be a generous and benevolent ruler, even offering Macbeth's servants rewards and his wife a diamond ring for being a 'most kind Hostess' (2.1.14), elaborating the language of hospitality and reciprocity already present in Shakespeare's text. To kill such a man, we infer from Banquo's comments, would be a gross injustice. It would necessitate Macbeth breaking his covenant with his king. Macbeth, however, prompted by Banquo to think on the witches' prophecies, attempts subtly to determine where his friend's loyalties truly lie. Can Banquo be relied upon to support Macbeth's claim to the throne when the time comes? Banquo's response is slippery: 'still keeping my bosom free, / And my Allegiances dear, I shall be councell'd' (2.1.26–7), he says. In chapter 21 of *Leviathan*, Hobbes had offered a series of scenarios in which a subject may be required to transfer their allegiance to a new sovereign, such as when taken prisoner and 'his means of life be within the Guards of the enemy'. Likewise, if the sovereign 'dye without known Kindred, and without declaration of his Heyre ... no Subjection is due'.[29] Duncan has recently

---

[26] Thomas Hobbes, *The Clarendon Edition of the Works of Thomas Hobbes*, vol. 4: *Leviathan: The English and Latin Texts (i)*, ed. Noel Malcolm (Oxford: Clarendon Press, 2012), 85.
[27] Hobbes, *Leviathan*, xi, 150. Allsopp (*Poetry and Sovereignty*, 47) explores a similar idea in *Gondibert* concerning Davenant's use of the word 'gnaw'.
[28] Allsopp, *Poetry and Sovereignty*, 16–17.
[29] Hobbes, *Leviathan*, 344.

announced his heir, of course, but Macbeth's plans are founded on the supposition that he will reach the throne unimpeded by framing Malcolm and his brother as the murdering conspirators themselves. However, Banquo's suggestion that he will 'keep his bosom free' is a problem for Macbeth: it goes against Hobbes's idea that we must yield up our free will to the sovereign in return for protection. He is keeping his cards close to his chest, and Macbeth cannot necessarily rely on his support. Banquo's murder is a direct result of Macbeth's inability to guarantee his loyalty.

These scenes establish Macbeth as a potential traitor, but they also show him to be a prospective sovereign. In another departure from Shakespeare, when Macbeth hears the bell that signals the moment to carry out the murder, he implores Duncan not to hear it, 'for 'tis a bell / That rings my Coronation, and thy Knell' (2.1.50). The line clearly foregrounds the theme of usurpation that runs throughout the play, and which is such an important trope of Restoration heroic drama. Macbeth's rise to power and the satisfaction of his ambition are predicated on his merciless treatment of Duncan, who must die for him to attain the crown.

Once Macbeth accedes to the throne, things quickly descend into darkness and despair, as he sets about consolidating his hard-fought but fragile hold on power. The central scenes establish Macduff as a potential heroic foil and threat to the 'bloudy Tyrants violence' (3.2.16), but, like Alphonso in *Rhodes*, he is not entirely without flaws himself. Macduff's claim that he wants 'not to Govern, but Protect' (3.2.40) Scotland would have raised images in the minds of Restoration audiences of the late Lord Protector, Oliver Cromwell, whose position was established by the Instrument of Government in 1653. In the closing moments of the play, the restored Malcolm orders that Macbeth's corpse be hung on 'A Pinnacle in *Dunsinane*, to shew / To future Ages what to those is due / Who others Right, by Lawless Power pursue' (5.9.32–4), just as Charles II had the bodies of Cromwell, Henry Ireton, and John Bradshaw exhumed and hung up at the Tower of London in 1660.[30] In the earlier scene, then, Macduff represents a character running the risk of following in the footsteps of unlawful usurpers like Macbeth and Cromwell. Macduff does appear, to his wife's distress, to harbour political ambitions of his own.

Macduff's political naivety is compounded by his irrational (and unmanly) fear of the witches in 2.5, and when he underestimates the extent of Macbeth's cruelty towards his wife and children in 3.6. Macbeth,

---

[30] On these contemporary parallels, see Richard Kroll, 'Emblem and Empiricism in Davenant's *Macbeth*', *English Literary History*, 57.3 (Winter 1990): 835–64.

he unconvincingly reassures his wife, 'cannot be / Possest with such unmanly cruelty' (3.6.11–12) as to harm innocent women and children. Lady Macduff, however, is more cynical. She recognises the brutal reality of Macbeth's tyranny: 'When Birds of stronger Wing are fled away, / The Ravenous *Kite* do's on the weaker Prey' (3.6.9–10).[31] Her death at the hands of Macbeth's henchmen only vindicates her reading of the political situation.[32] Like other characters in heroic poetry and drama, here Macduff is faced with a choice between private love (protecting his family) or public duty (protecting his nation). For example, in the fifth entry of *Rhodes*, Alphonso is forced to choose between saving Ianthe, who has disguised herself as a solider and joined the English forces fighting Solyman's army, and assisting his friend and comrade, Villerius: 'By staying here, you must Ianthe lose, / Who ventured life and fame for you, / Or your great master quite forsake' (5.103–8). Pitting martial honour against marital love, Alphonso eventually elects to go to his wife, sending the Admiral in his stead to support Villerius, but not before expressing doubts about the choice he has made. In the end, Alphonso is vindicated while Macduff, who makes the contrary choice – leaving his wife and children at the mercy of the tyrant to travel to Malcolm in England – is not. Macduff might be the closest the play has to an idealised hero, but he must pay a significant penalty to claim that role.

As a counterpoint, Macbeth too is presented with the stark choice between his public duty and his private obligations to his wife. In 4.4, as the English army approaches Dunsinane, Macbeth is caught between a desire to engage the enemy and to offer his support to Lady Macbeth, who has fallen into madness:

MACBETH *Seyton*, go bid the Army March.
SEYTON The posture of Affairs requires your Presence.
MACBETH But the Indisposition of my Wife
 Detains me here. (4.4.1–4)

Seyton insists that the enemy is fast approaching and that '*Scotland's* in danger' (4.4.5), but his commander-in-chief has more than external threats to worry about: 'So is my Wife, and I am doubly so. / I am sick in her, and in my Kingdom too' (4.4.6–7). Macbeth cannot decide what course of

---

[31] Cf. Davenant, *Gondibert*, 1.2.41: 'We blush to see our politicks in Beasts.'
[32] See Ted H. Miller, 'The Two Deaths of Lady Macduff: Antimetaphysics, Violence, and William Davenant's Restoration Revision of *Macbeth*', *Political Theory*, 36.6 (2008): 856–82; Anne Greenfield, 'D'Avenant's Lady Macduff: Ideal Feminism and Subversive Politics', *Restoration: Studies in English Literary Culture, 1660–1700*, 37.1 (2013): 39–60.

action to take, what fire he should fight first. Under pressure, he distractedly wrestles with his conscience:

> The Spur of my Ambition prompts me to go
> And make my Kingdom safe, but Love which softens
> Me to pity her in her distress,
> Curbs my Resolves. (4.4.9–12)

Earlier critics have dismissed this moment as 'superficial', even 'ludicrous', but, as I have suggested, this inner struggle is fully consonant with Davenant's heroic pattern elsewhere.[33] Consumed with self-doubt and paranoia, Macbeth prevaricates just like Macduff and Alphonso.

During the final battle, Lennox reports to Fleance and Donalbain that 'Some say he's Mad' (5.2.15) and that

> there is a Civil War
> Within his Bosom; which will hinder him
> From waging this successfully. None can
> Resist a forreign foe, who alwayes has
> An enemy within him. For each murder
> He weares a dagger in his Breast. (5.2.17–22)

Civil war rages within Macbeth's soul, as well as within the Scottish nation, and as so much early modern political philosophy stressed, a sovereign who brings about civil war immediately forfeits their right to rule because they are no longer protecting their subjects. In 5.3, Seyton betrays Macbeth, leaving his service just before the final battle. In an aside to the audience, he informs us that 'I am gone. / Not to Obey your [Macbeth's] Orders, but the Call of Justice' (5.3.42–3). Paralysed and paranoid, Macbeth can no longer guarantee the safety of his subjects and so irreparably breaks his covenant with his people. Seyton's rejection of Macbeth's authority presses home that, from this moment on, Macbeth is no longer sovereign.

This loss of power is anticipated in the earlier scene, also added by Davenant, in which Macbeth and his wife exchange their final words together. Here, Lady Macbeth explicitly blames her husband for Duncan's murder. Troubled and repentant, she begins to see the old king's 'fatal Ghost … Where e're I go' (4.4.28–9), in a parallel to Macbeth's visions of Banquo at the feast. Desperate, she accuses her husband of causing her mental disturbance:

---

[33] Raddadi, *Davenant's Adaptations*, 104; Hazelton Spencer, *Shakespeare Improved: The Restoration Versions in Quarto and on the Stage* (Cambridge, MA: Harvard University Press, 1927), 163.

> the strange error of my Eyes
> Proceeds from the strange Action of your Hands
> Distraction does by fits possess my head,
> Because a Crown *unjustly* covers it. (4.4.37–40; my emphasis)

That word 'unjustly' echoes Lady Macduff's earlier admonition to her husband, offering Lady Macbeth a (partial) moral redemption. It would seem, *pace* Hobbes, that there is an external standard of moral justice outside of the sovereign in the world of the play.

Macbeth himself emphatically protests, insisting that his wife first planted the idea of regicide in his head: 'had not your breath / Blown my Ambition up into a Flame / *Duncan* had yet been living' (4.4.51–3). Lady Macbeth retorts that his failure properly to govern the state as a 'just' monarch is a direct result of his failure properly to govern her as a husband, and therefore implies his masculinity is somehow compromised:

> You were a Man.
> And by the Charter of your Sex you shou'd
> Have govern'd me, there was more crime in you
> When you obey'd my Councels, then I contracted
> By my giving it. (4.4.53–7)

Finally, she begs him to give up his kingdom and 'with your Crown putt off your guilt' (4.4.58). His refusal to do so leads to his eventual downfall at the hands of Macduff – a man who has learned that he should have heeded his wife's advice when he had the chance. As Macduff deals the fatal blow, Macbeth finally comes to recognise his mistakes, bidding farewell to this 'vain World, and what's most vain in it, Ambition' (5.8.41).

While the many deaths witnessed in the play establish its tragic tone, Davenant does flirt with the tragicomic structures more usually associated with operatic heroic dramas.[34] *Macbeth* tempers the demise of its chief protagonist with an acknowledgement that better days are still to come for the newly restored Scottish monarch and his subjects. As Macduff states in the final scene: 'Now *Scotland*, thou shalt see bright Day again, / That Cloud's remov'd that did Ecclipse thy Sun' (5.9.17–18). We might compare this moment with Howard and Dryden's *The Indian Queen*, which culminates in the suicide of the usurping Zempoalla, but which nevertheless rejoices in its denouement as the true monarch is finally restored: 'Our clearest Sun-shine shou'd be mixt with rain', the hero, Montezuma, observes.[35]

---

[34] See Maguire, *Regicide and Restoration*, 151–62; Derek Hughes, 'Heroic Drama and Tragicomedy', in *A Companion to Restoration Drama*, ed. Susan J. Owen (Oxford: Blackwell, 2008), 195–210 (202–6).

[35] John Dryden, *The Indian Queen*, in *Works*, vol. VIII, 5.1.306.

The meteorological metaphor in both plays casts the usurpation of the villain as a terrible but momentary interruption, temporarily obscuring the eternal radiance of monarchy.

Moreover, in the closing lines added by Davenant, Macduff hopes that fortune will bless Malcolm's reign and the Scottish people, insisting that the darkness of Macbeth's tyranny will, in the end, serve only to highlight more strongly the new king's virtue:

> So may kind Fortune Crown your Raign with Peace,
> As it has Crown'd your Armies with Success;
> And may the Peoples Prayers still wait on you,
> As all their Curses did *Macbeth* pursue:
> His Vice shall make your Virtue shine more Bright,
> As a Fair Day succeeds a Stormy Night. (5.9.37–42)

In their earlier conversation in England, Malcolm alluded to his own moral deficiencies, disingenuously warning Macduff that he was 'so inclin'd / To Vice, that foul *Macbeth* when I shall rule, / Will seem as white as Snow' (4.3.36–8). Macduff now hopes that Malcolm will break the cycle of vice and oppression of the last eighteen years and rule successfully. In Orrery's *Henry the Fifth* (also 1664), Prince Hal, a loose-living heir who experiences a damascene conversation on his accession, represents a veiled reference to Charles II.[36] In Malcolm, *Macbeth* similarly gestures outwards to England's current political situation. By 1664, Charles was notorious for his sexual proclivities, much like Hal and Malcolm. Amidst the sincere jubilation of restoration, then, heroic plays like *Henry the Fifth* and *Macbeth* register royalists' genuine, if unspoken, concerns about the effectiveness and moral probity of their new monarch and what his reign will bring for the nation following a traumatic period of political, social, and religious upheaval.[37]

Supernatural Rivals: Theatrical Competition in 1663–1664

While I have suggested that Davenant's *Macbeth* incontrovertibly owes its allegiance to the heroic play, I do not mean that he sought simply to replicate the tried-and-tested idioms of *Rhodes*. As we have seen, his adaptation builds on the work of others like Orrery, Howard, and Dryden to develop a heroic dramaturgy that more properly suits its Restoration context, focusing more explicitly on questions of legitimate sovereignty and

---

[36] Boyle, *Henry the Fifth*, in *Dramatic Works*, vol. I, 165–224.
[37] See also Nicholas Jose, *Ideas of the Restoration in English Literature, 1660–71* (London: Macmillan, 1984), 44–66.

rightful rule that preoccupied contemporary audiences. As such, *Macbeth* represents a significant shift at a crucial moment in his company's history. We can see a concomitant shift too in the play's relationship to theatrical spectacle and the presentation of supernaturalism on the stage.

Davenant's adaptation makes extensive use of visual and musical spectacle. The 1674 quarto of the text notoriously closes the first scene with the witches exiting on wires, '*flying*' (1.1.10SD), and they enjoy substantial musical interludes, in which they sing and dance, in 2.5, 3.8, and 4.1. While it is difficult to establish from the surviving texts what actually occurred on stage in 1664 – the 1674 quarto likely reflects a later production at the Dorset Garden Theatre in 1673, and the Yale manuscript's relationship to any stage production is impossible to establish adequately – the witches seem to have sung and danced, if not quite taken off, at Lincoln's Inn Fields.[38] We have records attesting that the famed dancing master Luke Channel joined the Duke's Company in the 1664/5 season, and that he worked directly on *Macbeth*, but recent research by Tim Keenan and Andrew R. Walkling has convincingly demonstrated that Lincoln's Inn Fields did not have the technology to fly in the witches, as Dorset Garden could have done.[39] Instead, Davenant appears to have stuck to the basic wing-and-shutter configuration he had perfected in the 1650s to create his scenic spectacles.

How do these scenes of stage supernaturalism – singing and dancing, if not quite flying, witches – alter Davenant's heroic idiom as established in his Protectorate treatises and the various productions of *Rhodes*? Prior to *Macbeth*, Davenant strenuously argued against introducing supernatural elements into heroic poetry and drama. In the *Preface* to *Gondibert*, he criticises Virgil for leading his readers into 'conversation with Gods and Ghosts', which only 'deprives us of those naturall probabilities in Story, which are instructive to humane life'. Tasso, he writes, may have 'reviv'd the Heroick flame' with *Gerusalemme liberata* (1581), but he erred in including 'his Councell assembled in Heaven, his Witches Expeditions through the Aire, and enchanted Woods inhabited with Ghosts'. Such episodes do not serve Christian poets, Davenant stresses, but rather 'make

---

[38] The Yale manuscript copy of the play, dated to 1663 or 1664, contains all the songs and music cues found in Q1674, as well as the opening 'flying' direction and signals for machine effects at 3.8.21SD and 4.1.19SD. See Spencer, ed., *Davenant's Macbeth from the Yale Manuscript*, 38–54.

[39] On Channel, see John Downes, *Roscius Anglicanus*, ed. Judith Milhous and Robert D. Hume (London: Society for Theatre Research, 1987), 71. On the technological capacities of the respective theatres, see Tim Keenan, *Restoration Staging, 1660–74* (Abingdon: Routledge, 2017), 78–93; Walkling, *English Dramatick Opera*, 38–81.

a resemblance of Hell, out of the Dreames of frighted Women; by which they continue and increase the melancholy mistakes of the People' (4–6). Such statements need to be read in the context of the puritan 1650s, when suspicion of the supernatural was especially high; we should remember too that the *Preface* was addressed to the rationalist Hobbes. That said, none of the heroic works staged at Lincoln's Inn Fields prior to *Macbeth* contain magical characters or supernatural events, though all of Davenant's plays and adaptations make extensive use of scenery, music, and dance in non-supernatural contexts. Something appears to have happened over the winter of 1663/4 to prompt Davenant to reflect on his aversion to supernatural spectacle, and to alter his dramaturgical practice thereafter. But what?

I suggest that the answer essentially boils down to money and commercial competition. On 7 May 1663, Thomas Killigrew opened his new playhouse, the Theatre Royal in Bridges Street, with a production of John Fletcher's *The Humorous Lieutenant*.[40] Before this date, the King's Company had played in a converted tennis court in Vere Street, which did not have scenic technology of any kind. Plays were performed there largely in the same way they had been performed before 1642. Suddenly at Bridges Street Killigrew's company at last had at their disposal a fully functioning scenic theatre to rival Davenant's, which must have caused sincere alarm within the ranks of the Duke's Company; from now on, Davenant no longer enjoyed his monopoly on scenic spectacle, which had proved so popular with patrons like Samuel Pepys. According to Walkling, Bridges Street not only 'sported impressive changeable scenery on a par with that at Lincoln's Inn Fields', but it went even further: it 'incorporated the kind of advanced machine technology' used to create special stage effects 'that was not in evidence at the other house'.[41] Like Tasso's witches, Killigrew's actors could easily perform 'Expeditions through the Aire' using specialist machines, to the delight of spectators. For once, Davenant was trailing behind his rival.

The King's Company sought to demonstrate their new technological capabilities with the highly anticipated premiere of Howard and Dryden's *The Indian Queen*, staged in January 1664. This was an elaborately decorated production that presented audiences with stunning scenic effects, music, and costumes. John Evelyn saw it in February, describing it as 'a Tragedie well written, but so beautified with rich Scenes as the like had never ben seene here as happly (except rarely anywhere else) on a

---

[40] Van Lennep et al., eds., *London Stage*, vol. I, 64.
[41] Walkling, *English Dramatick Opera*, 61.

mercenarie Theater'.[42] Winn notes that with *The Indian Queen*, Howard and Dryden 'catered to the public taste for spectacle, which the new theatre was finally able to satisfy'.[43] Representing Dryden's first foray into the operatic heroic play, *The Indian Queen* was striking for its extensive use of machine and musical spectacle to present scenes of supernaturalism. This new dramaturgical convention bears most strikingly on Davenant's adaptation of *Macbeth*.

In 3.2, for example, Zempoalla, the Indian queen of the title, visits the 'dismal Cell' (3.2.2) of the prophet Ismeron after having a dream which she suspects relates to her recent usurpation of the throne. Zempoalla wants the prophet to call on the God of Sleep to '*tell / Great* Zempoalla *what strange Fate / Must on her dismal Vision wait*' (3.2.64–71). Ismeron proceeds to summon the God of Dreams with an incantation:

> *By the croaking of the Toad,*
> *In their Caves that make aboad,*
> *Earthy* Dun *that pants for breath,*
> *With her well'd sides full of death;*
> *By the Crested Adders Pride*
> *That along the Clifts do glide;*
> *By thy visage fierce and black;*
> *By the Deaths-head on thy back;*
> *By the twisted Serpents place'd*
> *For a Girdle round thy Waste;*
> *By the Hearts of Gold that deck*
> *Thy Brest, thy Shoulders, and thy Neck:*
> *From thy sleepy Mansion rise,*
> *And open thy unwilling Eyes,*
> *While bubling Springs their Musick keep,*
> *That use to lull thee in thy sleep.* (3.2.79–94)

At this point, the stage direction states that the '*God of Dreams rises*' (3.2.94SD) from under the stage.

Zempoalla's visit to Ismeron's cell is reminiscent of Macbeth's nocturnal sojourn to the witches' cave in Shakespeare's text (4.1), from where they conjure up their leader, Hecate, and the apparitions who will reveal the prophecies that eventually lead to Macbeth's downfall. Indeed, Shakespeare's play appears to serve as a direct source for Howard and Dryden's scene:[44]

---

[42] Quoted in Van Lennep et al., eds., *London Stage*, vol. I, 75.
[43] James A. Winn, *John Dryden and His World* (New Haven, CT: Yale University Press, 1987), 145.
[44] John Loftis explicitly draws out Howard and Dryden's indebtedness to Shakespeare's *Macbeth* in his commentary for the California edition; see Dryden, *Works*, vol. VIII, 303.

> Round about the cauldron go;
> In the poisoned entrails throw.
> Toad, that under cold stone
> Days and nights has thirty-one,
> Sweltered venom sleeping got,
> Boil thou first i'th' charmed pot …
> Fillet of a fenny snake,
> In the cauldron boil and bake;
> Eye of newt and toe of frog,
> Wool of bat and tongue of dog,
> Adder's fork and blind-worm's sting,
> Lizard's leg and howlet's wing,
> For a charm of powerful trouble,
> Like a hell-broth boil and bubble. (4.1.4–19)

The Scottish witches' recipe is more elaborate, but the essential ingredients are there in both plays: both incantations refer to toads, adders and serpents, bubbles and sleep; both are in a distinctive trochaic tetrameter, isolated from the plays' more familiar iambic pentameter rhythms; and both Dryden's God of Sleep and Shakespeare's apparitions partially satisfy their visitor's enquiries before descending below the stage only to be forcefully called back.[45] Finally, both Zempoalla and Macbeth are presented with a dramatic spectacle in which their respective fates are cryptically revealed: Zempoalla listens to a song 'suppos'd sung by Aerial-Spirits' (3.2.118SD), while Macbeth watches the procession of eight kings. Neither is calmed or reassured by these experiences; instead, their respective levels of fear, anxiety, and paranoia substantially increase from this moment on.

While it is impossible to determine whether Davenant began his adaptation before he became aware of Howard and Dryden's play or not, I suggest that Davenant turned to *Macbeth* in the winter of 1663/4 in an effort to counter the anticipated success of the King's Company's latest hit. If the scene in Ismeron's cell could delight and enthral audiences by so closely echoing Shakespeare's text, then Davenant surely intended to go one better by staging *Macbeth* itself, in heroic (i.e. operatic) form. With *Macbeth* among the nine Shakespeare plays allocated to the Duke's Company, Davenant could take advantage of the vogue for heroic drama by enhancing the Macduffs' scenes *and* expanding on the fascination with

---

[45] Intriguingly, Davenant adjusts the witches' incantations in his adaptation to iambic tetrameter ('Then round about the *Cauldron* go' (4.1.7)), possibly to distinguish prosodically the witches' speeches from their songs, which are trochaic.

supernatural spectacular in *The Indian Queen*, elaborating on the witches' songs that were already associated with Shakespeare's text.⁴⁶

The success of *The Indian Queen* may thus have caused Davenant to reconsider his commitment to a musical theatre in which human characters combine 'Musick and wholsome discourses' for the moral edification of audiences. Dramatic fashions and conventions evidently had changed since the Interregnum. In his theatrical miscellany *Playhouse to be Let*, produced in the summer vacation in 1663, Davenant has a musician propose to stage an 'Heroique Story / in *Stilo Recitativo*' in the vacant theatre. The playhouse manager quickly raises a concern:

> But do you think
> That natural? ...
> Suppose
> I should not ask, but sing, you now a question,
> And you should instantly sing me an answer;
> Would you not think it strange?⁴⁷

We might want to read this moment ironically, given that what follows in Act 3 of *Playhouse* is essentially a wholesale revival of *The History of Sir Francis Drake* in recitative. Nevertheless, whereas in the 1650s Drake, along with Alphonso and Ianthe in *Rhodes*, is free to sing without such self-conscious meta-theatrical qualification, by 1663 the idea of mortal characters singing for no good reason seems 'strange' to some, including the *Playhouse* theatre manager looking to secure a healthy return at the box office. By the Restoration, scenes of musical spectacle were once again being restricted to dramatic scenarios usually considered outside the normal parameters of verisimilitude, including scenes of supernaturalism.⁴⁸ Such musical conventions are reminiscent of theatrical practice in the Jacobean and Caroline periods and anticipate the way music is often deployed in the Dorset Garden dramatick operas of the 1670s.

---

⁴⁶ The songs 'Come away, Hecate' and 'Black spirits and white', found interpolated into 3.5 and 4.1 respectively of the folio edition of Shakespeare's text, derive from Thomas Middleton's *The Witch* (c. 1613–1616); Davenant kept and developed this material for his own adaptation. See Amanda Eubanks Winkler, '"Let's Have a Dance": Staging Shakespeare in Restoration London', in *The Oxford Handbook of Shakespeare and Music*, ed. Christopher R. Wilson and Mervyn Cooke (Oxford: Oxford University Press, 2022), 387–408 (391–2).
⁴⁷ William Davenant, *Playhouse to be Let*, in *The Works of S' William D'avenant* (London: Printed by T.N. for Henry Herringman, 1673), 67–119 (72); second pagination.
⁴⁸ Steven E. Plank, '"And Now About the Cauldron Sing": Music and the Supernatural on the Restoration Stage', *Early Music*, 28.3 (1990): 393–407; Amanda Eubanks Winkler, *O Let Us Howle Some Heavy Note: Music for Witches, the Melancholic, and the Mad on the Seventeenth-Century English Stage* (Bloomington: Indiana University Press, 2006).

When he sees *Macbeth* again in January 1667, Pepys tellingly describes its elaborate musical elements as 'strange'. Unlike the *Playhouse* manager, however, Pepys does not see this strangeness as in any way frustrating an overarching commitment to verisimilitude; on the contrary, the singing of the weird sisters was 'a *strange perfection* ... being most proper here, and suitable'.[49] The musical episodes in *Macbeth* are deemed 'proper' and 'suitable', we must suppose, because the witches are among that limited group of characters in Restoration theatre – the magical, the mad, and the melancholic – who are now permitted by convention to sing and dance onstage in a way that the heroic but mortal Sir Francis Drake and his comrades simply cannot without a meta-theatrical qualification.

Conclusion

Placing Davenant's adaptation of *Macbeth* in the wider context of its surrounding repertory allows us to appreciate its vitality as a piece of theatre more fully. The alterations made to the play bring it closely in line with the most popular genre of the period – the operatic heroic play or, in Walkling's formulation, spectacle-tragedy – while engaging directly in debates concerning contemporary politics and theatrical aesthetics. Moreover, such an approach reveals how the increasingly vigorous competition between the two theatre companies prompted Davenant to adjust his dramaturgical praxis in the 1663/4 season in ways previously unacknowledged by scholars who have only read his adaptation through its relationship to Shakespeare's text. With Killigrew's company benefiting materially from their investment in the new scenic theatre at Bridges Street, and thus from the fascination for theatrical supernaturalism in plays like *The Indian Queen*, Davenant abandoned the heroic aesthetic he had developed during the 1650s to present audiences with what they evidently wanted – which included singing and dancing witches. *Macbeth* thus represents a profound change in Davenant's thinking in 1664, both as a playwright and as a theatre manager. Further evidence of this sea-change comes when three years later, in 1667, Davenant collaborated directly with the mastermind behind *The Indian Queen*, John Dryden, on another Shakespeare adaptation, one equally obsessed with ambitious usurpers, magical conjurors, supernatural charms, and elaborate musical spectacle: *The Tempest, or the Enchanted Island*.

---

[49] Samuel Pepys, *Diary*, ed. Robert Latham and William Matthews, 11 vols. (London: G. Bell and Sons, 1970–1983), vol. VIII, 7 (emphasis added).

CHAPTER 3

More than a Song and Dance? Identifying Matthew Locke's Incidental Music for Macbeth

Silas Wollston

After attending a performance of *Macbeth* on 19 April 1667, Samuel Pepys recorded in his diary: 'though I have seen it often, yet is it one of the best plays for a stage, and variety of dancing and musique, that ever I saw'.[1] The enduring appeal of the play is evident from the number of productions that are recorded during the Restoration period and beyond. In his memoirs, the former prompter at the Dorset Garden theatre, John Downes, referred to a production in the 1670s: '*The Tragedy of Macbeth*, alter'd by Sir *William Davenant*; being drest in all it's Finery, as new Cloath's, new Scenes, Machines, as flying for the Witches; with the Singing and Dancing in it: The 1st Compos'd by Mr. *Lock*, the other by Mr. *Channell* and Mr. *Joseph Priest*; it being all Excellently perform'd, being in the nature of an Opera.'[2]

By 1702 two different musical settings of the play were vying for London theatregoers' patronage, one with music by John Eccles, and the other with music by Richard Leveridge; the latter proved the most popular and Leveridge's score continued to be performed throughout the eighteenth century and well into the nineteenth century. When Boyce came to publish it in 1770 however, he misattributed the music to Matthew Locke, probably on the basis of the reference made by Downes and unaware that a number of different musical settings had been composed. Confusion persisted throughout the nineteenth century and it was only in the 1960s that Leveridge's authorship was persuasively argued by Robert Moore and Roger Fiske.[3]

Nevertheless, some of the music by Matthew Locke that Downes referred to does appear to have survived: 'A Jigg called Macbeth', which perfectly fits the text of Davenant's song for the Witches 'Let's have a dance upon

---

[1] See www.pepysdiary.com/diary/1667/04/19/.
[2] John Downes, *Roscius Anglicanus*, ed. Judith Milhous and Robert D. Hume (London: Society for Theatre Research, 1987), 71.
[3] Robert E. Moore, 'The Music to *Macbeth*', *Musical Quarterly*, 47.1 (1961): 22–40; Roger Fiske, 'The *Macbeth* Music', *Music and Letters*, 45.2 (1964): 114–25.

the heath', is attributed to Locke (in a handwritten annotation) in a copy of *Musick's Delight on the Cithern* (1666).[4] Since Locke's surviving theatre songs were composed predominantly for the Duke's Company, the dance may relate to this company's performance of *Macbeth* in 1664; the earliest reference to music in a production is, however, found in Pepys's diary entry of April 1667 (as mentioned).[5] Another tune, 'The Witches Dance', which appears unattributed in *Apollo's Banquet* (1669), may also have been composed by Locke for productions of the play in the 1660s. So is that it? Is the sum total of Locke's surviving music for Restoration stagings of *Macbeth* no more than a song and, possibly, a dance? Can any of the instrumental music heard by Pepys at the 1667 production be identified within Locke's surviving theatre music?

The music that Locke composed for another Shakespearean adaptation, Shadwell's version of *The Tempest* produced by the Duke's Company at the Dorset Garden Theatre in 1674, serves to illustrate the format and purpose of a typical set of theatre ayres for a Restoration play. The music comprises five short instrumental movements which would presumably have been played shortly before the play began (divided into two groups, 'The First Musick' and 'The Second Musick') acting rather like the warning bells in modern theatres, a Curtain Tune that was played after the Prologue as the curtain rose, four Act Tunes (one for the end of each of the first four acts) and a concluding instrumental movement, presumably to be played before the Epilogue.[6] These pieces are scored in four parts for performance by a violin band – an ensemble of violin-family instruments in all sizes from treble to bass, like a small string orchestra but without double basses.[7] In

---

[4] The annotation is found in a copy in the Huntington Library. See Amanda Eubanks Winkler, ed., *Music for Macbeth* (Middleton, WI: AR Editions, 2004), xi, fn. 12. The same tune appears anonymously in *Apollo's Banquet* (1669) and is attributed to 'M. L.' in Thomas Greeting's *The Pleasant Companion* (London: Printed for John Playford, 1673).

[5] Davenant's Duke's Company performed *Macbeth* on 5 November 1664 at Lisle's Tennis Court, Lincoln's Inn Fields. The dance may date from a year earlier: a list of plays, under the date 3 November 1663, mentions 'Revived Play. Mackbethe'.

[6] These movements were published at the end of the score of Locke's music for 'English opera' *Psyche* (1675). The Act Tunes are almost certainly by Robert Smith (see later in this chapter).

[7] The violin band at the French court of Louis XIV, the famous 'Vingt-quatres Violons du Roi', became an emblem of French power and sophistication and was emulated across Europe. However, while the repertoire of the French ensemble was cultivated outside France, it was usually performed by much smaller ensembles. The violin band at the English court in 1660 was perhaps the only one outside France that had twenty-four official members; in practice, however, the operational strength of the band was usually twelve or fewer. The one documented occasion at which all twenty-four members performed together was for the signing of the Secret Treaty in Dover in 1670, a politically sensitive occasion at which it was clearly important to Charles that his violin band should be seen to match that of Louis XIV.

More than a Song and Dance? 63

1660, Matthew Locke had been appointed composer to the violin band at the court of Charles II and this ensemble accompanied dancing at court balls as well as ceremonial and public events, such as when the king dined in public. From 1665 onwards, the members of the court violin band also performed in the two commercial London theatres.[8] Performances by the band before the play began (which were presumably more extensive that the brief 'First' and 'Second Musick') became an attraction in their own right. The French philosopher Samuel de Sorbière, visiting a London theatre in 1664, commented that 'The Musick with which you are entertained diverts your time till the Play begins, and People chuse to go it betimes to hear it',[9] while Lorenzo Magalotti, accompanying the Grand Duke of Tuscany to England in 1669, wrote after going to the Bridges Street Theatre on 15 April: 'Before the comedy begins, that the audience may not be tired with waiting, the most delightful symphonies are played; on which account many persons come early.'[10]

Locke's music for *The Tempest* is the only set of theatre ayres that he published. Around a hundred other pieces for violin band by Locke survive in manuscript (Table 3.1, nos. 1–100).[11] Identifying which of these were used as theatre music is not straightforward. Initially, the outlook is promising, since just over three-quarters of them are found in a manuscript exclusively of Locke's music, which has the title 'The Rare Theatrical, & other Compositions'.[12] However, only twelve of

---

[8] On 20 March 1664/5, a warrant was issued 'to make up habits of several coloured silks for 24 violins, 12 of them being for his Majesty's service in the Theatre Royal, and the other 12 habits for his Majesty's service in his Highness the Duke of York's Theatre; and also 24 garlands of several coloured flowers to each of them'; Andrew Ashbee, ed., *Records of English Court Music* (Snodland: Andrew Ashbee, 1986), vol. I, 61.

[9] Samuel de Sorbière, *Relation d'un voyage en Angleterre* (Paris, 1664), 63, translated as *A Voyage to England* (London: Printed, and Sold by J. Woodward, 1709), 69.

[10] [Lorenzo Magalotti], *Travels of Cosmo the Third, Grand Duke of Tuscany* (London: Printed for J. Mawman, 1821), 190. The popularity of these performances appears to have led the enterprising violinist and band leader, John Banister, to organise the first public concerts in London from 1672 onwards. See Peter Holman, *Four and Twenty Fiddlers* (Oxford: Clarendon Press, 1993), 349.

[11] Seventy-eight pieces in US-NYp Drexel MS 3976, fifteen pieces in US-NYp Drexel MS 5061, and eight pieces in US-NYp Drexel MS 3849. The pieces in Drexel MS 3849 survive only in three parts, but I argue, principally on the basis of their inclusion in the bass partbook US-NH Filmer MS 7, that they are four-part pieces lacking a part. Concerning whether all of the pieces in Drexel MS 3976 were conceived for a violin band, see later in this chapter.

[12] US-NYp Drexel MS 3976. Holman has suggested that the title, which is in the hand of the manuscript's earliest verifiable owner, the Welsh harpist and antiquarian Edward Jones (1752–1824), may have been taken from the remains of an earlier binding. See Peter Holman's introduction to *Matthew Locke, The Rare Theatrical*, vol. 4, ed. Peter Holman, Music for London Entertainment, 1660–1800, Series A (London: Stainer and Bell, 1989), 9–10. The 'other Compositions' (i.e., non-theatrical compositions) referred to in the title of the manuscript include six sets of brawles.

Table 3.1 *Locke's violin-band music*

No.	Source, page	Title	Key	Type of 2nd part	3rd higher error [+] or C-clef	Concordance
1a–c	A, 1	*Brawles*	A	Indeterminate		*DM* (1665), no. 80, *AB* (c. 1669), no. 14, 'The Opera Tune', *TC* (1677), no. 6 'Gavat'
1d	A, 3	**Gavott [Act Tune]**	A			
2	A, 4	**The Fantastick [Curtain Tune]**	a	Low	+	
3	A, 7	Running Almand	a	Low		*PC* (1672, 1680, 1682), no. 26 'Gavot'
4	A, 8	Ayre	a	Indeterminate		*TC* (1677), no. 7 [a3 in g, first two sections only]
5	A, 9	Symphony	a	Indeterminate	+	
6	A, 10	Symphony	a	Indeterminate		
7	A, 11	**Act Tune**	a	Indeterminate		
8	A, 12	Jane Shore	A	Low		*AB* (1678), no. 73
9	A, 13	*Brawles*	Bb	Low	+	
10	A, 17	*Corant*	Bb	Indeterminate		
11	A, 18	*Saraband [& conclusion]*	Bb	Indeterminate		
12	A, 19	*Almand*	Bb	Indeterminate		
13	A, 20	*Galliard*	Bb	Low		
14	A, 21	**Lilk & Saraband [Curtain Tune]**	Bb	Low	+	Saraband: *C&D* (1659), pp. 12–13
15	A, 23	**Curtain Tune**	Bb	Indeterminate	+	*AB* (1678), no. 50 'A Theatre Jigg'; *DM* (1665), no. 76 'Antick Dance' [only 1st strain is concordant]
16	A, 25	Roundo	Bb	Indeterminate	+	
17	A, 26	**[Jig]**	Bb	Indeterminate		*1066*, ff. 11ᵛ–12
18	A, 27	**Curtain Tune**	Bb	Indeterminate		
19	A, 29	*[Ayre]*	C	High equal		*BC I*, no. 11 'Ayre' [a3]
20	A, 30	*[Saraband]*	C	High equal		*BC I*, no. 12 'Saraband' [a3]

21	A, 31	**Curtain Tune**	C	Low		
22	A, 35	Corant	C	Indeterminate		
23	A, 36	**Curtain Tune**	C	Indeterminate		
24	A, 38	[**Curtain Tune**]	C	Indeterminate		
25	A, 39	**Curtain Tune**	C	Low		
26	A, 43	**Curtain Tune**	C	Low		
27	A, 45	*Brawles*	C	Indeterminate		
28	A, 48	Saraband	C	Indeterminate		
29	A, 49	*Brawles*	c	High/low		
30	A, 53	[Ayre]	c	Low		
31	A, 55	[Ayre]	C	Indeterminate		
32	A, 56	[Hornpipe]	C	Indeterminate	+	*31431*, ff. 62ʳ–63
33	A, 57	*Brawles*	d	Low	+	
34	A, 60	[*Corant*]	d	Low	+	
35	A, 61	[*Corant*]	d	Low	+	
36	A, 62	Running Almain	d	Low	+	*Melothesia* (1673), p. 18 'Jig'
37	A, 63	Saraband	d	Low	+	
38	A, 64	Almand	d	Low	+	
39	A, 66	Corant	d	Low	+	
40	A, 67	Running Almand	d	Indeterminate		
41	A, [68/9]	[Jig]	d	Indeterminate	+	
42	A, 70	Almand	d	Low	+	
43	A, 71	Corant	d	Low		
44	A, 72	Ayre	d	Low		
45	A, 73	[Jig]	d	Low	+	
46	A, 74	Saraband	d	Low		
47	A, 75	Ayre	d	High equal		*BC II*, no. 8 'Ayre' [a3]
48	A, 76	[Galliard]	d	High equal		*BC II*, no. 9 'Galliard' [a3]
49	A, 78	Hornepipe	d	High equal		
50	A, 79	Gavot	d	Indeterminate		
51	A, 80	**Curtain Tune**	d	Low		
52	A, 82	[Jig]	d	Indeterminate		
53	A, 84	[Jig]	d	Indeterminate		

Table 3.1 (cont.)

No.	Source, page	Title	Key	Type of 2nd part	3rd higher error [+] or C-clef	Concordance
54	A, 85	[Jig]	d	High/low		
55	A, 85	Almand	d	Low	+	
56	A, 87	Corant	d	Low		
57	A, 88	**[Jig]**	d	Low		*AB* (c. 1669), no. 64 'She would if she could'
58	A, 89	Corant	d	Low	+	*1066*, f. 1ff.
59	A, 90	Almand	d	High/low		*1066*, f. 1ʳ, *5777*, f. 5ʳ, *44*, ff. 2, 10, 12, 14–16 [a3]
60	A, 92	Corant	d	Indeterminate	clef	*1066*, f. 1ʳ
61	A, 93	Saraband	d	Indeterminate		*1066*, f. 2
62	A, 94	Gavot	d	Indeterminate		*1066*, f. 2 'tune'
63	A, 95	**[Act Tune]**	d	Low		*5777*, f. 6 'tune'
64	A, 96	[?Act Tune]	d	Indeterminate		
65	A, 97	Brawles	D	Low		
66	A, 100	[Corant]	D	Low		
67	A, 101	[Corant]	D	Low	+	
68	A, 102	**[Curtain Tune]**	D	Low		See no. 72, A, pp. 108–10 [last two strains only]
69	A, 104	[Hornpipe]	D	Indeterminate		*AB* (1670), no. 34
70	A, 105	[Jig]	D	Indeterminate		
71	A, 106	**[Curtain Tune]**	D	High/low		
72	A, 108	**[Curtain Tune]**	D	Low		See no. 68, A, pp. 102–3 [lacking first strain]
73	A, 111	[Ayre]	D	Indeterminate	+	
74	A, 112	**[Curtain Tune]**	D	Indeterminate		*AB* (1670), no. 35 [variant of final strain]
76	A, 114	[Saraband]	D	Low		
77	A, 114	[Ayre]	D	Indeterminate		
78	A, 115	[Jig]	D	Indeterminate		

79	B, 1	Alman	g	Low		
80	B, 2	Corant	g	Indeterminate		
81	B, 3	Firk	g	Indeterminate		
82	B, 4	Alman	g	Low	clef	
83	B, 5	Corant	g	Low	clef	
84	B, 6	Firk	g	Low	clef	
85	B, 6	Running Alman	g	Indeterminate	clef	
86	B, 7	Corant	g	Low	clef	
87	B, 8	Saraband	g	Low	clef	
88	B, 9	Almand	g	Low	+	
89	B, 10	Saraband	g	Low		
90	B, 10	Jigg	g	Low		
91	B, 11	Tune Long Time	g	Indeterminate		
92	B, 12	Almand	g	Indeterminate		
93	B, 13	Galliard	g	Indeterminate		
94	C, 16ᵛ	[Curtain Tune]	g	High		*TC*, p. 5 [a3]
95	C, 17ʳ	[Ayre]	g	Indeterminate		*33236*, 11ʳ [a3]
96	C, 17ᵛ	[Ayre]	g	Indeterminate		*33236*, 11ʳ [a3]
97	C, 17ᵛ	[Introduction]	Bb	High		
98	C, 18ʳ	[Gavot]	Bb	High		
99	C, 18ᵛ	[Ayre]	Bb	Indeterminate		
100	C, 19ʳ	[Conclusion]	c/Bb	Indeterminate		
101	C, 21ʳ	[Introduction]	g	Indeterminate		*3849*, p. 3 'Almaine', 'Ayre'
102	C, 21ᵛ	[Galliard]	g	Indeterminate		*3849*, p. 4 'Ayre'
103	C, 22ʳ	[Gavot]	g	Indeterminate		*3849*, p. 4 'Ayre'
104	C, 22ʳ	[Sarabrand]	g	High		*3849*, p. 43
105	C, 22ᵛ	[Lilk]	g	Indeterminate		*3849*, p. 44; *TC* (1677), p. 29
106	C, 22ᵛ	[Curtain Tune]	F	High		*3849*, p. 44
107	*EO*, 71	[Conclusion]	g	High		*3849*, p. 45 'Jigg Almaine'
108	*EO*, 2	**Retornello with Violins**	D	Indeterminate		*EO*, p. 62 [Instrumental music in *The Tempest* (1674)]
						EO, pp. 63–4
						EO, p. 64
						EO, pp. 65–6
						EO, p. 67
						EO, pp. 68–70
						[Instrumental music in *Psyche* (1675)]

Table 3.1 (cont.)

No.	Source, page	Title	Key	Type of 2nd part	3rd higher error [+] or C-clef	Concordance
109	EO, 8	**Simphony at the descending of Venus**	a	Low		
110	EO, 31	**Symphony at the Parley of Venus and Mars**	G	Indeterminate		
111	EO, 52	**Symphony at the Descending of Apollo**	D	High		
112	EO, 57	**Symphony at the Descending of Jupiter**	D	High		

Identified theatre music in **bold** type; non-theatre music in *italic*.

Key

A US-NYp Drexel MS 3976
B US-NYp Drexel MS 5061
C US-NH Filmer MS 7

AB Apollo's Banquet (c. 1669–)
BC Locke, *The Broken Consort* (part one: I; part two: II)
C&D Locke, *Cupid and Death* (1659)
DM The Dancing Master (1651–)
EO *The English Opera* (1675)
PC *The Pleasant Companion* (1672–)
TC *Tripla Concordia* (1677)

44   GB-Ob Mus.Sch. MS C.44
1066 GB-Och Add. MS 1066
3849 US-NYp Drexel MS 3849
5777 GB-En MS 5777
31431 GB-Lbl Add. MS 31431
33236 GB-Lbl Add. MS 33236

these can be identified as theatre music on the basis of their titles, eight being labelled 'Curtain Tune', one as an 'Act Tune' and three others on the basis of titles in concordances.[13] Locke's Curtain Tunes do, however, have a distinctive multi-sectional form, in which duple and triple time sections are usually contrasted with one another. On the basis of this feature, a further six pieces in the 'Rare Theatrical' manuscript can be identified as Curtain Tunes, even though they are not labelled as such.[14]

But what of the other movements that made up a set of theatre ayres? With the sequence of movements found in *The Tempest* music in mind – First and Second Music, Curtain Tune, Act Tunes – one might expect each Curtain Tune in the 'Rare Theatrical' manuscript to be preceded and followed by its associated movements. However, it is clear from the order of parts of the manuscript that the original sequence of movements as performed in the theatre has not been preserved. For example, four Curtain Tunes appear as consecutive items on pages 36–44 (nos. 23–6). This is because the 'Rare Theatrical' manuscript is organised as an anthology, with all the pieces in the same key being placed together. Since the First and Second Music and Act Tunes for a play would quite often be in a different key from the Curtain Tune – as is the case with the music for *The Tempest* – the copyist would have had to dismember the theatre suites when creating the anthology.[15] Consequently, the sequence of movements in the manuscript is not necessarily of any significance when attempting to identify which pieces may have been used as preliminary music or Act Tunes. The only pieces that can confidently be linked to use in the theatre are the thirteen Curtain Tunes, the three Act tunes (nos. 1d, 7 and 63) and the two theatre Jigs (nos. 17 and 57) – a total of just eighteen pieces (in bold in Table 3.1).[16]

---

[13] Although no. 63 is entitled 'Curtain Tune' in the manuscript it does not have the multi-sectional form that characterises other Curtain Tunes; in a concordance it is simply labelled 'Tune' and this, in combination with its simple binary form, may indicate that it was used as an Act Tune. The theatrical pieces identified by titles in concordances are no. 1d 'The Opera Tune', no. 17 'A Theatre Jigg' and no. 57, which is labelled 'She would if she could', the title of George Etherege's play of February 1667/8; all three could have served as Act Tunes.

[14] Table 3.1, nos. 2, 14, 24, 68/72, 71, 74. One other multi-sectional piece that is probably a Curtain Tune is found in another manuscript (no. 94).

[15] The manuscript is evidently also incomplete, since it only contains music in four keys – A, Bb, C, D – the sections in G, E and F apparently having been lost at some stage.

[16] Jane Shore, the title of no. 8, was a mistress of Edward IV. She is a major character in *The True Tragedy of Richard III*, an anonymous play dating from *c.* 1590, and her story is central to the plot of Thomas Heywood's *Edward IV*, printed in 1600. This piece may relate to an adaptation from the 1660s or 1670s of one of these plays, or of Shakespeare's *Richard III*, possibly being used as an Act Tune. Alternatively, the music may set a traditional melody reflecting Shore's proverbial merry disposition and may have no theatrical link. The labelling of no. 64 as 'Tune' in the concordance GB-En MS 5777 might conceivably indicate that it was used as an Act Tune.

Since Locke appears to have been the 'house' composer to the Duke's Company, the theatrical movements in the manuscript presumably relate to the productions by this company from the 1660s and 1670s (Locke died in 1677). Locke's Curtain Tune for *The Tempest* famously depicts the rising and calming of the storm, so it is highly likely that he took care to match the mood of his music with the drama that it introduced, even if other composers did not.[17] The Curtain Tunes found in the 'Rare Theatrical' manuscript are musically highly characterised: many have a jokey, raucous feel to them, perfectly setting the scene for a Restoration comedy, while others are dark and intense, better suited to a tragedy. Frustratingly, none of the curtain tunes can be linked to a specific play with any certainty. There is, however, one possible exception.

Some of the musical features found in 'The Fantastick' (no. 2) appear to hint at the nature of its parent play, as does its title. The word 'Fantastick' (or 'phantastique') was used in the early seventeenth century to describe the strange and exaggerated gestures that were typical of the choreography of antimasque (or 'Antick') dances. Ben Jonson featured this type of devilish dance in the *Masque of Queens* (1609), in which witches are musically and physically represented as grotesque: 'with a strange and sudden music they fell into a magical dance full of preposterous change and gesticulation … dancing back to back and hip to hip, their hands joined, and making their circles backward, to the left hand, with strange fantastic motions of their heads and bodies'.[18] In the music for 'The Fantastick' (Music Example 3.1), Locke alternates long, held notes with livelier rhythmic sections, a feature that is also found in the 'Witches Dance' published in *Apollo's Banquet* (1669).[19] Although this feature is typical of antimasque dances more generally, the parallels between the two pieces are striking nonetheless.[20] 'The Fantastick' starts in the minor mode, but later modulates to the major mode for a triple-time section which is reminiscent of Locke's music to Davenant's witches song ('Let's have a dance'), where the lilting melody is combined with menacing lyrics. These shared musical

---

[17] For examples of composers who did not consider this to be necessary, composing serious minor-key music for comedies and major-key ones for tragedies, see Peter Holman, 'Introduction', in *Restoration Theatre Airs*, ed. Peter Holman and Andrew Woolley (Musica Britannica, forthcoming).

[18] Amanda Eubanks Winkler, *O Let Us Howle Some Heavy Note* (Bloomington: Indiana University Press, 2006), 30–1.

[19] The same features are also found in the 'Witches Dance', possibly by Robert Johnson, in *The Masque of Queens* (1609).

[20] Similar musical features are also found in the second strain of 'The Second Witches' Dance', GB-Lbl Add. MS 10444, no. 26, Ex. 3.6 in Peter Walls, *Music in the English Courtly Masque, 1604–1640* (Oxford: Clarendon Press, 1996), 142, and edited in full in Eubanks Winkler, *O Let Us Howle*, 33.

Music Example 3.1 'Low' writing for the second part in Locke's Curtain Tune 'The Fantastick', US-NYp Drexel MS 3976, pages 4–6

features suggest that the 'fantastick' stage action that Locke's music was presumably designed to accompany may well have been a witches' dumb-show and that this particular Curtain Tune may have been used for productions of *Macbeth*.

Since the music in the 'Rare Theatrical' manuscript is not preserved in the order in which it would have been performed, alternative methods are required to determine which other pieces in the manuscript might belong with 'The Fantastick' as incidental music to a play, possibly *Macbeth*. One possible method is suggested by another musical feature of 'The Fantastick', namely, the nature of the writing for the second part in the four-part texture. In this piece the writing for the second part appears to be better suited to a viola than a violin and could be called 'low': its range is closer to that of the third part than that of the first; the interval between the first and second parts often exceeds an octave, and the second part often crosses below the third (see Music Example 3.1, bars 2, 12, 17 and 25).[21] The use of violas on the second part is typical of French violin-band music and was adopted by the violin band at the English court during the 1630s, when it was directed by the Frenchman Etienne Nau. Locke presumably came across French music (and musicians) using this scoring during his time in the 'Low Countries' between 1648 and 1650, so the adoption of this instrumental practice by Locke for the newly reconstituted violin band at the English court in 1660 would be entirely understandable and would represent an expression of continuity with the practice of the band in the time of Charles I.[22] Furthermore, the make-up of the violin band at the English court in 1660 was described, in a document that is unfortunately now untraceable, as 'six violins, six counter-tenors, six tenors, and six basses'; the use of the term 'counter-tenors' for the instruments on the second part is strikingly similar to that used in an English court document from 1631 in which the term 'contrat[eno]r' is used.[23] The 'low' writing for the second

---

[21] Throughout the 'Rare Theatrical' manuscript, the second part is notated in the treble clef, but the prevalence of a particular copying error in which the music is notated a third too high indicates that the copyist was often working from exemplars in which this part was notated in a C1 clef. For more on 'third higher' errors, see later in this chapter.

[22] This may well be the scoring of the violin band depicted in the painting by Jerome Janssens of Charles II and his sister Mary dancing at the Hague in the late 1650s (see plate 6 in Holman, *Four and Twenty Fiddlers*). Locke's writing for the second part is nevertheless distinct from that of his French contemporaries, in the wide range of the part, the crossing of parts and the amount of rhythmic and melodic interest.

[23] The untraceable document is referred to in William Sandys and Simon Andrew Forster's *The History of the Violin* (London: William Reeves Bookseller, 1864), 146. Since the authors give no indication of the source of this information, it must be treated with great caution. However, some elements in this reference have the ring of authenticity. The division of the players into four groups, rather than the five of the pre-Civil War violin band, clearly matches the surviving repertoire, which is in four parts, a fact that may not have been known to Sandys and Forster at the time. The equal distribution, with six players on each part, also differs from the pre-war practice, in which treble and bass parts were more heavily doubled, but equal distribution would certainly suit Locke's more equally voiced, contrapuntal style of writing for the violin band. The vocal terminology used

part found in 'The Fantastick' is found in a further thirty-three pieces in the 'Rare Theatrical' manuscript and also in eight of the fifteen pieces by Locke in the manuscript US-NYp Drexel 5061; furthermore, in this source the second part is partly notated in a C-clef (C1) which is typically associated with the highest of the viola parts in French music. In addition, 'low' writing for the second part is also found in pieces by Locke's direct contemporary, John Banister, who played in the court violin band from 1660 onwards and directed it from 1662 to 1666. Fragmentary as it is, this musical, documentary and notational evidence appears to support the conclusion that violas, and not violins, were used on the second part of English violin-band repertoire when it re-formed at the Restoration. And since 'The Fantastick' uses this scoring, any reconstruction of a set of theatre dances associated with it would need to be chosen from other movements with a similar instrumentation.

By contrast, this 'low' style of writing for the second part is not found in the music of the younger generation whose compositional careers began in the late 1660s, namely Pelham Humfrey, John Blow and Robert Smith. In the works of these composers, the second part lies higher and is more suited to a violin. Examples of this sort of writing can be found consistently in the symphony anthems that Humfrey composed for the Chapel Royal from 1667 onwards and those of John Blow from 1670, as well as in Humfrey's court odes from the 1671 onwards. It can also be found in the sets of dances by Robert Smith that appear at the start of the manuscript US-NH Filmer MS 7 and which date from *c*. 1671.[24] This manuscript also contains seven movements by Locke which are not found in the 'Rare Theatrical' manuscript (nos. 94–100), as well as his music for *The Tempest*

---

to describe the two inner parts, 'counter-tenor' and ' tenor', is also typical of late seventeenth-century English sources: sometime in the early 1670s, the compiler of US-NHub Osborn MS 515 described the instrumentation of a five-part piece by Dietrich Becker as '2 treb. cont. ten. basse', and a page in James Talbot's manuscript (GB-Och Mus. MS 1187) which dates from the 1690s is labelled 'Violin Tenor & Counter Tenor'. See Robert Ford, 'Osborn MS 515: A Guardbook of Restoration Instrumental Music', *Fontes Artis Musicae*, 30.3 (1983): 174–84 (181). Unfortunately, it appears that Talbot did not gain access to a counter tenor violin to make measurements, since apart from the title, this page in the manuscript remains blank; see Robert Donington, 'James Talbot's Manuscript', *The Galpin Society Journal*, 3 (1950): 27–45 (30, 40). The English court document from 1631 is GB-Lpro, LC5/132, 242; see Holman, *Four and Twenty Fiddlers*, 234.

[24] This manuscript is a bass partbook, the sole survivor of a set of three partbooks. However, concordances with complete sets of parts make it a significant source. It appears to be a chronological sequence of dances and theatre suites; the second item is a set of dances composed by Banister 'for the new house', an apparent reference to the Dorset Garden Theatre, which opened in November 1671. A date around 1671 for Banister's pieces is supported by the concordance in GB-Och Mus. MS 1183, in which they are copied on to paper with pre-1671 watermarks. See Silas Wollston, 'The Instrumentation of English Violin-Band Music' (PhD, The Open University, 2009), chs. 5 and 7.

Sarabrand

Music Example 3.2 'High' writing for the second part in Locke's Sarabrand used in *The Tempest* (1674), published in *The English Opera, or, the Vocal Musick in Psyche* (London, 1675), pages 65–6

(1674): significantly, in six of these pieces his writing for the second part is, like that of his younger colleagues, 'high' and suited to a violin.[25]

In the Sarabrand (Music Example 3.2), the second part lies consistently close to the first, the lower limit of the second part is closer to that of the first part than that of the third, and the second part does not pass beneath the third part. Also, the highest note of the second part is g", which, if it were performed on a viola would require the use of third position, a technique that rank-and-file players in the English

---

[25] 'High' second parts are also found in the 'Symphonies' of Apollo and Jupiter in *Psyche* (1675). Evidence that Robert Smith may have composed the Act Tunes to *The Tempest* music is found in the manuscript US-NH Filmer 7: there is a terminal flourish at fol. 23 after Locke's Curtain Tune, and at fol. 24 the Third Act Tune is labelled 'Mr Rob Smyth'; the Fourth Act Tune and the Conclusion are missing in the manuscript. Furthermore, two copies of *The English Opera* omit the four act tunes and in 'the Yale copy' of the print, the Act Tunes are reportedly 'carefully marked in a contemporary hand with an "X"'. I have also argued that weak voice-leading in the Act Tunes are more characteristic of Smith than Locke. Curtis Price, *Music in the Restoration Theatre with a Catalogue of Instrumental Music in the Plays 1665–1713* (Ann Arbor: UMI Research Press, 1979), 260, fn. 20, acknowledging information supplied by Robert Ford. See also Wollston, 'The Instrumentation of English Violin-Band Music', 83–4, 241–3.

violin band had apparently not mastered.[26] The inescapable conclusion of this musical evidence is that there was a shift away from the use of violas on the second line towards the use of violins and that 'low' writing for the second part can therefore be identified as a feature of 'early' Restoration violin-band music, that is, music of the 1660s. The latest dateable example of 'low' writing for the second part is found in the theatre tune (no. 57) that Locke composed for Etherege's comedy *She would if she could*, which was first produced in February 1667/8.[27]

In the light of this evidence, Locke's use of 'low' writing for the second part in 'The Fantastick' suggests that, if it was used for *Macbeth*, it is more likely to have been associated with productions in 1660s than in the 1670s. This is in itself of limited significance. However, the conclusion that music with 'low' second parts are typical of Locke's violin-band writing up until at least 1668 enables the core of Locke's instrumental music from the 1660s to be identified and it is among these pieces that the other music that Pepys could have heard at the 1667 production of *Macbeth* – the 'ayres' before the show began and the tunes between the acts – are most likely to be found.

Dating repertoire on the basis of the presence of 'low' writing does, however, need to be treated with caution. This is because in four pieces in the 'Rare Theatrical' manuscript the writing for the second part has most or all of the characteristics of 'low' writing but also a highest note of g″ – the writing is in effect both 'low' and 'high'. One possible explanation for this is that these pieces are transitional, composed soon after the change from viola to violin on the second part had taken place, but before old habits had been abandoned.[28] A date around 1669 for two examples of such writing by Banister appears to support this interpretation.[29] There is

---

[26] The fact that between 1660 and 1685 English composers never wrote higher than the note c‴ for the first part in their violin-band music strongly suggests that the ability to shift into third position was not part of the regular technique of professional players.

[27] The melody of the dance appears in the first edition of the violin tune book *Apollo's Banquet*, dated to 1669, with the title 'She would if she could'. The four-part version can therefore be taken as an indication of the instrumentation of the violin band that played for the Duke's Company at the theatre in Lincoln's Inn Fields at that time.

[28] Locke may not have felt the need to abandon some features of 'low' writing at all, since they are entirely compatible with the use of a higher tessitura and allowing the second and third parts to cross freely often enables more satisfying voice leading. This may have been what Purcell found attractive in Locke's 'low' writing, echoes of which are found in some of his early overtures, including Z.771. See Silas Wollston, 'New Light on Purcell's Early Overtures', *Early Music*, 37.4 (2009): 647–55 (653–4).

[29] These are the first two pieces in a set of dances attributed to 'J.B.' in the manuscript GB-Lbl Mus. 142, 4–6, that includes a jig which was probably composed for Boyle's play *Guzman*, produced in 1669. The third piece in the set (on page 5), entitled 'Roundo', is a concordance of 'Don Gusman's Jigg' in *Apollo's Banquet* (1669), no. 160. See Holman's commentary in the Sotheby's sale catalogue, 21 May 1999, *Fine Printed and Manuscript Music* (London: Sotheby's, 1999), 51, item 95, where he states that the jig is by Smith.

also the possibility that some 'low' parts were written after the change, but happen not to make use of the newly available higher tessitura. In many cases, the upper limit of the second part appears to be governed by the tessitura of the first part, since Locke generally does not allow his second part to cross above the first.[30] In these cases, it has to be admitted that the highest note of the second part does not in itself allow the nature of the part (whether 'high' or 'low') to be determined, and it cannot be ruled out that pieces with the features of 'low' parts but no compositional opportunity to rise above f" (the highest note of viola parts) may date from the 1670s.

There is, however, another factor that may help to identify 'low' pieces with greater confidence. This is a particular type of error made by the copyist of the 'Rare Theatrical' manuscript in which the notes of the second part are copied too high by the interval of a third. The most likely explanation of this error is that in the exemplar from which the copyist was working, the second part was notated in the C-clef C1, in which all notes lie a third higher than in the treble clef, and he simply forgot to transpose them down a third to suit the new clef. 'A third higher' errors can therefore be interpreted as evidence of the use of a C-clef in the exemplar (as is the case with the pieces by Locke in US-NYp Drexel 5061), and consequently, since this clef is typically associated with the highest of the viola parts in French music, as evidence that the part was composed with a viola in mind. This type of error is found in twenty-four pieces in the 'Rare Theatrical' (see Table 3.1). Seventeen of these also have the features of 'low' second parts and the copying error can therefore be considered as corroborative evidence that the identification as a 'low' part is correct. Six of the other examples of this error are found in pieces in which the nature of the second part cannot be determined from the music itself, so the implication that they may well have been composed with a viola in

---

[30] This was common practice in French music, but not among English composers of the mid-seventeenth century: in the ayres of William Lawes and John Jenkins, the second part often acts as a descant *above* the main theme in the first part. The influence of this style post-1660 can be seen in the occasional use of 'descant' writing in the violin-band music of Banister (see, for example, GB-Och Mus. MS 1183, fols. 91–6 and 85–90, the latter composed 'for the New House', Dorset Garden Theatre, which opened in 1671) and as late as 1694, Purcell felt the need to make this recommendation: 'when you make a *Second Treble* to a tune, keep it always below the Upper Part, because it may [then] not spoil the Air'. The practice of allowing the second part to rise above the first may well have been one of the 'Barbarities' of which, according to Purcell, English music would gradually rid itself by studying 'a little of the French air'. See Purcell's contribution to the twelfth edition of John Playford's *An Introduction to the Skill of Musick* (London: Printed by E. Jones, for Henry Playford, 1694), 116; and Ian Spink, ed., *The Blackwell History of Music in Britain*, vol. 3: *The Seventeenth Century* (Oxford: Blackwell, 1992), 255. For Banister's music, see Wollston, 'The Instrumentation of English Violin-Band Music', 125–50, 228–38.

mind is particularly useful.³¹ The identification of 'low' second parts and 'a third higher' errors within individual pieces can also be helpful when trying to decide whether a sequence of consecutive movements within the manuscript does in fact constitute an original grouping.³²

Finally, when attempting to identify the theatre music within the 'Rare Theatrical' repertoire, it is worth considering whether any pieces can be ruled out. Four pieces are concordant with movements from Locke's 'Broken Consort', sets of chamber music composed for a small ensemble that mixed violins, viols and continuo instruments and performed at court in Charles II's private apartments in the early years of his reign. The distinctive call-and-response interplay of the two violin parts in these pieces sets them firmly within the pre-Restoration tradition of four-part repertoire developed by Charles Coleman, John Jenkins and William Lawes, and in this respect, they stand out from the rest of the music in the 'Rare Theatrical' manuscript.³³ The inclusion of these pieces in the manuscript could be explained by the fact that, along with the rest of the contents, they could be loosely described as 'four-part ayres', but on stylistic grounds I do not believe they are violin-band repertoire.³⁴ The other pieces that can probably be ruled out are the six sets of 'brawles', an Anglicised spelling of the French 'branles', the group dance that usually opened a court ball. Some of these are followed in the manuscript by corants and sarabands, and since these dances were also typically danced at court balls, they may belong with the brawles that precede them and may not have been used in the theatre. However, the Gavott which ends the brawles sequence in A major (no. 1d) also appears in another source under the title 'The Opera Tune by Mr Lock', indicating that it may have been used as an Act Tune in a theatrical production. This example suggests that dance music for court balls may well also have been used for other purposes in the theatre.

In conclusion, it appears that the 'Rare Theatrical' manuscript contains a large amount of violin-band music dating from the 1660s. On the

---

[31] In one other piece (no. 60) the second part is notated using a C-clef in a concordance (GB-Ob Mus. Sch. MS C.44).

[32] Only one grouping is indicated by a concordance, a five-movement sequence on 90–6 (nos. 59–63), beginning with an Almand, which is also found in the manuscript GB-Och Mus. MS 1066, fols. 1–6. The movement sequences used by Locke in his chamber music are also a potential guide.

[33] These pieces, and a fifth in the same style, are found on pages 19–20 and 47–9 of the manuscript. On the origin of this style, see David Pinto, *For ye Violls* (Richmond: Fretwork Editions, 1995), 43–52 and Holman, *Four and Twenty Fiddlers*, 253–8. Holman has suggested that the violin writing in these pieces is evidence of the influence of Italian émigré musicians and music in London, but I dispute this. See Wollston, 'The Instrumentation of English Violin-Band Music', 282.

[34] There is some evidence that pre-Civil War four-part repertoire was still being cultivated in Oxford in the 1660s, and that the 'Rare Theatrical' manuscript may have an Oxford origin; see Wollston, 'The Instrumentation of English Violin-Band Music', 120–3, 220–1.

basis of the 'low' writing for the second part, Locke's violin-band pieces in the manuscript US-NYp Drexel 5061 also appear to date from the 1660s. While relatively few pieces of the 'Rare Theatrical' repertoire can be confidently dated to the 1670s, the inclusion in the manuscript US-NH Filmer 7 of the seven pieces nos. 94–100 suggests that they have a theatrical origin and date from that decade, a conclusion that is also supported by the 'high' nature of the writing for the second part.[35] While it is not possible to identify any specific pieces that were used in the productions of *Macbeth* of 1664 and 1667, it is nonetheless extremely likely that some of those from the 'Rare Theatrical' manuscript with 'low' second parts were used for this purpose. Other pieces in the manuscript no doubt relate to plays performed by the Duke's Company in the 1660s; Locke has been identified as composer for a number of these, but it is also quite possible that some of the pieces were composed for plays for which we do not have evidence of Locke's involvement.[36] And while it is frustrating that the original groupings and order of movements were substantially lost as the manuscript was compiled, this situation does invite musicians today to use the 'Rare Theatrical' and its associated manuscripts as a resource to create theatre suites for any number of Restoration plays from the 1660s and 1670s, guided by the character of the music itself and taking note of the nature of the second part to achieve a degree of chronological refinement in the choice of movements.

Locke's music for *The Tempest* is rightly recognised as a landmark of programmatic theatre music, but due to the lack of a modern edition of the rest of Locke's instrumental theatre music, it has stood alone and without a wider context. Once the remarkable repertoire in the 'Rare Theatrical' is available to scholars and performers, I hope the use of Locke's music in theatrical productions will stimulate a greater appreciation of the riches of Restoration theatre and allow modern theatregoers to experience something of Pepys's theatrical enjoyment.

---

[35] On the basis of dateable repertoire, it appears that the contents of US-NH Filmer MS 7 were transcribed chronologically, a feature that it shares with other Filmer manuscripts. Locke's pieces nos. 94–100 appear between music from 1671 and his own music for *The Tempest* (1674). One play produced by the Duke's Company between those dates for which Locke has been identified as composer is Elkanah Settle's *The Empress of Morocco* (1673), so these pieces may relate to that production.

[36] In addition to Davenant's *Macbeth* (1664), Locke contributed music to the following plays: Davenant's *Love and Honour* (1661), Stapylton's *The Step-Mother* (1663), Davenant's adaptation of Shakespeare's *Henry VIII* (1663), Etherege's *The Comical Revenge, or Love in a Tub* (1664), Davenant's *The Rivals* (1664) and Etherege's *She would if she could* (1668). See table 1 in Holman, ed., *Matthew Locke, The Rare Theatrical*, 20–1.

CHAPTER 4

Cross-Dressing in Restoration Shakespeare: Twelfth Night *and* The Tempest

Fiona Ritchie

In her exploration of performing major roles in Shakespeare, *Brutus and Other Heroines*, actor Harriet Walter outlines a major issue in trying 'to dig back through the centuries to reach the original germ that motivated Shakespeare to write and which still moves us to perform his works'. In asking the key question 'What did Shakespeare mean?', women performers come up against an obstacle: 'He never meant *you* to play the part.'[1] Actresses first began wrestling with this problem over 350 years ago when in 1660 the first professional female performer appeared on the English stage. The ambiguous presentation of gender identity that resulted from boy actors playing female characters who assume male disguise within the world of the plays in which they appear has been the subject of much critical commentary.[2] But the advent of the actress and the eventual end to the practice of boy actors appearing in female roles did not necessarily eliminate opportunities for the exploration of gender issues in the seventeenth-century theatre. Through the practice of adaptation so popular in the period, complex engagement with questions of gender expression remained key to Shakespeare's works as they were performed on the Restoration stage. This chapter will explore cross-dressing in two

---

I am grateful to Jennifer Drouin and Nathan Richards-Velinou for their helpful comments on this chapter.

[1] Harriet Walter, *Brutus and Other Heroines: Playing Shakespeare's Roles for Women* (London: Nick Hern Books, 2016), 25. Walter makes these comments specifically in the context of her attempts to develop distinctive performances of three of Shakespeare's cross-dressing women.

[2] See for example Michael Shapiro, *Gender in Play on the Shakespearean Stage: Boy Heroines and Female Pages* (Ann Arbor: University of Michigan Press, 1994); Jean Howard, 'Crossdressing, the Theatre, and Gender Struggle in Early Modern England', *Shakespeare Quarterly*, 39.4 (1988): 418–40; Tracey Sedinger, '"If Sight and Shape be True": The Epistemology of Crossdressing on the London Stage', *Shakespeare Quarterly*, 48.1 (1997): 63–79; Jennifer Drouin, 'Cross-Dressing, Drag, and Passing: Slippages in Shakespearean Comedy', in *Shakespeare Re-Dressed: Cross-Gender Casting in Contemporary Performance*, ed. James C. Bulman (Madison, NJ: Fairleigh Dickinson University Press, 2008), 23–56. Drouin's article is particularly helpful in nuancing our understanding of this practice by distinguishing between the terms cross-dressing, drag, and passing.

Shakespeare adaptations of the period: William Burnaby's *Love Betray'd; or, The Agreable Disapointment* (1703), an adaptation of *Twelfth Night* that did not become a mainstay of the repertory and has been little studied, and John Dryden and William Davenant's *The Tempest; or, The Enchanted Island* (1667), one of the best-known and most enduring Restoration adaptations. I argue that the use of cross-dressing in Restoration Shakespeare is more complex than the traditional emphasis on its use as a means to sexualise the early actress suggests. This convention in fact allows for gender, sexuality, class, and race to be examined in and through performance.

In this chapter, I use cross-dressing as an umbrella term to denote the practice of performers appearing in the clothes of the opposite sex. In the early modern theatre, all female parts were cross-dressed in the sense that they were performed by boy actors dressed as women. Furthermore, Phyllis Rackin makes clear the significance of cross-dressing as a theatrical device in Shakespeare's work, noting that of the thirty-eight plays in the canon, ten involve characters donning clothes of the opposite sex. Cross-dressing is usually employed in the comedies and it is most frequently female characters that dress in male attire, most famously in *As You Like It* and *Twelfth Night* but also in *The Merchant of Venice*, *The Two Gentlemen of Verona*, and *Cymbeline*. In *The Taming of the Shrew* and *The Merry Wives of Windsor*, male characters dress as women. And in the history plays, three female characters probably appear in masculine battledress.[3]

Beth H. Friedman-Romell helpfully distinguishes between two key types of cross-dressing for women in the eighteenth-century theatre: breeches parts and travesty roles. The breeches' part entails a female character 'assum[ing] male disguise as part of the narrative structure of the play'.[4] In the travesty role, the actress performs a male character. John Harold Wilson notes that of 375 plays first produced between 1660 and 1700, 89 (almost one quarter) featured one or more breeches parts for women. Actresses performed travesty roles in a further fourteen plays. Furthermore, at least three plays were performed by all-female casts and many plays that featured breeches parts originally played by boy actors were revived. Thus, 'Almost every actress appeared at one time or another "dressed like a man"' and some became specialised or particularly famous in such roles.[5] Wilson's comment that cross-dressing was motivated by 'a desire to show off girls' legs' suggests that

---

[3] Phyllis Rackin, 'Shakespeare's Cross-Dressing Comedies', in *A Companion to Shakespeare's Works: The Comedies*, ed. Richard Dutton and Jean E. Howard (Malden, MA: Blackwell, 2003), 114–36.
[4] Beth H. Friedman-Rommel, 'Breaking the Code: Toward a Reception Theory of Theatrical Cross-Dressing in Eighteenth-Century London', *Theatre Journal*, 47.4 (1995): 459–79 (464).
[5] John Harold Wilson, *All the King's Ladies: Actresses of the Restoration* (Chicago: University of Chicago Press, 1958), 73. See also Elizabeth Howe, *The First English Actresses: Women and Drama, 1660–1700*

he reads the device as designed to titillate the male audience by objectifying the female performer.[6] However, more recent critics have issued important challenges to the idea of the Restoration actress as merely a sex object.[7] Paradoxically, the wearing of male dress directed attention to the female body of the actress as the breeches costume revealed her legs, usually covered by long and voluminous skirts. But women dressed in male attire were able to engage in a broader range of physical activities (for example, sword fighting), as their movement was not so conscripted as it was by their usual feminine garments.

A further important context is the popularity of Shakespeare on the Restoration stage. When the London theatres reopened in 1660, managers William Davenant and Thomas Killigrew turned to the plays of Shakespeare and other early modern dramatists to provide material for performance as professional playwriting had waned during the eighteen years in which the playhouses were closed. While some of Shakespeare's plays (notably *Hamlet* and *Othello*) were performed in versions relatively close to Shakespeare's text, other works were adapted to suit the taste of the times. The Restoration vogue for transvestism and the popularity of Shakespeare naturally came together: the Shakespeare plays which featured cross-dressing offered ready-made opportunities to see women in men's clothing, while adaptation offered a means to include further cross-dressing roles. *Twelfth Night*, arguably Shakespeare's most famous cross-dressing play, was performed using the 'original' text in the 1660s and four decades later was adapted by Burnaby as *Love Betray'd*. Although Burnaby's play eliminated one layer of cross-dressing by having the women's parts played by actresses, his adaptation did not remove as much of Shakespeare's gender-bending as one might anticipate. While Shakespeare's *Tempest* did not feature any cross-dressing (beyond the

---

(Cambridge: Cambridge University Press, 1992), 57. The most detailed exploration of cross-dressing in Restoration drama is by Jacqueline Pearson in *The Prostituted Muse: Images of Women and Women Dramatists, 1642–1737* (New York: Harvester Wheatsheaf, 1988), 100–18. Pearson concludes that 'Transvestite heroines are found in tragedy and comedy, as central or peripheral figures' in the plot and notes that while cross-dressing can be 'used for erotic effect', the device can also offer critiques of male behaviour or allow a 'serious and far-reaching examination' of women's place in society (*Prostituted Muse*, 117–18). Candy Schille notes that casting women in male roles was a gimmick that proved 'an effective and titillating appeal to consumerism'. Candy B. K. Schille, '"Man Hungry": Reconsidering Threats to Colonial and Patriarchal Order in Dryden and Davenant's *The Tempest*', *Texas Studies in Literature and Language*, 48.4 (2006), 280.

[6] Wilson, *All the King's Ladies*, 83.

[7] In addition to the work of Leigh and Rosenthal cited later in this chapter, see Deborah C. Payne, 'Reified Object or Emergent Professional? Retheorizing the Restoration Actress', in *Cultural Readings of Restoration and Eighteenth-Century English Theater*, ed. J. Douglas Canfield and Deborah C. Payne (Athens: University of Georgia Press, 1995), 13–38.

fact that Miranda, the only female character, was played by a boy actor), Dryden and Davenant saw fit to add two new parts that were performed as travesty roles: Hippolito, a male character played by an actress, and Sycorax, a female character played by an actor. An examination of these two adaptations reveals how the advent of the actress altered the use of cross-dressing in Shakespeare's works.

Samuel Pepys records attending three performances of *Twelfth Night* in the 1660s but describes it as 'silly' and 'one of the weakest plays that ever I saw on the stage'.[8] Prompter John Downes, however, says the play 'had mighty success by its well Performance' and further comments that 'All the Parts being justly Acted Crown'd the Play.'[9] But while Downes lists several roles and actors, he makes no mention of Viola/Cesario or the actress who played that part, suggesting that *Twelfth Night*'s cross-dressing was not a major draw. Pepys does not mention this aspect of the play either, though on other occasions he comments favourably on seeing actresses in breeches.[10] The *London Stage* contains only these three records of performance in unadapted form until the play was revived in January 1741. In the interim, Burnaby adapted *Twelfth Night* as *Love Betray'd; or, The Agreable Disapointment* in 1703. Having authored three previous comedies and several epilogues for plays by other writers, Burnaby now turned his hand to Shakespeare adaptation.[11] The preface to *Love Betray'd* acknowledges his debt: 'Part of the Tale of this Play, I took from *Shakespear*', Burnaby writes, 'and about Fifty of the Lines; Those that are his, I have mark'd with Inverted Comma's, to distinguish 'em from what are mine'.[12] Despite his attempts to clarify the nature of his borrowings in the printed text, readers will also note speeches that echo Shakespeare, even if they are not direct quotations. Burnaby uses much of Shakespeare's plot (itself taken from Plautus and an Italian play, *The Deceived*) but changes some of the characters, for example conflating

---

[8] See 11 September 1661, 6 January 1662/3, 20 January 1668/9, *The Diary of Samuel Pepys: A New and Complete Transcription*, ed. Robert Latham and William Matthews, 9 vols. (Berkeley: University of California Press, 1970), vol. II, 177; vol. IV, 6; vol. IX, 421.

[9] John Downes, *Roscius Anglicanus*, ed. Judith Milhous and Robert D. Hume (London: Society for Theatre Research, 1987), 54.

[10] See for example the entry on 23 February 1662/3 (Pepys, *Diary*, vol. IV, 56).

[11] For Burnaby's theatrical writing, see *The Dramatic Works of William Burnaby*, ed. F. E. Budd (London: Eric Partridge at the Scholartis Press, 1931).

[12] Preface, in [William Burnaby,] *Love Betray'd; Or, The Agreable Disapointment* (London: Printed for D. Brown ... F. Coggan ... W. Davis ... and G. Strahan, 1703), [n.p.]. Budd's text of *Love Betray'd* does not include lineation so this chapter cites page numbers from the 1969 Cornmarket Press facsimile edition of the 1703 printing of the play. Subsequent page references appear parenthetically in the text.

Malvolio and Sir Andrew Aguecheek into a new figure named Taquilet, and rechristening everyone except Cesario and Sebastian.[13]

While Viola's name is mentioned a couple of times at the beginning and end of the text, the dramatis personae and speech prefixes employ the name Cesario exclusively. This choice to emphasise the male identity of the character suggests that Burnaby is principally concerned with the character when dressed as a man. Three new female characters are added: Laura (Viola's servant, now in the employ of the Duke), Emilia (confidante to Olivia, who is now called Villaretta), and Dromia (an old woman in love with Drances, the counterpart to Sir Toby). Burnaby therefore responds to the paucity of female parts in Shakespeare's play by creating roles for the women in the Lincoln's Inn Fields company and uses these characters to explore women's feelings on love through a variety of conversations and interactions. Indeed, the addition of female roles was a practice initiated by early Restoration adapters such as Dryden and Davenant, who add to their version of *The Tempest* a sister and confidante for Miranda. Katherine West Scheil, one of few scholars to have written on this play and one of even fewer to have taken it seriously, claims that the cross-dressing elements in adaptations like this one 'are not developed beyond Shakespeare's originals, except in their use of actresses' to perform them.[14] However, Scheil's reading fails to address the question of what happens when actresses instead of actors play these breeches parts. Played by a woman, Burnaby's Cesario uses the duel scene to question assumptions about bravery and gender. Having an actress play Cesario opposite an actor as Moreno reduces the homoerotic resonance of the ending of the adaptation but the final scene retains a considerable amount of ambiguity about sexuality. Furthermore, Burnaby adds a scene in which Cesario extends their cross-dressing by disguising themself as a doctor, passing as a male professional.[15]

The Latin epigraph on the play's title page, 'iam te sequetur' or 'soon she will follow you', pinpoints a major change made by Burnaby in this adaptation. Viola's motivation for dressing as Cesario and entering Orsino's

---

[13] Sir Toby is now Drances and is much less harsh than Shakespeare's character. Villaretta (Olivia) has a sentimental transformation absent in *Twelfth Night*. Orsino is now Moreno and Antonio becomes Rodoregue. Burnaby uses the spelling Cæsario.

[14] Katherine West Scheil, *The Taste of the Town: Shakespearian Comedy and the Early Eighteenth-Century Theatre* (Lewisburg, PA: Bucknell University Press, 2003), 252. Barbara Murray's important essay on *Love Betray'd* is discussed later in this chapter.

[15] In this chapter I attempt to mitigate the complexities of pronoun use for characters who dress as the opposite sex by using the gender neutral 'they/them'.

service in Shakespeare's play is explained in Burnaby's version as driven by love. In a conversation with Laura towards the start of the play, Cesario tells us that they first saw the Duke in France and they have loved him for the past two years. Now 'unable longer to endure the torture of my Wishes' (11), Viola has left her brother Sebastian to come to Venice, where Moreno (i.e. Orsino) is Duke. Having changed her name to Cesario and produced a letter 'as from one his Highness knew in *Paris*, to recommend me for his Page', Cesario has been welcomed by Moreno, who 'lik'd my Person; calls me pretty Youth; makes me sing to him, and sometimes kisses me' (12). Cesario is unhappy not because (or not only because) Moreno's affection is based on misgendering but because Moreno also professes love for Villaretta (Olivia). Cesario can therefore use their position as Moreno's messenger to discourage rather than encourage Villaretta's affection for the Duke in the hopes of winning Moreno for themself. The crystal-clear reason of pre-existing love offered for Cesario's disguise posits female to male transvestism as a valid means for a character to fulfil their desires, although the implication is that the woman beneath the disguise will ultimately be revealed. Although cross-dressing often has this effect in Shakespeare, the reasons for characters like Viola and Rosalind to adopt male clothing are usually reactive rather than proactive and lie mainly in the protection that passing as a man offers to a woman alone in society.[16] While Viola's love for Moreno may seem to ground the play firmly in a heteronormative world, Barbara Murray demonstrates that the epigraph's classical intertextuality subverts this. The quotation is taken from Horace's 'To Gabinius', which invokes the beautiful boy Gyges as more attractive to a man than his mistress, and which also echoes Aphrodite's promise to Sappho ('If she flees now, soon she shall pursue').[17] Same-sex desire is thus clearly indicated from the start of the play.

The early scene between Laura and Cesario contains further elements of exposition. Laura underscores the resemblance between the siblings, perhaps because now that Cesario is played by a woman and Sebastian by a man it is harder to make them look alike: 'Lord, Madam!' she says 'you

---

[16] For example, Shakespeare's Viola, shipwrecked and alone in Illyria, first wishes to serve Olivia in order that she 'might not be delivered to the world' (1.2.44) but when the Sea Captain tells her Olivia will admit no visitors, she instead requests his help to 'Conceal me what I am' so that she can serve Orsino instead (1.2.56). She has no prior knowledge of Orsino (or Olivia) but seeks to protect herself since as a woman she cannot go about alone in the world. In this chapter I cite Shakespeare's works from the Folger Digital Texts of the plays.

[17] Barbara A. Murray, '"Strange Star": Same-Sex Love and William Burnaby's *Love Betray'd or The Agreeable Disapointment* (1703)', *English Studies*, 93.2 (2012): 183–4.

look so like your Brother when you laugh, and in these Cloaths too, that, I vow, I can't tell but you are my Master *Sebastian*, all this while' (11). Cesario further emphasises the likeness – '"Twould puzzle one of better sense than thee, *Laura*, to distinguish it' – and offers a piece of physical proof, 'the only apparent difference between us', a mole on the arm (11).[18] Finally, Laura's concern about Viola's breeches disguise is revealed as based in anxiety about class as well as gender. As the scene opens, Cesario urges Laura 'Prithee Wench, lay by thy Fears' and the latter retorts 'Alas! Madam, it grieves me to think that my Lady must be a Servant, that may be so waited on! To be a Page, and wear Breeches too!' The stage direction following this speech tells us that Laura then '*weeps*' (10). Cesario's response is to emphasise the liberty gained by the ruse: 'This Servitude is Freedom, for it brings me to the Man I love' (10).

Like their Shakespearean counterpart, Burnaby's Cesario becomes involved in a duel with Taquilet (the character who amalgamates Sir Andrew and Malvolio). As in *Twelfth Night*, Cesario is unwilling to enter into combat and is branded a coward by their opponents, but this reluctance to fight is presented as perfectly reasonable as their opponent offers no clear-cut offence that could lead to a duel; rather Taquilet (like Sir Andrew) issues a challenge based on his own jealousy and is egged on by Drances (as is Sir Andrew by Sir Toby). While in both versions it is Viola/Cesario who is accused of cowardice, the texts make clear that their opponents are even more fearful: Sir Andrew offers up his horse in order to get out of the duel once he hears what a 'firago' (3.4.286) his opponent is and Taquilet claims he can 'feel [Cesario's] Sword already quite thro' my Midriff' before the latter has even drawn (33).[19] Burnaby's Cesario proclaims themself 'no Fighter' but encouraged by Taquilet's timidity ('that Fellow is certainly as great a Coward as my self') draws their sword with the challenge 'Villain look to your Life' (33), thus seeming to display bravery. This has comic results: Taquilet '*runs over*' to Drances in a panic proclaiming 'O Lord! The Devil! I'm kill'd' (33). But when Drances draws on Cesario, the page trembles, stammers, and eventually kneels to beg for mercy. It is only at this point that Taquilet draws because he now realises Cesario is not a threat. The joke in this scene is not so much on

---

[18] The use of the mole as evidence picks up on a moment at the end of Shakespeare's play in which Sebastian and Viola realise their shared parentage as both assert that their father had a mole upon his brow (5.1.254–5). It also echoes *Cymbeline*, in which Iachimo uses his knowledge of a mole on Imogen's breast to try to prove to Posthumus that he has been intimate with his wife.

[19] Shakespeare's use of 'firago', a term typically applied to women, constitutes a nod to the audience about Cesario's true identity as a woman.

Cesario's cowardice but on Taquilet's and the punchline is his comment that Cesario should expect 'after affronting a Man of my Courage ... to be run thro' the Body, and have thy Skin pull'd over thy Ears' (33). Taquilet's faintheartedness is further underlined by the arrival of Rodoregue (who parallels Shakespeare's Antonio): when he draws his sword, Taquilet '*jumps back*' in fear, uttering in an aside 'O Lord! I'm a dead Man yet' (33). As this moment is not found in the equivalent scene in Shakespeare but added by Burnaby, the implication is that the adapter wants to emphasise Taquilet's cowardice just as much as, if not even more than, Cesario's. To an even greater extent than Shakespeare, Burnaby undermines the idea that bravery is implicitly tied to gender.

In Shakespeare's play and in the adaptation sword fighting is clearly supposed to serve as the epitome of masculine behaviour. While Burnaby's Cesario may ultimately fail to prove themself a man at duelling, the discussion between Cesario and Laura following this moment makes clear that they have proved themself a lover. Cesario laments to Laura that 'One can't have to do with Breeches ... without mischief' (36), mischief that includes not only the duel but the fact that Villaretta has fallen for Cesario despite their role as Moreno's envoy: 'For tho' I pleaded for *Moreno*, yet I gain'd for my self – I sigh'd for him, but she sigh'd for me!' (37) This dialogue also sets up the following scene, in which Cesario dresses as a physician and succeeds in performing a professional male identity. Cesario tells Laura that her happiness depends on being certain of Villaretta's 'disaffection to my Lord *Moreno*' (37). Laura proposes the doctor disguise because Villaretta has just sent for the Duke's physician but 'tho' Ladies frequently send for him, yet she never did before, and since your Ladyship's so good at Disguises, I'll dress you up, and you may pass upon her for him, which is a sure way to get into her Secrets' (37). Cesario then becomes 'so fir'd with this Physical Enterprize, that I must pursue it' (37). As Villaretta prepares for the doctor's arrival, Emilia urges her to 'sit down, and look sick' or the doctor 'won't feel your Pulse' (37). While Villaretta doubts that the doctor will be able to do anything for her, Emilia urges her 'Never doubt his Skill! ... you must use him like your Confessor, and tell him the bottom of your Heart' (38). Cesario is thus able to diagnose Villaretta's 'Languishness' and 'touch[] the very Spring of [her] Disease' (40) and Villaretta readily confesses that her love for Cesario is what ails her.

Meanwhile, Emilia (Villaretta's companion) decides that she wants to get in on the act and asks the doctor what might remedy her own ailment, 'a trembling at my Heart in a Morning' (39). Cesario makes a blustering reply: 'O! Madam, the only thing in the World, are my Drops! and

Blooding and Vomiting, or so –' (39). Despite the fact that Cesario displays a complete lack of medical knowledge, they are still able to fool Villaretta, who does not recognise that the doctor is the page with whom she is in love. Appearing convincingly as a doctor, who would probably have been an adult man, would arguably be more difficult for a woman than appearing convincingly as a page, who was usually a younger male. The scene thus provides us with further evidence of Cesario's skill in cross-dressing. Given the new emphasis in Burnaby's version of *Twelfth Night* on Viola/Cesario's pre-existing love for the Duke, the doctor scene and its test of whether Villaretta genuinely loves Cesario and spurns Moreno performs an important function in the plot. Cesario can now be certain that Moreno's feelings for Villaretta are unrequited and is free to pursue their own romantic interest in the Duke.

In the final scene of *Love Betray'd*, the plot is wound up as in Shakespeare's play, with Villaretta realising she has married Cesario's brother Sebastian and Cesario outed as Viola and promised in marriage to Moreno. Burnaby's handling of the denouement is somewhat different than Shakespeare's, however. Firstly, the scene offers repeated revelations of Cesario's gender identity before it is finally accepted. Burnaby thus emphasises that Cesario has successfully passed as a man throughout the play, perhaps because (as in the emphasis on Cesario's physical resemblance to Sebastian in the first act, mentioned earlier) he realised that a Restoration audience might require more convincing that a woman could be mistaken for a man now that an actress rather than a boy actor was playing this role. Secondly, Burnaby ups the stakes with increased threats of violence to Cesario. Shakespeare's Orsino threatens to kill the page offstage whereas Moreno draws his sword on Cesario in front of Villaretta and the other characters. As Moreno '*Offers to Stab*' Cesario, Villaretta '*steps between*' and then Laura '*Enters and holds his [Moreno's] Arm*' (56).[20] This leads to a striking visual tableau as the truth about Cesario's identity is revealed by Laura, who weeps (again) as she declares that Cesario is 'A poor unhappy Woman!' (56) Moreno admits to being 'confounded' but is not convinced (56). When the Priest testifies to having performed a marriage ceremony between Villaretta and Cesario (or so he thinks), the stage directions tell us that Villaretta '*looks pleas'd*', Cesario '*Astonish'd*', and Moreno '*Enrag'd*' (57). The Duke once more tries to stab Cesario but Laura again holds him back and urges that Cesario 'be search'd first, and you'll be satisfy'd' (57).

---

[20] Villaretta's actions here form part of the sentimental transformation of the character that critics like Scheil have observed.

Before this can come to pass, Sebastian enters and recognises his sister in Cesario. The truth is finally revealed beyond all doubt when Cesario '*Shows the Mole on her Arm*' as 'evidence' in case Sebastian 'shou'd discredit my account' (59). Class again comes into play here as Cesario alludes to their shame at being discovered not because they are dressed as a man but because they are taking on the role of a servant:

> You call up all the shame into my Cheeks;
> I've strove to hide that secret from the World,
> For what I do, dishonours what I am,
> My Family is Noble, and my Country
> The most Civiliz'd — (59)

Moreno then somehow remembers that Sebastian is wellborn and asserts that 'if *Cesario* be his Sister, / I must claim a part in this days fortune' (60). A masque (on which more later), dedicated to Cesario, who 'has blest us all' (61), is then introduced to celebrate the nuptials, although no details are provided in the text. Finally, Moreno speaks the closing lines of the play, which offer a moral (something completely lacking in Shakespeare): 'That Honesty is still the care of Providence!' (61)[21] This is more than a little problematic, because the disguised Cesario's pursuit of Moreno can hardly be said to be honest (and Moreno himself arguably shows a similar lack of integrity when he quickly switches his affections from Villaretta to Cesario at the end of the play).

As scholars have noted, the revelation at the end of *Twelfth Night* that the boy Cesario is actually the woman Viola in disguise does not fully restore heteronormativity to the world of the play.[22] Orsino proposes to Viola and asks her to assume female dress again: 'Give me thy hand; / And let me see thee in thy woman's weeds' (5.1.285–6). Viola responds that the sea captain who first rescued her from the shipwreck has her 'maid's garments' (5.1.288) but the captain never returns and the text does not indicate that Viola dons women's clothes again. Orsino's last lines before Feste's song closes the play reveal a continued slippage between genders:

> Cesario, come;
> For so you shall be, while you are a man.
> But when in other habits you are seen,
> Orsino's mistress and his fancy's queen. (5.1.408–11)

---

[21] The moral is further expanded to include Rodoregue ('good will wait upon a worthy action') and Sebastian ('Fortune can't long stain an honest Friendship').

[22] Drouin notes that 'since the promised marriage is not part of the play proper and there is no onstage renunciation of drag, there is no confirmation of the reinstatement of gender norms' ('Cross-Dressing, Drag, and Passing', 45).

Although the Duke alludes to his subsequent union with Viola, the audience is left with the visual image of Orsino united in marriage with Cesario, her male alter ego.

Given the tendency of Restoration adapters of Shakespeare to simplify and to clarify, we might expect *Love Betray'd* to erase the gender ambiguity and reinforce heteronormative couplings as the conclusion to the play. In some ways, the play does so: the fact that Burnaby's Cesario is performed by a woman tones down the homoeroticism of the union between Orsino and Viola, who, though now revealed as a woman, in Shakespeare is still played by a male actor. Even so, much ambiguity remains in *Love Betray'd*. Burnaby's Moreno never asks Cesario to assume women's clothes again and proposes marriage with lines that preserve the slippage between the two characters:

> My Heav'n! my *Viola*! my *Cesario*!
> Let the dear Name survive – tho' I discharge
> The service – And now you are
> Your Masters Mistress! (60)

Again, class is revealed as a key issue involved in cross-dressing. Moreno liberates Cesario from servitude but not necessarily from presenting as a man. Villaretta then adds to the gender confusion with her lines to Moreno: 'I Marry'd *Cesario*, my Lord, as well as you; / *Sebastian* is my second Husband' (60). This line presumably means both that Villaretta thought she had married Cesario initially but subsequently found out that she was married to Sebastian and that Villaretta's and Moreno's families are now united as each has married one of the siblings. Yet one might also be tempted to read these lines as somewhat orgiastic in the context of the play's gender-bending, as Villaretta expresses a marital and potentially sexual connection with a woman (Viola/Cesario) and two men (Sebastian and Moreno).

In addition to the allusions present in the play's epigraph, Murray notes that the epilogue also 'offer[s] a code which directs readers to celebration of the delight and the passion of same-sex love'.[23] This slippery text contains several ambiguities, including the idea that husbands might be wilfully ignorant of their partners' gender identities. In marriage, 'The Knot is Wove with so much subtlety, / That 'tis the Husband's Interest not to see' the 'tender Secrets' that might be hidden from him.[24] He might

---

[23] Murray, '"Strange Star"', 185.
[24] Epilogue, in Burnaby, *Love Betray'd* [n.p.].

therefore instead 'Live in Ignorance' since 'He can't our Shame, without his own disclose'. The epilogue affirms the connection between gender identity and disguise and concludes by celebrating the play's outcome, asserting that 'No disappointment ever was so kind; / Or Woman so much cheated to her mind!' But whether this agreeable disappointment refers to Villaretta's satisfaction at gaining Sebastian in marriage or her pleasure at having wooed Cesario is uncertain.

In addition to the ingenious consideration of gender and sexuality offered by adaptations that reworked Shakespeare to showcase the actress, another key facet of Restoration Shakespeare was the use of music and spectacle. In his preface to *Love Betray'd*, Burnaby claimed that he intended the last act to feature a masque 'but the House neglect[ed] to have it Set to Musick'.[25] Scheil explains that the audience of the period would have expected 'a wealth of ancillary entertainments' including music and dancing in addition to a five-act play.[26] Dryden and Davenant's *Tempest* was particularly popular for its songs, and the operatic version prepared by Thomas Shadwell that succeeded it in 1674 added additional music and spectacle. Charles Gildon's *Measure for Measure*, performed at Lincoln's Inn Fields in 1700, also set a precedent for this type of entertainment by including four musical interludes in the form of Henry Purcell's *Dido and Aeneas* broken up into segments. A recent predecessor to *Love Betray'd* was Granville's *The Jew of Venice*, an adaptation of *The Merchant of Venice* first staged in 1701 and continually popular until 1741. This play featured an elaborate masque of Peleus and Thetis performed for Antonio, Bassanio, Gratiano, and Shylock at the end of Act 2 and detailed over six pages in the play as published. That Burnaby may have had this play in mind in developing his own Shakespeare adaptation is also suggested by the inclusion of the doctor scene, which parallels Portia's cross-dressing as a lawyer in the trial of Shylock and similarly allows Cesario to successfully perform as a male professional.

[25] Preface. In fact, Burnaby suggests that the management's oversight with regard to the masque caused the play to fail. Indeed, there is little evidence of *Love Betray'd* being staged. The *London Stage* surmises a date of first performance in February 1703 because the script was published on the eleventh of that month (with the conventional 'as it was acted at the theatre' formula on the title page) and presumably it had at least a short run then. The title page proclaims that it was acted at Lincoln's Inn Fields; that is, by Betterton's Company. The play was subsequently revived on 1 March 1705 for the benefit of George Pack and Lucretia Bradshaw (who probably played Pedro and Villaretta). All performance information is taken from the open access and open source London Stage Database, londonstagedatabase.uoregon.edu. It should be noted that the records of performance in the Restoration likely only account for a small fraction of the performances that actually took place before newspapers began printing regular theatre advertisements in 1706.
[26] Scheil, *Taste of the Town*, 146.

In contrast to Burnaby's version of *Twelfth Night*, Dryden and Davenant's *Tempest* had an extremely long stage history: versions of this adaptation held the stage from 1667 until 1838.[27] As well as the addition of music and spectacle to this version, its success was also, I argue, a result of its addition of transvestite roles to Shakespeare's drama in a bid to capitalise on the new explorations of gender identity made possible by the advent of the actress. Dryden and Davenant add several new characters, including the male role of Hippolito, which was played by an actress, and the female role of Sycorax, which was generally played by an actor.[28] These are travesty roles, in which performers play characters of the opposite sex, rather than breeches parts, in which female characters assume male disguise as part of the plot of the play.[29] Hippolito is a man who has never seen a woman and parallels Miranda, the woman who has never seen a man. This new character also provides a love interest for Dorinda, the sister created for Miranda. Sycorax is here Caliban's sister and is wooed by Trincalo. Travesty roles offer another method of exploring gender identity, particularly through the interplay between the different sexes of actor and character. These roles demonstrate that cross-dressing can have resonances that go beyond objectifying and sexualising the Restoration actress by dressing her in male attire.

The play's prologue draws attention to the use of cross-gender casting by asserting that the theatre's 'dearth of Youths' has forced 'One of our Women to present a Boy', a 'transformation ... / Exceeding all the Magick

---

[27] In this chapter I focus on the Dryden and Davenant text (first performed in 1667 and published in 1670), not Shadwell's version, which added even more music.

[28] While no cast lists survive from early performances, the *London Stage* (following Wilson, *All the King's Ladies*, 166) conjectures that Jane Long played Hippolito. Mary (Moll) Davis is often mentioned as a possible performer of the role but according to Pepys she played the part of Ariel (*Diary*, vol. IX, 422). We do not know who acted Sycorax in the Restoration but performance records for the eighteenth century show that the part was played by a large number of actors. The appearances of Mrs Miller in the role at Bartholomew Fair in August 1749 seem to have been an anomaly, as does the performance of Hippolito by Theophilus Cibber on 7 January 1723. The implications of having actresses perform spirit roles such as Ariel are explored by Amanda Eubanks Winkler, 'Sexless Spirits? Gender Ideology and Dryden's Musical Magic', *The Musical Quarterly*, 93.2 (2010): 297–328. Schille comments on the connotations of Hippolito's name ('"Man Hungry"', 277).

[29] Friedman-Romell defines travesty roles as those in which 'the actress assumes a male role for extra-textual reasons' and offers 'the performer's ... desire to display virtuosity in a male part' as one such rationale ('Breaking the Code', 464). I extend this concept to include female roles played by male actors. In the case of Hippolito and Sycorax, the actors' motivation for cross-dressing may not have been strictly extra-textual as it is likely that these parts were written to be acted by performers of the opposite sex and part of the effect of the play depends on this cross-dressing. Defining Hippolito and Sycorax as travesty roles allows us to distinguish between cross-dressing undertaken by a character as part of the plot (the breeches part) and cross-dressing undertaken by a performer as part of the play but not intrinsic to its narrative structure (the travesty role).

in the Play'.³⁰ What is more, unlike plays with breeches roles in which the cross-dressed female character ultimately doffs her male disguise, in this drama we are instructed not to 'expect in the last Act to find, / Her Sex transform'd from man to Woman-kind' (87). Confirmation of the already known sex of the actress is therefore withheld in an erotics of deferral. The gender-bending of the character of Hippolito and the actress who played him continues as the speaker asserts that 'What e're she was before the Play began, / All you shall see of her is perfect man' (88). Thus the prologue insists on Hippolito's/Long's masculinity and even in its sexualising final couplet – 'Or if your fancy will be farther led / To find her Woman, it must be abed' (88) – continues to entertain the possibility that the spectator might be attracted to the female actor because of her performance of masculinity. In the case of Hippolito, this masculinity consists of a voracious sexual appetite and eagerness to engage in physical combat, as we shall see.

The play manifests a pronounced interest in sexuality in both the plot and the numerous sexual innuendos and double entendres of the dialogue. Jocelyn Powell sees Pepys's emphasis on the innocence of the adaptation (he proclaimed it 'the most innocent play that ever I saw') as evidence that in performance the play avoided being overly bawdy; but we might instead read the diarist's comments as protesting too much.³¹ While the characters, especially Miranda, Dorinda, and Hippolito, are presented as innocent (indeed, their extreme naivety is where much of the humour lies), the play's comic effect depends on the audience members' awareness of and experience in sexual matters. In addition to this emphasis on sexuality, Lori Leigh points out that Dryden and Davenant considered sexual politics to be key to the play.³² Thus the changes they made to the text further emphasise this theme. In Dryden and Davenant's version, Caliban has attempted to rape not just Miranda but both sisters. His

---

³⁰ John Dryden and William Davenant, 'The Tempest; or, The Enchanted Island' (1670), in *Shakespeare Made Fit*, ed. Sandra Clark (London: Everyman, 1997), 79–185 (87). Subsequent references are to this edition and appear parenthetically in the text. The prologue's claim is somewhat disingenuous as although Hippolito is a male role, it was probably written to be performed by an actress. Dryden and Davenant's preface to the play mentions the new character of Hippolito, 'the Counterpart to Shakespear's Plot ..., a Man who had never seen a Woman', but says nothing about casting (Preface, 84). But in the prologue the fact that Hippolito is played by an actress becomes clear. The prologue could have been written after the rest of the play and the casting of an actress as Hippolito introduced then. But as manager of the theatre company that performed it, Davenant would have been alive to the possibilities that travesty performance could offer as he wrote the play.

³¹ See 7 November 1667 (Pepys, *Diary*, vol. VIII, 522). Jocelyn Powell, *Restoration Theatre Production* (London: Routledge & Kegan Paul, 1984), 74.

³² Lori Leigh, *Shakespeare and the Embodied Heroine: Staging Female Characters in the Late Plays and Early Adaptations* (Basingstoke: Palgrave Macmillan, 2014), 68.

wish to 'peopl[e] … this Isle with *Calibans*' (1.2.268) therefore suggests his desire to dominate the island by mastering its female inhabitants and to ensure his claim to the land through procreation, 'an exercise of the power principle', as Candy Schille would have it.[33] Likewise in the comic plot, Trincalo conspires to woo Sycorax so that he can 'lay claim to this Island by Alliance' (2.3.222). Caliban aids him in winning her over, telling Sycorax, 'You must be kind to him, and he will love you' and Trincalo, 'I prithee speak to her, my Lord, and come neerer her', leading Trincalo to praise Caliban as 'a rare Pimp' (3.3.27–8, 33).[34] While Caliban may seem to promote the relationship between Trincalo and Sycorax in order that he might drink the sailors' 'immortal Liquor' (3.3.55), in the context of his comments on the attempted rape of Prospero's daughters it is clear he realises 'that females may be currency in power negotiations among men'.[35] Furthermore, Trincalo's subsequent proud declaration that he has 'Espous'd the lawful Inheritrix of this Island' and can therefore 'claim a lawful Title' (3.3.119, 122) to the nation shows that he too understands the importance of forging relationships with native women in order to claim sovereignty.

In addition to the cross-gender casting, there are also parallels between Sycorax and Hippolito in that both have uncontrollable sexual appetites. Having met and fallen in love with Dorinda, Hippolito learns that there are other women in the world and expresses his desire to 'have all of that kind, if there be a hundred of 'em' (3.6.53–4). Likewise, when Stephano, Ventoso, and Mustacho re-enter in Act 4, Sycorax asks Trincalo (no doubt with sexual undertones) if she should meet them and 'be kind to all of 'em, / Just as I am to thee' (4.2.10–11). She then quickly switches her affections to Stephano who asks her 'wilt thou leave him, and thou shalt be my Princess?' to which she agrees, 'If thou canst make me glad with this Liquor' (4.2.133, 134). Hippolito's voracious sexual appetite leads to a duel with Ferdinand over Miranda in which Hippolito is seriously wounded but ultimately saved by the intervention of Ariel's application of a 'purple Panacea' and 'Weapon-Salve' (5.1.55, 79). Hippolito repents: 'The fault / Was only in my blood; for now 'tis gone, I find / I do not love so many' (5.2.45–7) and the expected pairings of Miranda with Ferdinand and Hippolito with Dorinda are brought to fruition at the play's conclusion.

---

[33] Schille, '"Man Hungry"', 282.
[34] The allegation of incest between Sycorax and her brother (4.2.107–9) is both further proof of her libidinality and an obstacle to Trincalo's attempts to assert his claim to the island by coupling with her.
[35] Schille, '"Man Hungry"', 282.

Sycorax's fate is rather different. As the characters prepare to leave the island at the end of the play, she tells Trincalo 'I'le to Sea with thee, and keep thee warm in thy Cabin' but he refuses: 'No my dainty Dy-dapper … You are partly Fish and may swim after me. I wish you a good Voyage' (5.2.250, 251–3). Sycorax is thus not 'subsumed into the patriarchal order' but 'abandoned by it' once Trincalo no longer needs her.[36] The resolution of the drama thus requires that male-to-female transvestite performance is encoded as monstrous and irredeemable, while the sexual transgressions of the female-to-male travesty role are corrected and resolved by the end of the play.

Furthermore, although the ending of the play promotes multiple pairings amongst the characters (Miranda and Ferdinand, Dorinda and Hippolito, Ariel and his spirit love Milcha), it 'unhitches the interracial coupling of Trincalo and Sycorax'.[37] As a white European, Hippolito's sexual excesses can be redeemed, but as a racialised Other, Sycorax's cannot. Hippolito's recuperation is brought about by a duel with Ferdinand, a scene with no counterpart in Shakespeare which the adapters have deliberately added. In the Restoration *Tempest*, sword fighting and sexuality are again linked (as in *Twelfth Night/Love Betray'd*) when Ferdinand and Hippolito duel over Hippolito's assertion that his 'inclinations are to love all Women' (4.1.289), including Miranda. On one level, the combat is ridiculous and laden with double entendres: when Hippolito asks for an explanation of what a duel is, Ferdinand responds 'You must stand thus, and push against me, / While I push at you, till one of us fall dead' (4.1.312–13). This sexual innuendo might be read as heteronormative, as an actress and an actor physically grapple with each other on stage, or homoerotic, given that both characters are male. But despite his lack of experience, Hippolito is more than willing to fight: he proclaims himself 'ready' and urges Ferdinand to cut to the chase, 'Come, come this loses time, now for the Women, Sir' (4.3.3, 6–7). Though Hippolito is declared 'unskilful' (4.3.14) and ultimately defeated, the actress playing the part eagerly engages in stage combat.[38]

That the juxtaposition of male character and female role might have engaged and inspired women in the audience to imagine possibilities for

---

[36] Schille, '"Man Hungry"', 278.
[37] Susan B. Iwanisziw, 'The Shameful Allure of Sycorax and Wowksi: Dramatic Precursors of Sartje, the Hottentot Venus', *Restoration and 18th-Century Theatre Research*, 16.2 (2001): 3–10 (10).
[38] Leigh (*Shakespeare and the Embodied Heroine*, 91) notes the contrast with Viola in *Twelfth Night*, to which I would add that while Dryden and Davenant's Hippolito is certainly much braver and more enthusiastic about fighting than Viola, Burnaby's Cesario is somewhat more courageous than their Shakespearean counterpart.

behaviour other than the feminine norm is suggested by Laura Rosenthal's discussion of Margaret Cavendish's response to a cross-dressed female performer she saw in Europe during the Interregnum. Cavendish writes of an Italian woman who acted men's roles 'so Naturally as if she had been of that Sex' and further praises the fact that she appeared 'more used to Handle a Sword than a Distaff'.[39] Rosenthal notes that this cross-dressing 'fascinates Cavendish for its liberating and (arguably) erotic possibilities' at the same time as the performer's femininity (Cavendish also praises her graceful dancing) also engages her interest.[40] Though Rosenthal does not make the link with Hippolito in her discussion of *The Tempest* in this article, the appeal of both the cross-dressed female mountebank performer and the actress playing the male role of Hippolito lies in the fact that femaleness is visible through the male attire, that cross-dressing can be emancipating, and that both enthusiastically engage in the typically masculine physical pursuit of sword fighting.

Hippolito's excessive libido is the force that must be controlled to bring about a harmonious ending to the play and the monogamous outcome for Hippolito's character might be construed as Dryden and Davenant's way of containing female sexuality. However, Leigh points out two flaws with this reading.[41] Firstly, this interpretation does not fully acknowledge that while Hippolito's unbridled desire is rendered on stage by an actress, this concupiscence actually stems from a character who is male. Secondly, the character's sexual desire is for another woman (Dorinda) or women – he asserts he is 'made for twenty hundred' of them (4.1.273) – and because Hippolito is played by an actress this passion therefore has a homoerotic (and specifically a lesbian) charge. This is further emphasised by the fact that Dorinda reciprocates this desire: she says their touching of hands 'makes me sigh just so' and gives her 'a pleasing grief' (2.5.66–7, 68). The fact that the adaptation puts female same-sex desire on full display might be interpreted as a way to further sexualise Restoration actresses by pandering to voyeuristic heterosexual male fantasies of lesbian sex. However, the possibility remains that such a display was appealing to women in the audience, as Cavendish's fascination with the cross-dressed female performer suggests.

---

[39] Quoted in Laura J. Rosenthal, 'Reading Masks: The Actress and the Spectatrix in Restoration Shakespeare', in *Broken Boundaries: Women and Feminism in Restoration Drama*, ed. Katherine M. Quinsey (Lexington: University Press of Kentucky, 1996), 201–218 (201).
[40] Rosenthal, 'Reading Masks', 201.
[41] Schille claims that both Murray and Rosenthal interpret the play in this way ('"Man Hungry"', 277–8). For the counterargument, see Leigh, *Shakespeare and the Embodied Heroine*, 89.

Leigh's argument that we must fully consider the gender of both actor and role can be extended to the character of Sycorax. J. Douglas Canfield writes of Sycorax as 'the exotic other, representing European male wish fulfillment: unlimited sex with native women in the colonies'.[42] One might, then, expect this character to offer sexual titillation in performance but Canfield's reading fails to acknowledge that the role of this native woman is played by a man. Susan Iwanisziw notes that although Sycorax's racial identity is never clarified, she is a comic-grotesque figure who is 'mocked by an ethnic humor predicated on her giant size, opportunistic sexuality, and essential ignorance'.[43] Casting a male actor in this part is, then, a deliberate way to emphasise this joke. The interplay of character and actor in *The Tempest*'s travesty roles is thus more complex than is suggested by the idea that the use of cross-dressing was a means to exploit the Restoration actress in order to titillate male members of the audience.

Recent scholarship has nuanced our understanding of the Restoration actress's onstage agency and the public recognition of her professional status while still acknowledging that the use of cross-dressing in Restoration drama could at the same time sexualise the actress as playwrights took advantage of the new commodity of the female performer. If the breeches-clad Restoration actress is presented as an object of enjoyment for the male spectator's gaze, we might expect that cross-dressing in Restoration Shakespeare adaptations would reinforce heteronormativity as the inevitable and desired outcome of cross-dressing. However, in the case of *Love Betray'd*, Burnaby preserves and at times enhances the gender ambiguity of *Twelfth Night* to a surprisingly large degree and the play seems more concerned with delineating class distinctions than gender difference. The travesty roles created by Dryden and Davenant in their version of *The Tempest* are also more complex than a reading of theatre history that posits early actresses as mere sex objects would suggest. The part of Hippolito allows the actress to engage in liberating masculine behaviour and to explore sexual desire for multiple other women. The casting of a male actor as Sycorax, while intended as a grotesque joke, raises important issues about the period's understanding of women's place in the colonial project. Exploring cross-dressing in Shakespeare adaptations of this period therefore offers us an important way to shed new light on the performance of gender, sexuality, class, and race on the Restoration stage.

---

[42] J. Douglas Canfield, *Heroes and States: On the Ideology of Restoration Tragedy* (Lexington: University Press of Kentucky, 2000), 141.
[43] Iwanisziw, 'Shameful Allure', 10.

CHAPTER 5

Performing Restoration Shakespeare in the Eighteenth Century

James Harriman-Smith

Restoration adaptations of Shakespeare's plays continued to appear on English stages throughout the eighteenth century.[1] Like any collection of performances, however, the eighteenth-century performance of Restoration Shakespeare was never static nor homogenous: lines written in the Restoration were cut or altered; 'restorations' from Shakespeare's own texts were made; and hundreds of other accommodations and alterations took shape, meeting the daily demands of changing companies, theatres and audience tastes. This chapter focuses on the fate of one piece of Restoration Shakespeare in particular, Nahum Tate's *The History of King Lear*, which added a love plot between Edgar and Cordelia, cut the Fool, and concluded with the survival of Lear, Gloucester, and Cordelia. This adaptation was first performed early in 1681 and then remained in theatrical repertoires well into the nineteenth century, undergoing many changes in the process.[2] It is these changes that interest me here, and my discussion of them relies heavily on a promptbook that came to light in 1979.[3] Held in the British Library – and recently digitised and made available online – this promptbook was made for the Theatre Royal at Drury Lane, one of eighteenth-century London's two patent theatres, then under the control of James Lacy and the actor-manager David Garrick.[4] The promptbook,

---

[1] To give a few examples: William Davenant's *Macbeth* (1664) was still being performed at Covent Garden and at Drury Lane in the 1798/9 season; John Dryden's *The Tempest; Or, The Enchanted Island* (1667) was staged twice at Drury Lane in both the 1797/8 season and the 1798/9 one; and Dryden's *All for Love* (his 1677 adaptation of *Antony and Cleopatra*) appeared three times at Covent Garden in the early years of the 1790s. All data from the London Stage Database, londonstagedatabase.usu.edu.
[2] Lynne Bradley, *Adapting King Lear for the Stage* (London: Routledge, 2016), 46 – see this volume for a more detailed account of the development of *King Lear* than I am able to give here.
[3] Vanessa Cunningham, *Shakespeare and Garrick* (Cambridge: Cambridge University Press, 2008), 123.
[4] [Nahum Tate and David Garrick], *The History of King Lear, A Tragedy: As it is now acted at the King's Theatres. Revived, with Alterations, by N. Tate* (London: Hitch et al., 1756). British Library: C.119.dd.22.

98   JAMES HARRIMAN-SMITH

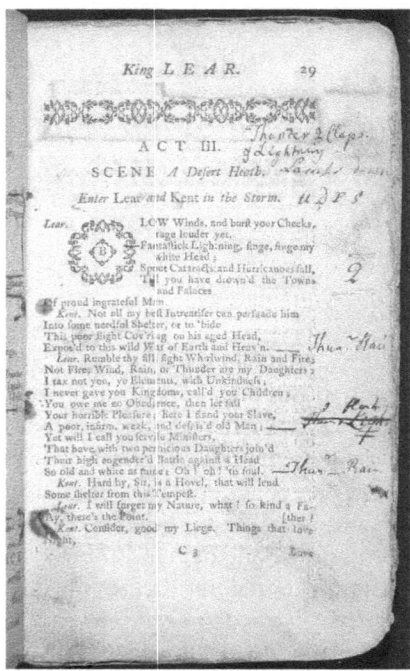

Figure 5.1 *The History of King Lear, A Tragedy: As it is now acted at the King's Theatres. Revived, with Alterations, by N. Tate* (London: Hitch et al., 1756), page 29. © The British Library Board (C.119.dd.22)

an extract of which is shown in Figure 5.1, is an annotated copy of a 1756 printing of Tate's *Lear*.[5]

In what follows I use this source and others to show the variety of ways that Garrick and his contemporaries might refashion a piece of Restoration Shakespeare. Out of such variety emerges a distinctive set of critical priorities that both extend Tate's own position and offer us today new ways of thinking about Shakespeare's work and its reception. A key theme throughout is the importance of sequence and contrast: the Jacobean *Lear* offers only illusory relief to break its grim vision of a cruel world, but Tate's adaptation provides a much more optimistic combination of light and dark moments. Garrick and others in the 1700s inherit Tate's

---

[5] 'David Garrick's Annotated Copy of *The History of King Lear, an Adaptation by Nahum Tate*', The British Library, www.bl.uk/collection-items/david-garricks-annotated-copy-of-the-history-of-king-lear-an-adaptation-by-nahum-tate.

emotional chiaroscuro and draw on the affordances of their stages to augment and enrich it, notably through their ability to balance large- and small-scale effects.

Such an argument must begin with an acknowledgement of the challenges and potential of its main source. Edward Langhans's description of the annotated copy of Tate's *Lear* contends that it is 'far too sloppy to have served in a performance': while the annotations 'begin carefully enough', 'they turn into rough notes' by the end of the second act; most scene changes are marked, but 'there are no descriptions of settings'; and entrances and exits are indicated erratically.[6] On top of this, three different people appear to have written notes: Garrick's hand is joined by that of Richard Cross (Drury Lane's prompter until 1760) and perhaps also that of Ralph Harwood (prompter in the 1780s).[7] Based on this evidence, Langhans hypothesises that Garrick bought this edition of Tate's adaptation as soon as it was published, intending to use it in preparing a production of the play. However, he then 'became interested in further alterations' and another copy of Tate – now lost – was used for the 1756 performance.[8] This supposition explains the appearance of annotations by Cross and Garrick, but not those by Harwood (presuming his to be the third hand). Instead of providing further arguments, however, Langhans concludes his analysis by pointing out that the alterations recorded in this book are very different to those that appear in the 1773 Bell's Shakespeare edition of *King Lear*, which – like many plays in this series – was published with the claim of having been set from the Drury Lane promptbook. Ultimately therefore, Langhans takes this annotated 1756 text to be 'a step toward the 1773 Garrick alteration', with perhaps some additional, unexplained marks from Harwood after Garrick's death.[9]

Several other critics have also commented on this promptbook, emphasising how much it remains a piece of Restoration Shakespeare. Reiko Oya observes that 'the relationship between this text and Garrick's staging is not clear', noting that lines apparently restored by Garrick from the Jacobean *King Lear* as early as 1753 are not restored in this text.[10] Vanessa Cunningham makes a similar point, but also notes that this promptbook's

---

[6] Edward A. Langhans, *Eighteenth Century British and Irish Promptbooks: A Descriptive Bibliography* (New York: Greenwood Press, 1987), 164–5.
[7] Langhans, *Eighteenth Century British and Irish Promptbooks*, 164.
[8] Langhans, *Eighteenth Century British and Irish Promptbooks*, 165.
[9] Langhans, *Eighteenth Century British and Irish Promptbooks*, 165.
[10] Reiko Oya, *Representing Shakespearean Tragedy: Garrick, the Kembles, and Kean* (Cambridge: Cambridge University Press, 2011), 193–4.

restoration of a mere ten lines from Shakespeare's play confirms a hypothesis first made by Arthur John Harris in 1971: that Garrick's *Lear* – even though it was trumpeted as a return to the Jacobean text – was actually nothing of the sort, and that it was instead George Colman who made the first major revisions of Tate's *Lear* for his Covent Garden production in the late 1760s.[11] Harris made this argument in response to George Winchester Stone's assertion that 'the force of Tate was vastly qualified after his play had held the stage for sixty years' by both the arrival of Garrick (who first played Lear in 1742 at the age of twenty-four) and the changes the actor-manager made to it thereafter.[12] Harris's position, confirmed thirty years later by Cunningham's use of the British Library promptbook, is the opposite of Stone's and might be presented as the idea that Garrick, perhaps more than we expect, performed a Restoration Shakespeare version of *King Lear*'s text.[13]

Yet while the annotated 1756 edition of *Lear* indicates Garrick's proximity to a Restoration version of Shakespeare's tragedy, it remains, as Langhans and Oya show, a challenging source to work with. The promptbook is a palimpsest. Speeches from Goneril and Edmund at the start of Tate's fifth act were first marked up with cuts and cues for scene changes, exits and entrances, but then later excised completely.[14] Other parts of the play seem to have been cut and then later re-included, with the word 'In' written next to them.[15] The brevity and simplicity of these later overwritings makes it all but impossible to identify their maker or their precise date, but they are hardly unexpected: Jane Freeman reminds us that attitudes to *King Lear* changed over the course of the eighteenth century, with audiences criticising the play's lack of pomp in 1747 and praising the exact same thing in 1772.[16] The layering of this particular promptbook, unmentioned by Freeman, might thus be considered as just one more piece of evidence to support the mutable tastes of the theatrical public.

As a palimpsest whose annotations are difficult to date, attribute or even explain as part of a project to restore Shakespeare, this promptbook has received limited attention. Yet such challenges might be recast as

---

[11] Cunningham, *Shakespeare and Garrick*, 123.
[12] George Winchester Stone, 'Garrick's Production of *King Lear*: A Study in the Temper of the Eighteenth-Century Mind', *Studies in Philology*, 45.1 (1948): 89–103 (103).
[13] Arthur John Harris, 'Garrick, Colman, and King Lear: A Reconsideration', *Shakespeare Quarterly*, 22.1 (1971): 57–66 (63).
[14] Tate and Garrick, *History of King Lear*, 57–8.
[15] For example, Tate and Garrick, *History of King Lear*, 28.
[16] Jane Freeman, 'Beyond Bombast: David Garrick's Performances of Benedick and King Lear', *Restoration and 18th Century Theatre Research*, 14.2 (1999): 1–21 (9).

opportunities, if we consider that although this source doesn't tell us exactly how eighteenth-century theatre professionals handled Restoration Shakespeare, it does demonstrate – perhaps over quite a long period – the variety of ways in which the theatre of the 1700s returned to the adaptations of the late seventeenth century. In other words, this is a text to think with, in that it offers a complex and imperfect trace of multiple attempts to think through Tate's *Lear*. As such, I argue we might learn two things from it: both something about the scope of Garrick and his contemporaries' thinking about Restoration Shakespeare and something about how that thinking operated on a scene-by-scene and line-by-line progress through Tate's text. Such a study of this promptbook, supplemented here with appeals to other pertinent sources from across the eighteenth century, reveals the range and subtlety of the period's engagement with Restoration Shakespeare, at both micro and macro levels. A renewed consciousness of that diverse and complex engagement has a lot to offer to our work on eighteenth-century, Restoration, and even Jacobean drama.

Practicalities

A promptbook is a practical document. Annotations in this 1756 edition of Tate's *Lear* record, for example, who speaks last, who says what and how much, when a performer should prepare to enter, when scenes change and how, and much else besides. As is true of all promptbooks, however, such practical concerns are also deeply intertwined with the work of interpreting the play. In this section I thus demonstrate how a careful attention to the 1756 promptbook, despite the ambiguities of this text's historical usage, still offers us reason to revise several critical commentaries on Garrick's renditions of Restoration Shakespeare. Following Restoration and eighteenth-century performance tradition, which emphasised the striking moments of a play, this part of my argument gathers evidence by moving in chronological sequence from one key 'point' in Tate's work to the next: from Lear's cursing of Goneril, to Lear's raving on the heath, and then on to Lear's recovery from madness in the arms of his daughter Cordelia, before the two of them are sent to prison.[17]

---

[17] For more information about acting 'points', see William B. Worthen, *The Idea of the Actor: Drama and the Ethics of Performance* (Princeton, NJ: Princeton University Press, 1984), 72; Lisa A. Freeman, *Character's Theater: Genre and Identity on the Eighteenth-Century English Stage* (Philadelphia: University of Pennsylvania Press, 2002), 31–2.

The Curse

A great number of the many eighteenth-century accounts of Garrick's performance as King Lear refer to the moment when Lear curses Goneril. In his *Dramatic Miscellanies* (1785), Thomas Davies compares Garrick's performance to those of his rivals and predecessors, recording how the actor-manager's 'preparation' for this speech 'was extremely affecting': by 'throwing away his crutch, kneeling on one knee, clasping his hands together, and lifting his eyes towards heaven', Garrick 'presented a picture worthy the pencil of Raphael'.[18] John Shebbeare, writing in 1755, also contrasted Garrick's version of this point with other actors, remembering how 'All is so forcibly and interestingly expressed, with attitude and action so becoming to the occasion, that … astonishment seizes me that a Goneril has power to go off stage unblasted at this imprecation.'[19] Davies and Shebbeare are both celebrating the same moment in Garrick's performance, but that moment appears also to have evolved during the second half of the eighteenth century. In his 2001 study of Garrick, Jean Benedetti quotes from Shebbeare's account and observes that lines from Lear's speech included in Shebbeare's book are not found in 'Garrick's own adaptation, published in 1773'.[20] What Benedetti ignores, however, is that these lines do appear in the annotated 1756 edition of Tate, and so open up the possibility of using this text alongside the 1773 edition to reveal how this iconic point in the play was nevertheless still subject to a revealing range of possible reinterpretations of the Restoration text.

Consider, for example, the last line before Lear calls upon nature to make his daughter sterile. As printed in 1756, there is an exclamation from Goneril here: 'Mark ye that', which interrupts Lear's rising anger and potentially distances both daughter and audience from it.[21] This line is altered by hand in the promptbook to read 'We fear you not', a change that does not appear in Bell's edition (where the line is cut altogether) but one which does make the moment far more combative, and so also makes Shebbeare's comment on Goneril's defiant response to her father's imprecation all the more understandable. That said, both Bell's edition and the annotated 1756 copy of *Tate* agree on the deletion of Goneril and Albany's lines at the end

---

[18] Thomas Davies, *Dramatic Miscellanies, Consisting of Critical Observations on Several Plays of Shakespeare, with a Review of His Principal Characters, and Those of Various Eminent Writers, as Represented by Mr Garrick and Other Celebrated Comedians* (London: Davies, 1783), vol. II, 280.
[19] John Shebbeare, *Letters on the English Nation by Battista Angeloni, A Jesuit, Who Resided Many Years in London* (London, 1755), vol. II, 289.
[20] Jean Benedetti, *David Garrick and the Birth of Modern Theatre* (London: Methuen, 2001), 104n.
[21] Tate and Garrick, *History of King Lear*, 17.

of King Lear's curse.[22] After the monarch has said 'How sharper than a serpent's tooth it is / To have a thankless child', any further comment before the end of the scene would detract from the pathos of the moment and from Garrick's performance. Although it is not cited by her, this cut fits with Vanessa Cunningham's analysis that 'Garrick shares, and expects his audience to share, Lear's view of himself as "a man / More sinned against than sinning"'.[23] The cut also fits Jean Marsden's view that, in eighteenth-century performance of Restoration Shakespeare, 'the spectacle is emotion not special effects'.[24] What Francis Gentleman called, in his footnotes to the 1773 edition, the 'melting' conclusion of this curse 'into a modulated shiver of utterance' is all the stronger for the changes made to Tate's text, changes already explored in manuscript annotations that indicate both when to end the scene and how much to involve Goneril in this moment.[25]

The Storm

While these changes support Marsden's claim that emotion and not special effects generate the spectacle of this eighteenth-century version of a Restoration play, other key points in the 1756 promptbook complicate her position. Indeed, one might even emphasise the practicalities of staging the curse to suggest that this moment had its own 'special effects'. The British Library promptbook tells us that the prompter should ring for the end of Act 1 as Albany enters and hears Lear's mounting rage.[26] This allows for the curtain to fall directly upon Lear's exit, and so for the alignment of the monarch's dismissal of his daughter and the theatre's release of its public, some of whom may even have heard the prompter's bell tolling out the climax of this part of the performance. Such alignment, however, is a small and hardly conclusive example. The indications given by the promptbook for the storm scene that opens Tate and Garrick's third act offer much stronger evidence for the idea that eighteenth-century approaches to this play did not simply favour sentiment over special effects but rather sought instead to use the material affordances of the stage to amplify emotion to the utmost.

[22] Tate and Garrick, *History of King Lear*, 17; William Shakespeare, *Bell's Edition of Shakespeare's Plays*, ed. Francis Gentleman (London: Cornmarket, 1969), vol. II, 20.
[23] Cunningham, *Shakespeare and Garrick*, 127.
[24] Jean I. Marsden, 'Improving Shakespeare: From the Restoration to Garrick', in *The Cambridge Companion to Shakespeare on Stage*, ed. Stanley Wells and Sarah Stanton (Cambridge: Cambridge University Press, 2002), 21–36 (33).
[25] Shakespeare, *Bell's Edition of Shakespeare's Plays*, 2:20n.
[26] With the instruction, 'Act Ring': Tate and Garrick, *History of King Lear*, 17.

As with the curse, there are many accounts of the performance of the storm. Thomas Wilkes's description of it in his *General View of the Stage* (1759) is cited by Kal Burnim as a particularly powerful account of 'the effect of Garrick's actions with his Lear now on the verge of madness':[27]

> I never see him coming down from one corner of the Stage, with his old grey hair standing, as it were, erect upon his head, his face filled with horror and attention, his hands expanded, and his whole frame actuated by a dreadful solemnity, but I am astounded, and share in all his distresses ... Methinks I share in his calamities, I feel the dark drifting rain, and the sharp tempest.[28]

As well as evidence of Garrick's ability to project powerful sentiment, Wilkes's account also supports my argument that theatrical special effects amplify emotional experience. The 1756 edition's annotations – unavailable to Burnim and unmentioned by Marsden, but reproduced here in Figure 5.1 – suggest an entry for Lear and Kent at 'UDPS' – that is, from the upper door on the prompt side (stage left) – and so from the furthest corner of the stage, as Wilkes himself recorded.[29] The 'dark drifting rain' and the 'sharp tempest' are also present in these promptbook markings: 'Thunder 2 Claps of Lightning' appears at the top of the page, with 'Lamps down' immediately below it.[30] Both notes refer to special effects: lowering the stage lights to darken the stage, and translating the storm (including the rain) into a series of sonic effects, from rumbling thunder to the crash of lightning.

To judge by the placement of the annotations on the promptbook page, these noises were apparently intended to occur at specific points during the scene's opening speeches. Lear's second outburst is, for instance, framed by calls for '__Thun & Rain'.[31] This framing, when considered with those effects that open the scene, has a powerful effect. In both instances, Lear seems to talk into the storm: he shouts 'Blow winds, and burst your Cheeks' into the opening salvo of noise, and 'Rumble thy fill, fight Whirlwind, Rain and Fire' into the second set of thunder. The projected *mise en scène* of this passage is effectively a dialogue between monarch and weather, a dialogue that, at some point in its history, one of the contributors to this promptbook considered extending. Here is my transcription of the speech in question:

[27] Kalman A. Burnim, *David Garrick, Director* (Pittsburgh: University of Pittsburgh Press, 1961), 146.
[28] Thomas Wilkes, *A General View of the Stage* (London: Coote and Whetstone, 1759), 234–5.
[29] Tate and Garrick, *History of King Lear*, 29.
[30] Tate and Garrick, *History of King Lear*, 29.
[31] Tate and Garrick, *History of King Lear*, 29.

```
_____Thun_&_____Rain
LEAR Rumble thy fill, fight Whirlwind, Rain and Fire;
I tax not you, ye Elements, with Unkindness;
I never gave you Kingdoms, call'd you Children;
You owe me no Obedience, then let fall
Your horrible Pleasure; here I stand your Slave,                    flash
A poor, infirm, weak, and despis'd old Man _____  Thun.&Light.  ≠
Yet will I call you servile Ministers,
That have with two pernicious Daughters join'd
Their high engender'd Battle against a Head
So old and white as mine; Oh! Oh! 'tis foul. _____Thun_&_____Rain³²
```

Next to the lines 'You owe me no Obedience, then let fall / Your horrible Pleasure; here I stand your Slave, / A poor infirm, weak, and despis'd old Man', there is a cancelled call for thunder and a flash of light. If that special effect had been maintained then it would have been the scene's sole instance of the storm seeming to respond to Lear, rather than anticipating his orders. We might expect some noise at this point, given the amount of thunder elsewhere in this scene; but the absence of such a special effect, and a noticeable absence at that, makes the pathos of the moment all the more powerful. Lear has ordered the sky to 'let fall / Your horrible pleasure' and it has apparently ignored him. The 1756 promptbook, by placing a call for the storm's response and then, sometime later, cancelling it, thus shows a rejected alternative *mise en scène*, a *mise en scène* that would have had less pathos. We might then note the absence of any call for thunder during Lear's second speech in Bell's Shakespeare of 1773, which suggests that the storm continued to ignore Lear's orders late into Garrick's career as well.³³ The bookends of thunder, however, remain constant.

It is worth comparing these markings to those in the promptbook for George Colman's version of Tate's *Lear* at Covent Garden (*c.* 1767–1773), which, while departing from the Restoration text far more than Garrick, is nevertheless very close to it when Act 3 opens on the heath.³⁴ Here too we find that the monarch's second speech in the scene is framed by thunder and lightning (see Figure 5.2).

---

[32] Tate and Garrick, *History of King Lear*, 29.
[33] Shakespeare, *Bell's Edition of Shakespeare's Plays*, 2:37–8.
[34] [Nahum Tate and George Colman], *The History of King Lear, As it is performed at The Theatre Royal in Covent Garden* (London: Baldwin and Becket, 1768), 34. This interleaved promptbook is held at the Folger Shakespeare Library (shelfmark PROMPT Lear 43). I follow the Folger catalogue in my dating of this promptbook. Available through Adam Matthew, *Shakespeare in Performance: Prompt Books from the Folger Shakespeare Library*.

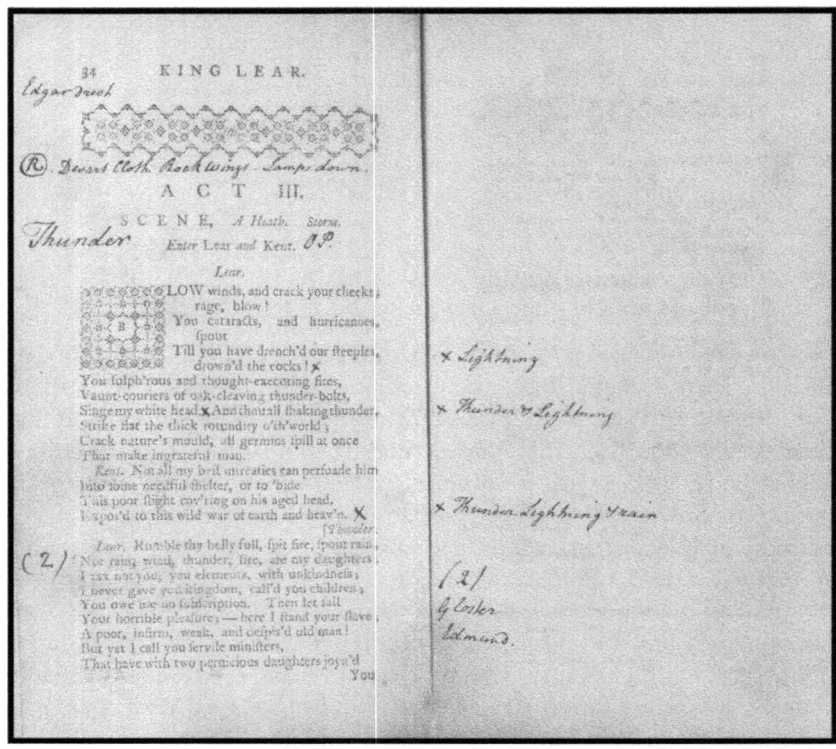

Figure 5.2 *The History of King Lear: As it is performed at The Theatre Royal in Covent Garden* (London: R. Baldwin and T. Becket, 1768), page 34 ‖ facing page 34. At the Folger Shakespeare Library Call #: PROMPT Lear 43.

Annotations to the start of the scene, however, indicate that Lear's opening speech (to which Colman restored several lines from Shakespeare's text) was twice punctuated by the elements. No such meteorological punctuation appears in the rough markings on the Drury Lane text. While such a difference does not necessarily mean that Colman and Garrick's actual renditions of this scene were always distinct across the eighteenth century, it does, once again, indicate the subtlety and range of eighteenth-century engagement with Restoration adaptations of Shakespeare. Colman's heavy use of thunder and lightning in the opening moments of this act might well have made the absence of any thunder and lightning in response to Lear's demand that the heavens 'let fall / Your horrible pleasure' all the more striking and pathetically ironic. Once more, then, we see how special effects are aligned with sentiment, both in their presence and, for those spectators sensitive to Lear's efforts to interact with the storm, the felt presence of their absence.

It is not just the sounds of thunder and lightning that amplify the emotion of the heath scenes during the eighteenth century. Both the promptbook for Colman's *Lear* and the British Library's annotated copy of Tate's play reveals the impact of scene changes. In the Colman promptbook there is a note for 'Desart Cloth. Rock Wings. Lamps down' at the top of Act 3.[35] The next scene takes place in Gloucester's castle ('Picture / Borders / Lamps up'), after which we return to the heath, finding ourselves in a part of it with 'Waterfall' and 'Hovel'.[36] This sequence of settings suggests that Colman's heath scenes take place on a deep stage, one which was then hidden by the intervening domestic scene, and then discovered anew with a 'waterfall' and 'hovel' added to it. That the outdoor scenes should take place on a larger visible acting space is hardly unsurprising, but this does not mean we should discount the impact of an alternation between a large and small space, or the symbolism of having a dialogue between Gloucester and his traitorous bastard son Edmund take place among scenery that, for the audience, is only barely hiding the savagery of the heath. Indeed, Edmund's last words 'The younger rises when old doth fall' gain even more power as their hateful articulation seems to call up the very heath and thunder that his father has desperately gone out into.

The details of the Colman promptbook allow us to picture its staging quite clearly, but the same argument might also be made for the one marked less assiduously by Garrick and Cross (and maybe Harwood too). While this text never marks settings, it does mark scene changes, using a variety of circular symbols joined by lines.[37] Mapping these markings to the demands of the play suggests the need for an absolute minimum of five scene configurations (two exterior, two interior and a prison), and the same alternation in Act 3 between a large and small acting space as found in Colman's promptbook. Furthermore, the depth of Garrick's heath stage is also supported by Wilkes's recollection of the actor-manager 'coming down from one corner of the Stage' in the storm scenes. That entry could, of course, have taken place at either the start of Act 3 or after the brief scene

---

[35] Tate and Colman, *History of King Lear*, 34.
[36] Tate and Colman, *History of King Lear*, 35–6.
[37] These markings occur on the following pages, Langhans describes them as 'cues [for] scene changes' (Langhans, *Eighteenth Century British and Irish Promptbooks*, 164). The variation between dotted and undotted circles is not fully consistent with the apparent use of flats. Tate and Garrick, *History of King Lear*, 7, 9, 15, 18, 19, 20, 22, 23, 24, 29, 30, 33, 41, 44, 45, 48, 49, 55, 58, 59, 62.

in Gloucester's castle. There is no way to be certain. The rough annotations on the 1756 copy give no further information, although they do raise a different question. Halfway through a long speech by Lear in the second heath scene, someone has placed a mark traditionally used for an entrance: '//////'.[38] The only person who could possibly enter here is Edgar as Poor Tom, but this character has no lines for half a page. Perhaps this is a cue to enter into the hovel through a trap (and thus invisibly), or perhaps this is an aborted idea and Edgar takes up his place while the interior scene hides the heath backdrop. No matter how we interpret the marking, though, the range of possibilities all point to an attempt to have Edgar's 'Five Fathom and half, poor Tom' surprise the audience and thus have them share the surprise of Kent as, from somewhere on a deep and darkened stage, a mad voice rings out.

For all the impact of Edgar's lines, King Lear remains as much at the centre of this second heath scene as in the first. Leigh Woods draws on several accounts of Garrick's performance of this scene to argue that here, as elsewhere in this actor's career, he presented a play's 'hero as a domestic, sensory, mobile, and oddly vulnerable creature', in marked contrast to 'the peerless, static, and monolithic portrayals' of characters implied by 'critical accounts of the Restoration players and their immediate successors'.[39] With reference to two 1747 accounts of Garrick's Lear, Woods points specifically to how the actor played with straw during the hovel scene, and claims that such business 'captured Lear's habitual resort to his own power' and thus exemplifies Garrick's ability to '*objectify* complex states of mind, supporting and embellishing the surface of the spoken text'.[40] Such 'small physical details' parallel Garrick's efforts in other tragic roles, like Hamlet, to produce a 'scaled down' character to his public.[41] Woods's argument is fascinating, and finds an echo in Freeman's later claim that '[b]y moving beyond the old bombastic style of tragic acting, and by paying attention to the details of Lear's pain, Garrick continued to deepen his understanding of Lear's experience'.[42] The study of promptbook evidence allows, however, for some additional nuancing of Freeman and Woods's positions. The Colman promptbook notes, for example, the need to clear 'straw' from the stage, and so suggests that Garrick's stage business was

[38] Tate and Garrick, *History of King Lear*, 34.
[39] Leigh Woods, 'Crowns of Straw on Little Men: Garrick's New Heroes', *Shakespeare Quarterly*, 32.1 (1981): 69–79 (69).
[40] Woods, 'Crowns of Straw on Little Men', 74.
[41] Woods, 'Crowns of Straw on Little Men', 72.
[42] Freeman, 'Beyond Bombast', 18.

powerful enough to be imitated at Covent Garden.[43] While confirming the success of what Woods and Freeman describe, one should however note that such 'small physical details' and the scaling down of Lear do not take place in a vacuum: as already discussed, these pathetic passages also made use of the amplifying potential of the London patent stages. Lear may well have played with straws, but he seems to have done so in a cavernous space with 'lamps down'. The littleness of these acts is significant, but it is a littleness that is productively in tension with the grandeur of other staging decisions.

One might be tempted to call such grandeur the grandeur of Restoration Shakespeare. As discussed in the 'Introduction' to this volume, the large-scale spectacle possible on an indoor stage with machines and movable scenery was central to the distinct identity of Restoration theatre and helped secure its success. Music, perhaps most obviously in Thomas Shadwell's operatic adaptation of *The Tempest* (1674), was an important part of this too,[44] and music plays a key role in the annotations found on the 1756 edition of Tate's *King Lear*, again demonstrating how this palimpsestic thinking through of the play found productive combinations of special effects and sentimental stage business. Lear's recovery from madness and his recognition of Cordelia is another one of this work's most famous passages, or 'points'. Woods argues that Garrick's decision (recorded by Davies in 1781) to put 'his hand upon the cheeks of Cordelia' as he asked 'Be your tears wet?' is the perfect counterpart to the character's distracted playing with straws, another instance of the actor-manager physicalising emotional states through a small but highly resonant action.[45] Woods does not note, however, that several sources indicate that this moment was introduced with theatre-filling music.

The Recovery

John Burgoyne recalled, in the preface to his *Lord of the Manor* (1781), the power of this music to produce an 'increase of sensibility' as the tragedy's final act began with 'the mute group of Cordelia and the aged parent

---

[43] A note at the start of the fifth act reads 'See that Stage is free from Straw' (presumably that used by Lear earlier in the play): Tate and Colman, *History of King Lear*, 59.

[44] For a discussion of the peculiar generic indeterminacy created by such music see: Claude Fretz, '"marvellous and surprizing conduct": The "Masque of Devils" and Dramatic Genre in Thomas Shadwell's *The Tempest*', *Restoration: Studies in English Literary Culture, 1660–1700*, 43.2 (2019): 3–28.

[45] Woods, 'Crowns of Straw on Little Men', 74.

asleep in her lap'.⁴⁶ Annotations to the 1756 edition of Tate suggest how such a moment, as a mixture of special effect and sentimental gesture, was envisaged. The original text of Tate's play places Lear's recovery at the end of Act 4. In the 1756 printing, however, we find handwritten instructions to ring for the end of this act when Edgar defends his father from Tate's version of Shakespeare's Oswald.⁴⁷ The curtain then falls with a rewritten version of lines addressed to Gloucester by his son: originally 'come, your Hand. / Far off methinks, I hear the beaten Drum; / Come, Sir, I will bestow you with a friend', the audience instead hears words that, shorn of concern for military manoeuvres, simply articulate a child's care for his parent: 'come, your Hand / Come, Sir, I will bestow you in a Place of Safety'. When the next act begins we do indeed find ourselves in a place of safety, just with a different pairing of parent and child. Furthermore, a manuscript note at the bottom of the promptbook page requests 'Curtain slow – with soft Musick'.⁴⁸ Such music would not be out of place on the Restoration stage, and here, once more, in conjunction with the rearrangement of the play's acts, amplifies a moment of sentiment to the status of moving spectacle.

There is perhaps another, more practical concern behind the manuscript changes marked on this copy of Tate (changes that were maintained in the 1773 'from the Drury Lane promptbook' printing of Garrick's *King Lear*). By moving the monarch's recovery to the start of Act 5, the actor playing Lear received more time offstage in the wake of the demanding mad scenes of the heath. The performer's own recovery could be as much of a concern as King Lear's. Indeed, both Freeman and Cunningham note that Garrick himself performed the part of the mad monarch relatively few times later in his career, perhaps because of how exhausting this role was for him.⁴⁹ Garrick frequently mentions how much energy certain performances took from him, although this may well have been as much a savvy publicity strategy as an apology.⁵⁰ Regardless, the new opening of Act 5 responds, as so many of the matters discussed in this section, to practical as well as aesthetic requirements. Benedetti's analysis of Garrick's *Lear* has already

---

⁴⁶ John Burgoyne, *The Lord of the Manor* (London: Evans, 1781), 13. See also the discussion of Garrick's use of music in Michael V. Pisani, *Music for the Melodramatic Theatre in Nineteenth-Century London and New York*, Studies in Theatre History and Culture (Iowa City: University of Iowa Press, 2014), 3–4.
⁴⁷ Tate and Garrick, *History of King Lear*, 55.
⁴⁸ Tate and Garrick, *History of King Lear*, 54.
⁴⁹ Cunningham, *Shakespeare and Garrick*, 129–30; Freeman, 'Beyond Bombast'.
⁵⁰ See Leslie Ritchie, *David Garrick and the Mediation of Celebrity* (Cambridge: Cambridge University Press, 2019), 107, 128.

demonstrated this with a description of how the play's prison scenes were staged: using Tate Wilkinson's memory of the production's scenery, and Burnim's identification of what the 'prison' backdrop may have looked like, Benedetti observes that the recorded details of performance keep Lear out of sight when he has no lines, again giving the performer needed recovery time while also managing the audience's engagement with the action.[51]

I discuss this prison scene in more detail in the following section, 'Contrasts, Foils and Transitions'. For now, it is enough to note how it too brings together practical concerns and a complex balance between large- and small-scale effects. Wilkinson notes the use of straw in the prison: a neat echo of the straw found in the hovel on the heath, and another marriage between sentiment and the affordances of the patent theatre stage.[52] As we move through each of the 'points' of *King Lear*, eighteenth-century materials, especially the 1756 annotated edition of Tate, record how emotion and spectacle unite in an eighteenth-century thinking through of a Restoration Shakespeare text. Rather than necessarily testifying to what actually happened on a given night some time in a hundred-year period, these sources instead illuminate the range of interpretations available, a range which has its limits and its own distinctive shape of possibilities. As critics have noted, these possibilities include a great deal of sentiment and sentimentalisation, of smallness and of scaling down, but they combine, I argue, such things with a certain grandeur too, an amplification of sentiment through special effects that range from the use of music, sound and light to the timing of entrances, exits and curtains. This combination of the big and the small, visible in the practical thinking of the promptbooks, now demands our attention as part of a distinctive and revealing aesthetic strategy.

Contrasts, Foils and Transitions

Modern criticism of the relationship between Tate's *Lear* and Garrick's reworking of it appears to fall into two camps. On one hand, Lynne Bradley claims that Tate 'puts considerable effort into making the play more consistent and seemly', something that Garrick's alterations continued even as his own public discourse about restoring Shakespeare's text

---

[51] Burnim, *David Garrick, Director*, 149–50; Benedetti, *David Garrick and the Birth of Modern Theatre*, 108.
[52] Tate Wilkinson, 'Original Anecdotes Respecting the Stage, and the Actors of the Old School, with Remarks on Mr Murphy's "Life of Garrick"', *Monthly Mirror*, 13 (February 1802): 122–124 (124).

produced a means of satisfying his audience's 'desire for the *appearance* of authenticity without having to be remotely authentic'.[53] On the other hand, Oya has argued that Garrick ultimately 'crammed Tate's happy-ending tragedy' with additional material and so 'overwhelmed the audience without fail' and despite 'the textual and emotional inconsistencies' such cramming entailed.[54] Oya's attention to Garrick's 'inconsistencies' and Bradley's to Tate and Garrick's 'consistency' both, however, share a common source in a key aesthetic issue for eighteenth-century adaptation of Restoration Shakespeare: the extent to which performance aimed to exploit contrasts for spectacular and emotional effect. Oya touches on this when she observes how Garrick's inconsistencies 'overwhelmed' theatregoers, and, although Bradley's overarching theme is Garrick and Tate's total reworking of Shakespeare, she too recognises the 'tremendous amount of rewriting ... needed to recreate Shakespeare in a contemporary mould'.[55] According to a letter sent to Garrick in 1763, this 'contemporary mould' clearly had ample space for powerful contrasts of emotion.

> Such violent starts of amazement, of horror, of indignation, of paternal rage, excited by filial ingratitude the most prodigious; such a perceptible yet rapid gradation, from those dreadful feelings to the deepest frenzy ... These, sir, are some of the great circumstances which so eminently distinguished your action two nights ago.[56]

This letter was written by Garrick's friend, Dr George Fordyce. Although thus hardly without bias, it nevertheless testifies to an aesthetic approach that valued the powerful performance of varied emotions. Garrick excels because, in his rendition of the curse on Goneril, he moves clearly but rapidly between 'amazement', 'horror', 'indignation', 'rage' and 'frenzy'. With the help of other witnesses to Garrick's performance of his alteration of Restoration Shakespeare, it is easy to identify other such passages of extreme affective contrast. At the end of the heath scenes of Act 4, for instance, Garrick's Lear fell asleep on stage and so set calm slumber against the ravings of his dialogue with Edgar.[57]

---

[53] Bradley, *Adapting King Lear for the Stage*, 64–5.
[54] Oya, *Representing Shakespearean Tragedy*, 18.
[55] Bradley, *Adapting King Lear for the Stage*, 65.
[56] David Garrick, *The Private Correspondence of David Garrick with the Most Celebrated Persons of His Time Now First Published from the Originals, and Illustrated with Notes, and a New Biographical Memoir of Garrick*, ed. James Boaden (London: Colburn and Bentley, 1831), vol. I, 154 – for reasons of brevity, my quotation heavily abridges the original letter.
[57] This information is available in the Harvard promptbook of Garrick's *King Lear*, discussed by Burnim here: *David Garrick, Director*, 148.

There is no direction for Lear to sleep on the heath in the printed text of Tate's play. Yet while the Restoration drama lacks this specific contrast, it too demonstrates a deep interest in sequence, and especially those sequences which produce starkly different emotions on stage. In Tate's preface and prologue he first observes that Shakespeare's original play lacks such sequencing, calling it both a 'Heap of Jewels unstrung' and – shifting the metaphor for the play's prologue – a 'Heap of Flow'rs', which now 'shall chance to wear / Fresh beauty' since they have been 'strung by this course [sic] Hand into a new arrangement'.[58] Crucially, then, Tate presents his rewriting of Shakespeare's play as something more complicated than the addition of a romance between Edgar and Cordelia and the substitution of a happy ending: these changes are part of a resequencing of the drama, and, specifically, a newly strung sequence that balanced light and dark material. A digression in John Hill's *The Actor* on the performance of *King Lear* points out how effective this could be.

> There is not perhaps on the stage a more moving scene than that of Edgar's discovering himself to Cordelia, Shakespear [sic] meant the mad things that precede it principally as foils to it; and 'tis in this sense that the player we are commending in the part performs it.[59]

Hill's work was published in 1750, but it does not distinguish between Tate's text and its Jacobean source, and instead simply calls the play's author 'Shakespear' (as many eighteenth-century theatregoers also did).[60] Yet Tate's changes to the plot allow scenes of madness to follow scenes of love as part of a sequence of contrasts. Hill praises this sequence, and – to judge from the promptbook evidence – Garrick was careful to preserve it and so remain close to his Restoration predecessor.

Hill calls the products of sequencing events of contrasting emotional resonance 'foils'. He does not only identify them occurring at the level of scenes but also at a much smaller scale. Continuing his discussion of Edgar, Hill notes that 'the real beauties of the part' emerge when the character pretends to be mad and speaks with Lear in the hovel, since these speeches entail both 'frantic action' and – most importantly – a 'change to reason', producing a foil-like 'contrast of … passionate and affecting speeches' that, in Hill's view, allowed the actor Lacy Ryan to charm 'the

---

[58] Tate and Garrick, *History of King Lear*, A2ʳ, A3ʳ.
[59] John Hill, *The Actor: A Treatise on the Art of Playing* (London: Griffiths, 1750), 293.
[60] The eighteenth-century process by which Shakespeare's name and authorship became marketable (still underway when Hill is writing) is traced in Michael Dobson, *The Making of the National Poet: Shakespeare, Adaptation and Authorship, 1660–1769* (Oxford: Oxford University Press, 1992), 99–133.

more judicious part of an audience'.⁶¹ From material discussed elsewhere in this chapter, we might add other instances of foiling to this example: the falling asleep at the end of the hovel scene, the cursing of Goneril, and even King Lear's speech into the storm, as the use (or absence) of sound effects and other spectacular devices gave different meanings to the character's imprecations.

One final, and especially revealing, instance of this principle of sequence occurs during the happy ending of Tate (and Garrick's) *King Lear*. In Shakespeare's tragedy, King Lear enters in the final scene carrying the dead Cordelia in his arms and we learn that the patriarch was too weak to save his daughter from those sent by Edmund to kill her. In the Restoration *Lear*, and in both Garrick's and Colman's reworkings of it, the audience visits the prison where the monarch and his daughter are incarcerated and witnesses instead one final flaring of the old man's strength as he fights off the assassins long enough for Edgar and Albany to save the day. To use Hill's terms, such salvation serves as a 'foil' to what precedes it and thus pleases the audience as so many other altered scenes were meant to do. At the same time, however, Tate, Garrick and Colman all retain some of Shakespeare's language at this point, relying on the change of plot to change its meaning. The speech in question runs as follows:

> GENTLEMAN Look here, my lord, see where the generous king
> Has slain Two of 'em.
> LEAR   Did I not fellow?
> I've seen the day, with my good biting faulchion
> I cou'd have made 'em skip: I am old now,*
> And these vile crosses spoil me; out of breath!
> Fie, oh! Quite out of breath, and spent.⁶²

I take my text from the 1773 Bell's Shakespeare edition of *King Lear* (set from the Drury Lane promptbook), where Gentleman has placed an asterisk upon the phrase 'I am old now', drawing his reader's attention to what he describes as 'a transition, which often furnishes, as audiences have experienced, an admirable stroke for acting merit'.⁶³ This is another moment of a foil, where Lear's pathetic recognition of his weakness is, for eighteenth-century audiences, balanced with the fact that he nevertheless had just enough strength to save his child from death. Yet, because Restoration

---

⁶¹ Hill, *The Actor*, 291.
⁶² Shakespeare, *Bell's Edition of Shakespeare's Plays*, 2:77.
⁶³ Shakespeare, *Bell's Edition of Shakespeare's Plays*, 2:77n.

and eighteenth-century writers have chosen to retain Shakespeare's words here, this passage also allows us a window back into the Jacobean text, where the 'transition' has a very different impact: it intensifies the despair of the moment by adding to it this father's haunting realisation of his own impuissance.

Lear's failure to save Cordelia is but one of a host of things that turn from bad to worse in Shakespeare's tragedy. The king banishes Kent and then Cordelia too. Cornwall puts out one of Gloucester's eyes and then, despite the servant's intervention, the other too. Edgar talks his father out of suicide only for the two of them to encounter Lear mad. Edmund loses the duel with his brother, but then reveals his order for the execution of the king and his daughter. These sequences differ from the foils of Tate and Garrick, since they hold out a vision of a better future only to dash it with an even crueller reality. Shakespeare's characters even comment on this pattern: Edgar intones 'the worst is not / So long as we can say "This is the worst"' when he encounters his blinded father, and Kent greets Lear's arrival with Cordelia's corpse by asking 'Is this the promised end?' only to see his monarch struggle on yet further before eventually dying.[64]

Neither Kent nor Edgar's lines was ever spoken on the Restoration or eighteenth-century stage, and perhaps it is Shakespeare's piling of worse upon worse that Tate referred to when he described the 'heap' of material in this play that needed to be strung anew. Tate and his eighteenth-century successors do, after all, seem to have recognised that Shakespeare's sequencing had no place on their stages. Even Colman, who controversially cut the love plot between Cordelia and Edgar, still retained the happy ending of the Restoration text, and so confirmed an eighteenth-century attitude to Shakespeare's tragedy most famously articulated by Samuel Johnson when, in the notes to his 1765 edition of *King Lear*, he recorded his shock at Cordelia's death.[65] We also find this attitude of hostility towards unremitting tragedy expressed in more general terms in the period. Hill, again in *The Actor*, argued that the best tragedy 'suspends for a few moments the rage, or the misery of the principal characters to better engage the theatregoer in what follows'.[66] Henry Home, Lord Kames, says something

---

[64] William Shakespeare, *King Lear*, ed. R. A. Foakes (London: Thomson Learning, 2006), 305–6, 386.
[65] William Shakespeare, *The Plays of William Shakespeare in Eight Volumes*, ed. Samuel Johnson (London: J. and R. Tonson, 1765), vol. VI, 159; for further discussion of this comment, see Freya Johnston, 'Samuel Johnson', in *Great Historians: Dryden, Pope, Johnson, Malone*, ed. Claude Rawson (London: Continuum, 2010), 115–59 (143, 149, 152).
[66] Hill, *The Actor*, 20.

similar in his *Elements of Criticism* (1762) when he observes the need for a dramatist to include 'seasonable respite' which, rather than distracting an audience from a tragedy, will instead 'relieve the mind from its fatigue; and consequently prevent a wandering of thought'.[67]

Looking back from the perspective of Restoration and eighteenth-century adaptations, it becomes immediately evident that while there is contrast in Shakespeare's play, it is within material of increasingly darker shades. Tate's *Lear* of the late seventeenth century articulates the aesthetics of contrast he created in terms of both addition and contrast: he sets off Shakespeare's dark beauties with the lightness of a love plot and a happy ending. Garrick's *Lear* (and, to a lesser extent, Colman's) inherits this principle of contrast, of foiling at the level of scenes and within individual speeches, but also adds to it in two ways: Garrick's own practice makes Lear's transitions into star turns, and writers of the mid-eighteenth century also come to understand such moments as a necessary element in the affective economy of a tragedy.

In the case of Tate's *King Lear*, promptbooks and other sources reveal – if not with any certainty – the precise events and features of eighteenth-century performances of Restoration Shakespeare, at least the range of ways that Garrick, Colman, and others put their own mark upon a seventeenth-century play. These included an attention to the practical possibilities of the stages of Drury Lane and Covent Garden (entrance timings, the use of discovery, the choice of where to end an act), and, beyond this, clear efforts to combine spectacle and sentiment, to place crashes of thunder in such a pattern as to generate ironic pathos in the storm, or to represent the return of reason to the monarch with soft music and a rising curtain. Often, such combinations entailed the connection of objects on markedly different scales, from the smallness of a single gesture to the grandeur of a scene change or sound effect that filled the theatre.

These productive theatrical tensions between the sentimental and the spectacular lead us to observe a set of fundamental differences between the Jacobean, Restoration, and eighteenth-century *King Lear*. Tate claimed his adaptation did not merely add a love plot, but also gave to Shakespeare's tragedy a new pattern, transforming a heap of material into a garland. Garrick's *King Lear* extends this, producing – with the help of all the techniques and choices we find recorded in the promptbooks –

---

[67] Henry Home, Lord Kames, *Elements of Criticism*, ed. Peter Jones (Indianapolis: Liberty Fund, 2005), vol. II, 421.

a chiaroscuro experience of sublime, spectacular tragedy and domestic sentiment whose littleness not only touches its audience deeply but also, as Kames, Hill, and other theorists observed, provided that public with necessary emotional respite. As for Shakespeare's play, it emerges from this analysis as newly bleak and profound. Seen through Restoration and eighteenth-century eyes, the Jacobean drama operates through the denial of relief, stretching its audience, like its hero, ever longer on the rack of its tough world.

CHAPTER 6

An Actor's Perspective on Restoration Shakespeare
Louis Butelli

The veteran Folger Theatre actor Louis Butelli played Duncan in the Folger's 2018 production of Sir William Davenant's Macbeth. *The production was part of 'Performing Restoration Shakespeare', a research project funded by the Arts and Humanities Research Council in the United Kingdom and led by Queen's University Belfast. Richard Schoch, the project's Principal Investigator, interviewed Butelli on his experience of performing Restoration Shakespeare today.*

RS: *Louis, you are no stranger to Shakespeare, not least because of your long association with Folger Theatre and the Folger Shakespeare Library. Before you became involved in the production of Davenant's* Macbeth, *what did you know about Restoration Shakespeare?*

LB: Before I got involved in this production, I knew exactly zero about performing Restoration Shakespeare – so I asked some friends to help light the way for me. Dr Michael Witmore, Director of the Folger Shakespeare Library, reminded me that, 'theatre is this amazing art form; it's designed to just vanish as soon as it happens, which is why it's so powerful. And the Restoration is important … it was a really muscular moment in theatre history where Shakespeare's plays were taken apart and put back together again in a new way.'[1]

That was enough for me. I was in.

RS: *What's different about the role of Duncan in Davenant's version of* Macbeth?

LB: In Shakespeare's great play, Macbeth kills Duncan offstage somewhere between Acts 1 and 2, and that is the last we see of the King. Case closed and, in that version, I can go out for dinner before curtain call. *Macbeth*

---

[1] Louis Butelli, interview with Michael Witmore, Director, Folger Shakespeare Library, Washington, DC, 13 December 2019.

An Actor's Perspective on Restoration Shakespeare 119

Figure 6.1 The witches (Emily Noël, Rachael Montgomery, Ethan Watermeier) and Duncan (Louis Butelli) in Act 2, Scene 5 of the Folger Theatre's 2018 production of Sir William Davenant's *Macbeth* (dir. Robert Richmond).
Set design by Tony Cisek and costume design by Mariah Hale.
Photograph by Brittany Diliberto.

aficionados might be surprised to know that in Davenant's adaptation of *Macbeth*, the bloodied ghost of the murdered Duncan appears in Act 4, Scene 4 to stalk Lady Macbeth. She confesses this haunting to Macbeth during the scene, saying 'his fatal Ghost is now my shadow and pursues me Where e're I go'. Davenant really liked plot symmetry, so Macbeth and Lady Macbeth both get their own ghost.

RS: *In the true Restoration spirit of rewriting Shakespeare, the director Robert Richmond made some other changes to the role of Duncan. What else did you do in the production?*

LB: In our show, Robert had me appear two more times as Duncan's reanimated corpse or, as we affectionately called him, 'Zombie Duncan' [see Figure 6.1]. In Act 2, Scene 5, my body was dragged on-stage and brought back to unholy 'life' by a trio of singing, dancing witches – one of whom was visibly pregnant – bearing rusty garden tools and covered in blood, singing that they 'rejoice when good kings bleed'. I appeared to Lady Macbeth as the ghost again in Act 5, Scene 1 for her mad scene. This time, I hovered behind her and handed her the bloody knives used to murder Duncan with which she would, presumably, commit suicide offstage.

Perhaps most surprising of all would have been the fact that not only was I playing Duncan and 'Zombie Duncan', I was also playing the Warden of Bedlam Asylum. The frame for the entire production was that Davenant's *Macbeth* was being performed by the inmates of Bedlam, the mental asylum in London, two weeks after the Great Fire of London in 1666. In our 'Bedlam performance' of *Macbeth*, the inmates/actors replace the theatrical prop knives with real knives, so that during the dumbshow of Duncan's murder in the performance, the Warden is *actually* killed. At this point, the inmates take over and, as Robert said in his program notes, 'we are transported into a dark, ruthless world of violence and mayhem. Bedlam ensues!'[2]

At this point, quite rightly, you might be thinking, 'what?'

RS: *The meta-theatrical Bedlam frame, although it's clearly indebted to Peter Weiss' play* Marat/Sade *(1963), is also very specific about the Restoration, with allusions to Bedlam and the Great Fire of London, which happened just two years after the first performance of Davenant's* Macbeth. *With so much historical consciousness and awareness in the framing concept, how did you, the other actors, and the director think about Restoration acting style?*

LB: Some of the most complicated conversations amongst the team sought agreement upon an authentic Restoration 'acting style'. For theatre practitioners these days, such issues are dealt with at the moment of an actor's audition. If one's style doesn't fit the piece, one simply isn't hired. Here, we were all hired before a style was agreed upon.

What, then, *is* a 'Restoration' style of acting? I'm not sure that it's possible to actually know. Certainly, the scholars helped immensely by sharing images from their research of performances past, including the pictures of different hand gestures in John Bulwer's *Chirologia* from 1644. There were many of us – our director, actors, and scholars alike – who felt that the large, demonstrative gestures from such pictures might be considered as templates for our own performances.

The difficulty, of course, is that we can't actually see *how* Restoration actors moved from one gesture to another. Fluidly? Mechanically? Subtly? Further, we can't know for certain if a 'Restoration performance' was

---

[2] Robert Richmond's director's note can be read in its entirety here: www.folger.edu/events/macbeth/directors-notes.

entirely composed of stylised gestures; or, if the artist creating the image simply chose the most dynamic moment of a given performance to paint. This is not to disregard the importance of all of the clues that history gives us, just to say that, once armed with the images, we then had to actually *do* something with them.

That in mind, we spent numerous hours of rehearsal experimenting with movement. Some sessions, we would confine ourselves to using only the actual gestures we found in the images. Some sessions, we would take a single gesture and abstract it variously. Some sessions we would imagine the 'volume' of a particular gesture and play with turning the 'dial' up and down on it. Additionally, because we had set our production in an asylum, we spent some time imagining the ways in which cognitive issues might cause someone to use physicality in surprising and extreme ways.

Experimentation of this sort is what I love about the theatre: when there are no rules, you invent them, like children at play. Even more satisfying was the scholars' presence, participation, and delight in the experiment, calling out suggestions and even trying out gestures themselves. I hope I'm not speaking out of turn by suggesting that some of the scholars may have found themselves moving their bodies in ways they hadn't ever before, and are perhaps pleased they never have to do so again.

In the end, I believe we arrived at a place wherein scenes could be played truthfully, with heightened emotion reflected with expanded physicality. Is that a Restoration acting style? I don't know, but it was quite gratifying to perform.

RS: *You make a good point about the limitations of evidence from theatre history. That's a perspective that scholars understand very well. And yet the theatrical past comes to us only through such documents, however partial and imperfect they are. Did you undertake any research yourself at the Folger on Restoration theatre, including acting practices?*

LB: Yes, because I was hungry to know more. Who, I wondered, was Davenant's own leading actor? Who played Macbeth in his show, and what could we learn about a Restoration style of acting from him?

We know that the diarist Samuel Pepys was an avid theatregoer, and we know that he frequented the theatre in Lincoln's Inn Fields where Davenant's company performed in the 1660s. He saw Davenant's original *Macbeth* on multiple occasions, writing in his diary on 19 April 1667: 'So to the playhouse …. Here we saw "Macbeth" which, though I have seen it often, yet it is one of the best plays for a stage, and variety of dancing and musique, that ever I saw.'[3]

I adore S. Pepys the 'fanboy', but we don't learn much here about the actual acting, apart from how much he seemed to enjoy all of the singing, dancing, and 'musique' in Davenant's work.

RS: *When Pepys saw* Macbeth, *the title role was played by Thomas Betterton, the Duke's Company's leading male actor. What does Pepys say about Betterton as Macbeth?*

LB: Well, we get two more diary entries, the first on 16 October 1667: 'To the Duke of York's house .... I was vexed to see Young (who is but a bad actor at best) act Macbeth in the room of Betterton, who, poor man! Is sick: but, Lord! What a prejudice it wrought in me against the whole play, and everybody else agreed in disliking this fellow.' And then a few weeks later, on 6 November: 'To a play ... "Macbeth" which we still like mightily, though mighty short of the content we used to have when Betterton acted, who is still sick.'[4]

My first encounter with Thomas Betterton, then, esteemed actor of the day, shareholder in Davenant's company, and later a theatre manager in his own right, was indirect, as he was out sick for at least two performances, replaced in at least one of those by the – allegedly inferior – Young, poor man.

RS: *It's fascinating that Pepys identified the role of Macbeth so closely with Betterton, so much so that he was always disappointed when a different actor took the role. And yet Pepys's comments are still frustrating: we know that Pepys thought Betterton was a great actor, but we don't know why he thought that. What was so special about Betterton's acting?*

LB: Right. What made Betterton so good? Why was he a better actor than Young? Was there an approach he used, unique to his time, that made him great? There is no easy answer.

Is it even possible to get close to Betterton's performance? Colley Cibber, who saw Betterton on the stage many times over nearly two decades, really tried to describe how the great actor worked.

---

[3] Samuel Pepys, *Diary*, 19 April 1667, quoted in *Pepys on the Restoration Stage*, ed. Helen McAfee (New Haven, CT: Yale University Press, 1916), 318.
[4] Pepys, *Diary*, 16 October 1667 and 6 November 1667, quoted in *Pepys on the Restoration Stage*, ed. McAfee, 71, 214.

In his *Apology for the Life of Mr. Colley Cibber* (1740), when he remembers those performances from fifty years earlier, Cibber sets up a comparison between a hypothetical 'mis-guided' actor performing Hamlet's soliloquy 'O, that this too, too solid flesh would melt' and Thomas Betterton playing the same. As Cibber imagines it, the first (not so good) actor 'has thrown himself into all the straining Vociferation requisite to express Rage and Fury and the House has thundered with Applause; though the misguided Actor was all the while (as Shakespeare terms it) tearing a Passion into Rags'.

The reference to Hamlet's advice to the players is interesting here. Cibber then says that, if one was to actually examine the text of the 'beautiful Speech', and consider a genuine encounter with a melancholy ghost, one might find that it requires a more delicate, quiet approach, which is exactly how he remembered that Betterton had played the part. Let me read the passage from Cibber:

> This was the Light into which Betterton threw this Scene; which he opened with a Pause of mute Amazement! then rising slowly, to a solemn, trembling Voice, he made the Ghost equally terrible to the Spectator as to himself! and in the descriptive Part of the natural Emotions which the ghastly Vision gave him, the boldness of his Expostulation was still governed by Decency …. But alas! to preserve this medium between mouthing, and meaning too little, to keep the Attention more pleasingly awake, by a tempered Spirit, than by mere Vehemence of Voice, is of all the Master-strokes of an Actor the most difficult to reach. In this none yet have equalled Betterton.[5]

RS: *Cibber always praised Betterton's acting, but do you think he's a reliable or impartial eyewitness?*

LB: Hard to say. Cibber was nearly seventy when he wrote the *Apology*, and he was writing about performances that happened back in the 1690s, when he was himself a young man in his twenties, and new to the theatre business. So, I suspect that nostalgia couldn't have helped but influence his assessment of Betterton's performances, because they were so much associated with Cibber's own youth. I mean, the songs we learn as children, in the arms of a parent, sit differently with us when we're grown than do the songs 'the kids are listening to these days' on Spotify. I say this because, for an actor, any attempt to generate a performance guided only by nostalgia does not give the entire truth. We accept nostalgia as part of an emotional blueprint

---

[5] Colley Cibber, *An Apology for the Life of Mr. Colley Cibber, Comedian* … 2nd ed. (London, 1740), 84.

for a performance, but an effective performance must connect with our *current* emotional truth, the communicative modes of the *present* moment, and the room we co-inhabit *right now*, whenever that may be.

Cibber's quote then, I think, does not help us to better understand Restoration-style acting, if such a thing exists as distinct from acting in any other period. While the quote does imply that Cibber himself seemed to prefer what we might today call 'naturalism' – in the sense of conveying the truth of our emotional experience rather than a stylised representation – that particular term also seems not to have been meaningful to Restoration actors. He also, perhaps, contradicts himself a few pages later, when he suggests that it's better for an actor to do too much rather than too little because, in his estimation, the worst theatrical sin is to be boring:

> I mean that dangerous Affectation of the Monotone, or solemn Sameness of Pronunciation ... for of all Faults that so frequently pass upon the Vulgar, that of Flatness will have the fewest Admirers. That this is an Error of ancient standing seems evident by what Hamlet says, in his Instructions to the Players, viz. 'Be not too tame, neither,' &c .... He that feels not himself the Passion he would raise, will talk to a sleeping Audience.[6]

Here, returning to Hamlet's 'advice to the players' to arrive at an opposite conclusion, Cibber seems to be begging actors not to be, if I'm reading him right, boring. He seems to crave some vocal and emotional fireworks and, while demonstrative gestures are again not mentioned, one can only imagine that some physical manifestation of said fireworks would have been inevitable.

RS: *The passages you cite from Samuel Pepys's* Diary *and Colley Cibber's* Apology, *among the best eyewitness accounts of Restoration theatre, really show the difficulty of knowing what Restoration acting was really like. Even the people who saw Restoration actors in the flesh found it difficult to write about. To bring our conversation back to the Folger production of Davenant's* Macbeth: *In the end, what decision did the director and the cast come to about invoking or drawing upon Restoration acting style, whatever that might mean?*

LB: As we continued to rehearse, it was apparent to all of us that generating an 'authentic' Restoration style of acting would be, by any metric, a huge compromise. Given more time in which to work, we could have kept digging and exploring very happily. However, there were also other pressing concerns, such as learning the lines, the blocking, the fight choreography, and discovering our characters and relationships with our scene partners.

[6] Cibber, *Apology*, 85.

As Ian Merrill Peakes, our own Macbeth, opined to me, 'There is no definitive "Restoration" style. Our attempts at it only served to have us taking a few illogical stabs at a style beyond our grasp. There was no unifying vocabulary to ground us and so we ended up agreeing on a slightly heightened version of playing. That is to say, we played it mostly with our own sensibilities and tried to just tell the story we had.'[7]

Still, as implied by Ian's use of 'play', our experimentation with acting styles taught us tons. Whether or not the look of our performances ultimately matched the images we used for our gestural play, the very fact that the scholars had introduced the material into the room, that all of us pushed ourselves out of our comfort zones and worked with physicality that felt unnatural, and that we took every single suggestion from every member of the team seriously – all that interplay between scholars and actors ended up baked into the cake of our production.

That, I suppose, is part of the collaborative alchemy that makes the theatre beautiful to me as an art form. Would our audience in 2018 be aware of the amount of work and thought and scholarship that went into this or that hand gesture? Perhaps, perhaps not. But as Michael Witmore said to me, regardless of style, 'the most authentic part of the performance is the organic connection of the actors to the story'.[8]

RS: *The rehearsal schedule for Davenant's* Macbeth *was accelerated, just three weeks instead of the customary four. After the first week or so in which lots of different staging choices were explored, including period style, the moment inevitably came for the director to decide what's in and what's out, so that the production as a whole could cohere. What was that final stage of rehearsal like?*

LB: For those watching the clock, we spent the next ten days swirling around in a tornado of our director's drive, our actors' experimentation, our musicians' precise tinkerings, our designers' ingenuity, and our producers' increasingly less gentle suggestions that time was of the essence. Our scholars, who certainly understand the nature of a deadline, helped us immeasurably to narrow our focus to the urgency of compromise and committing to a single choice, as it were, right now. The time had come to stop thinking and to start *doing*.

We've discussed the difficulty of 'knowing' a Restoration-era actor's performance. I suspect it is also difficult to know what the mood within a

[7] Ian Merrill Peakes, text message to Louis Butelli, 12 December 2019.
[8] Butelli, interview with Witmore, 13 December 2019.

Restoration-era theatre company was like when they approached opening night. I find it hard to believe that it would have been any less exhilarating for them than it was for us. So, as the clock ran down, we did what any theatre company does: pull together, prioritise time, and call a moratorium on anything that might distract from the urgent task of readying the show to open.

Our final ten days were spent in technical rehearsals and previews. This is the time where every department is expected to be ready to deliver. Actors are more solid on their choices, gestures, and choreography through the show. Sets and props have built the world and are running around to be sure that everything looks right and works right. Costumes have put clothes on everybody and are frantically adjusting hems, accessories, and wigs. Lights and sound are paramount; most of the tech rehearsal is for the designers to tweak how the production looks and sounds. Through it all, scholars are watching everything from the darkened auditorium, making contextual notes and finding connections between scholarship and our artistic practice that, more often than not, we practitioners don't even notice until the scholars write about it in a newspaper or an essay after the fact. What a thrill to have those humans in the room during the process itself!

Our musicians had taken up residence onstage, and they had a very stressful job indeed. They needed to hear each other and the actors, they needed to keep their instruments in tune and scores up to date, even as things were changing around them constantly – and they needed to provide what was, arguably, the most 'authentically' Restoration part of the entire evening. Richmond and musical director Bob Eisenstein placed the six musicians on stage in the 'inner above', a sort of balcony at the back of the stage, and their playing of both full songs and underscoring added immeasurably to the story. Including violins, viola, cello, harpsichord, percussion, and bagpipe, the soundscape was a vital character in the show.

For us actors, having been asked not only to inhabit our characters but to do so through a particular stylistic prism, I'll say with some modesty that we did what we always do; we accepted our given circumstances, we allowed the feeling of the music and the design and the reality inside the unreality to wash over us and inhabit us, and we brought everything we could of our flesh and blood selves, and our most privately held emotional truths, out on to the stage.

Perhaps Restoration performers and audiences didn't conceive of 'naturalism' in the same way that we do today. Still, I suspect that any audience at any time feels a jolt in their spine when they experience something onstage that feels truthful to them, something that they recognise as themselves, their loved ones, their communities. It is our job as actors, when we have jobs, to bring the truth of the human condition no matter what the production.

RS: *Some of the production's design elements were informed or inspired by Restoration theatre practice, even though the Folger Theatre itself a hybrid version of Elizabethan and Jacobean theatre architecture. Could you talk a bit about the design choices for Davenant's* Macbeth?

LB: Set designer Tony Cisek refit the stage entrances and 'inner below' of the Folger Theatre with iron bars and gates, and wooden scaffolding, evoking Bedlam as both performance space and prison. He also created an aerial installation of dirty rags that could be rearranged by pulleys to create any number of shapes, helping to move us from location to location. The idea was to evoke a 'do-it-yourself' system of Restoration-style moving scenery with depth and perspective. Tony also rigged a semi-circular 'shower curtain railing' across the mid-stage on which two large canvas curtains were hung. These curtains could be pulled together to create a large 'movie screen', for want of a better term. From behind this screen, we could create a variety of shadow 'special effects' with lighting instruments, found objects, and actors' bodies. In this way we presented Duncan's murder, the appearance of Hecate, and a mad, murderous chorus of Bedlam inmates [see Figure 6.2].

In consultation with the lighting department, Tony also hung several large iron 'chandeliers' and sconces throughout the space, and placed practical lanterns along the forestage, accurately representing the candlelight used in a Restoration theatre [see Figure 6.3]. Finally, Tony built out the downstage lip of centre stage to install a small trap door covered with an iron grate, with enough room beneath it to install a fog machine and lighting instruments, evoking a witches' cauldron from which 'evil spirits' emerged through the course of the evening.

Costume designer Mariah Hale acknowledged the vital importance of clothing in Restoration theatre – we know that Charles II loaned his own coronation robes to the Duke's Company to be used as costumes – while seeking to keep us located in our theatrical asylum. With the exception of Duncan, the 'Warden', who was bewigged, and dressed impeccably to resemble Charles I, the murdered king who would have been very much in the original audience's mind, everyone else wore items that seemed to be

Figure 6.2 Duncan's murder in the Folger Theatre's 2018 production of Sir William Davenant's *Macbeth* (dir. Robert Richmond), with Louis Butelli (Duncan), Kate Eastwood Norris (Lady Macbeth), and Ian Merrill Peakes (Macbeth). Set design by Tony Cisek and costume design by Mariah Hale. Photograph by Brittany Diliberto.

on loan from a filthy storehouse somewhere in the bowels of the building. The clothes were authentically of the period, but craftily ill-fitting, and increasingly dirty as the show went on.

RS: *Davenant's* Macbeth *was first staged in 1664 by the Duke's Company, then still under Davenant's leadership. Restoration acting companies, and the Duke's Company especially, were small tightly knit organisations, in which some actors (like Thomas Betterton) remained for decades, playing the same roles opposite the same other company members. Do you think any of that professional stability remains for an actor today?*

LB: How thrilled Restoration actors must have been! As a theatre practitioner in the twenty-first century, I can say that it is the dream of many of us to work inside a 'repertory' company – that is, to have an artistic family with whom the work of creating and performing plays is perpetual. While I've been lucky enough to experience something similar at the Folger, mainly, we actors in the twenty-first century are 'hired guns', moving as

An Actor's Perspective on Restoration Shakespeare 129

Figure 6.3 Ian Merrill Peakes as Macbeth in the Folger Theatre's 2018 production of Sir William Davenant's *Macbeth* (dir. Robert Richmond).
Set designer Tony Cisek used tattered sheets to suggest the wing-and-drop sets used in the English Restoration theatre. The production's musicians are visible in the upper gallery. Costume design by Mariah Hale. Photograph by Brittany Diliberto.

nimbly as possible from gig to gig. Indeed, it can sometimes seem as if most of the job consists of finding the next job.

That said, for Davenant's *Macbeth*, I reunited with actor Ian Merrill Peakes (Macbeth), with whom I'd worked on four shows previously; Karen Peakes (Lady Macduff), with whom I'd worked on two shows; and Kate Eastwood Norris (Lady Macbeth), with whom I'd worked on one show. Ian and Kate had played opposite each other as Macbeth and Lady Macbeth at the Folger in 2008, in a production directed by Aaron Posner and the artist and magician Teller. Also, Karen Peakes, Ian's partner, played Lady Macduff in the same 2008 production, at which time she was pregnant with their son Owen. To come full circle, Owen himself played alongside us in Davenant's *Macbeth* as both Fleance and a bird-headed embodiment of Hecate. He was brave and heroic and did a fantastic job.

In this way, with such familiarity (literal here) amongst the acting company, we could come close to sharing an experiential and emotional language to tell our story. A feeling of profound trust in an ensemble is required for us actors to make ourselves vulnerable enough to be truthful. While I am reluctant to assign twentieth- and twenty-first-century psychology to actors of the seventeenth century, surely Davenant's company, Shakespeare's company, and any other company would know the importance of trust and truthfulness to performance. After all, they still had to go out in front of an audience, say lines that they'd learned, and risk being booed or hissed off the stage, which sometimes did happen.

As for me, I also reunited with director Robert Richmond, with whom I've been collaborating theatrically since 1998.[9] Of all of us, he was the individual for whom the clock counting down towards opening night was ticking loudest. It was he who was required to pull together the various strands of Davenant's *Macbeth* into what we hoped would be a cohesive whole that pleased the audience.

RS: *Classical actors like you are certainly used to having a dramaturg in the rehearsal room. But I suspect it was a new experience for you to rehearse with nine scholars in the room. What was that experience like? What did you learn from it?*

LB: Yes, theatre artists and practitioners are very much accustomed to the company and contributions of scholars in their work. It is standard operating procedure to have a dramaturg, often a practising academic, on staff for any show, classical or contemporary. In my experience at the Folger, particularly in working on Shakespeare's plays, the presence of the dramaturg at the table is beyond reassuring. The dramaturg – at the Folger this is most frequently the brilliant Michele Osherow from the University of Maryland, Baltimore County – provides research on the play itself, and context for whatever production and design choices the director has made in framing the play.

In Michele's case, she is present for all of the 'table work' – the several days of reading and discussion with the whole company literally sitting around a table. She returns periodically as we get up on our feet to begin staging, and is present again for all of technical rehearsals, previews, and opening. She writes a scholarly essay which is included in the show's programme, returns to performances to moderate post-show discussions, and is generally 'on call' to answer questions and provide further research. For me, she has been something of a celebrant of the work – never scolding, never correcting – and just seems to make everybody around her feel smarter and more confident.

---

[9] Full disclosure: I must mention here that Richmond is my longest and most treasured theatrical co-conspirator and one of my closest friends; together we have created work for countless thousands across the United States and other countries, and we co-created my solo show *The Gravedigger's Tale*.

On Davenant's *Macbeth*, we were blessed with not one dramaturg, but with a room full of scholars with a wide variety of specialisations. Whatever questions arose in the exploration of our piece, they would inevitably intersect with one or another scholar's area of expertise, running the gamut from gender and sexuality to the ways in which trapdoors were used during the Restoration. Ultimately, the experiment here was not to have multiple dramaturges on hand; rather, the experiment was to fully integrate actors, musicians, designers, and scholars into a singular entity.

Most fascinating about this experiment was an immersion in a broad spectrum of methodologies. To be very reductive, at the outset it felt to me that each department could be abbreviated as such: the producers were money-based, the scholars were fact-based, the actors were faith-based, the designers were detail-based, and the musicians were all precision. As with any family, we were committed to each other and to accommodating a variety of personalities and approaches to a common pursuit. If it took us all some time and patience to learn to speak each other's languages, so be it. That negotiation itself then became part of the work of art.

As I said at the beginning of our conversation, I came to the project with zero knowledge of Restoration Shakespeare. Through the process of rehearsal, in conversation with scholars during coffee breaks or out for beverages after work, the world of the Restoration opened up for me. In running our show and chatting with audiences afterwards, I learned that our own curiosity and diligence in building the piece had indeed been passed along, at least to the friendly audience members I encountered. In returning to the Folger to read and study up for our conversation, I realised that, though I now had more knowledge of Restoration Shakespeare, I had barely scratched the surface, and I gained even more respect for the scholars working on our show.

To put it another way, the scholars bravely walked into 'our world', the professional stage, but we had not returned the favour by visiting the library, the stacks, the deep rabbit hole of book after book, the lonely laptop. In some small way, I hope that my own forays into researching Restoration theatre can repay their bravery with some of my own.

As we come to the end of our conversation, deep in the throes of a global pandemic, with so many things shut down, including the theatre, I would feel remiss if I didn't state the obvious: Restoration Shakespeare has happened before, and I believe with all my heart that it will happen again.

CHAPTER 7

Staging Restoration Shakespeare with Restoration Music

Robert Eisenstein

Robert Eisenstein, Artistic Director of Folger Consort, was musical director for the Folger's 2018 production of Sir William Davenant's Macbeth. *The production was part of 'Performing Restoration Shakespeare', a research project funded by the Arts and Humanities Research Council in the United Kingdom and led by Queen's University Belfast. Amanda Eubanks Winkler, the project's Co-Investigator, interviewed Eisenstein on his experience of performing Restoration Shakespeare with Restoration music.*

AEW: *Robert, could you start by telling us about the place of music in the English Restoration theatre. Even for scholars, it's easy to forget just how much the Restoration theatrical experience was saturated with music.*

RE: That's right. After the Duke's Company and the King's Company were established by a patent from Charles II in 1660, they both enjoyed access to court musicians: the string players were known as 'the 24 violins', after the precedent set by Louis XIV at Versailles. Under the guidance of composers Matthew Locke and John Banister, these court musicians performed in the afternoons for the two new theatre companies, with the twenty-four string players divided between them.

Music was a feature of pretty much every stage production mounted in London between 1660 and 1700. That was most obviously true for dramatick operas like Davenant's adaptation of *Macbeth* (1664), with music by Matthew Locke. But music was included in the performance of all sorts of plays, whether as curtain tunes, entr'actes, instrumental music for dance, songs interpolated into dramatic scenes, choruses, processions, and special effects such as drums, bells, and bird calls.

We need to remember that a Restoration theatregoer's experience often began with instrumental music, not with words spoken by an actor. Before the curtain tune started (like an overture today), the band might well have been playing some other music, maybe not composed for the specific play being performed, but something to keep the audience entertained while they waited for the play to start.

Though it seems odd to audiences today, Restoration audiences were totally accustomed to productions that had interpolated masques or masque-like scenes that might not have been directly connected to the plot and action of the play. Yet these scenes often had the some of the production's most interesting music and often featured choruses, orchestral pieces, dances, and of course elaborate costumes, machines, and scenery. To modern directors, these scenes or masques can feel like an unwelcome interruption to the play. In Thomas Shadwell's adaptation of *The Tempest* (1674) there is a Masque of Devils and a Masque of Neptune. In Charles Gildon's version of *Measure for Measure* (1700), Purcell's *Dido and Aeneas* is performed in its entirety, although divided into four court entertainments staged for Angelo. In Davenant's *Macbeth* – a play we will talk about – there are extensive scenes for the witches, chorus, and orchestra.

AEW: *On the one hand, there's strong documentary evidence that music was a mainstay of Restoration theatre production; but on the other hand, there's much less evidence about which particular music was played. Could you tell us about the surviving examples of Restoration theatre music?*

RE: Considering that we don't know much about the music for the 600 or so different plays performed in the Restoration, it's remarkable that we know a lot about the music for Shadwell's 1674 adaptation of *The Tempest*, because it survives almost entirely intact. Most of the string music was composed by Matthew Locke. (He was appointed by Charles II as composer to his band of twenty-four violins.) The 1674 production of *The Tempest* also featured songs by Pelham Humfrey and John Banister, the latter having been the director of the court string band between 1662 and 1666. The songs by Banister and (possibly) Humfrey were probably used in the earlier 1667 version of *The Tempest* and then retained for the more elaborate 1674 production at Dorset Garden.

There's also a useful manuscript ('The Rare Theatrical & Other Compositions by Mr Mathew Lock') that contains a lot of string band music, including pieces labelled as curtain tunes. Locke composed music for more than a dozen plays, and this source may include most of it. The manuscript could well include music used in Shakespeare adaptations, but we don't know for sure because it doesn't ascribe any of the music to specific plays and because the music is organised according to key, not in 'suites'. I refer readers to Silas Wollston's chapter in this volume, 'Identifying Matthew Locke's Incidental Music for *Macbeth*' for much more valuable information about this source as well as the 24 Violins. Wollston concludes, as we did for our staging of *Macbeth*, that 'The Rare Theatrical' is a valuable source for modern revivals of *Macbeth* and indeed other Restoration plays.

Gildon's *Measure for Measure*, first performed at Lincoln's Inn Fields in 1700, is a special case. The production included Henry Purcell's famous short opera *Dido and Aeneas*, which was divided into four 'Musical Entertainments' that, in the world of the play, were performed at court for Angelo.

Purcell was the greatest English theatre composer in the later seventeenth century, and we have songs and incidental music by him for a number of plays and dramatick operas. In my work with Folger Consort, we've used music he composed for *Abdelazar or the Moor's Revenge*, *Dioclesian*, *King Arthur*, and, most famously, *The Fairy Queen*, anonymously adapted (perhaps by Thomas Betterton) from *A Midsummer Night's Dream*.

There is also music for the Davenant *Macbeth*, which was heard by 1664. Some of the Locke tunes from 'The Rare Theatrical' were likely used in the early production and there are several extant dances by Locke in other sources as well. Later music by John Eccles (*c.* 1695) and Richard Leveridge (1702) survives too, and the latter score was used in revivals well into the nineteenth century.

All these musical sources for Restoration Shakespeare can be reasonably used in modern productions of those Restoration adaptions, but they're not the only valuable historical sources for modern stage directors and music director to consider. Indeed, in both the Folger production of Davenant's *Macbeth* (2018) and Folger Consort's semi-staged concert version of Gildon's *Measure for Measure* (2016), we drew upon a range of period music and other music that seemed appropriate to our specific productions. Historically precise materials are a starting point for creative work, not an end point.

AEW: *Can you talk a bit more about Folger Consort's concert version of Gildon's* Measure for Measure? *That performance arose from a 2014 Folger scholar-artist workshop on Restoration Shakespeare that Richard Schoch and I directed, in which we collaborated with you and other Consort members.*

RE: Gildon's version of *Measure for Measure* was actually a revision of Davenant's *The Law against Lovers* (first performed in 1662, but not published until 1673), which was itself a conflation of *Measure for Measure* and *Much Ado About Nothing*. In making his adaptation, Gildon, who focused only on *Measure for Measure* in his own adaptation, followed Davenant's practice of revising and simplifying Shakespeare's text, removing language that Restoration audiences would have found objectionable. In particular, he altered the role of Isabella to present her as an unambiguously virtuous character.

For our concert version, we were fortunate to have Richard Clifford as our director and Sir Derek Jacobi as Angelo. We performed at the Kennedy Center in Washington, DC, and also with Napa Valley Shakespeare in northern California. Our goal in creating the concert performance, which used an abbreviated version of Gildon's play, was to give a sense of what it would have been like to move from the dramatic text to extensive musical interludes (the segments from Purcell's *Dido and Aeneas*) and back again. In a way, dispensing with costumes, blocking, and scenery puts these transitions into clear relief, focusing on the considerable ability of wonderful actors in the absence of the usual theatrical accoutrements and the usual visual component of a period string band.

Selecting the particular excerpts from the play to include was of course a balancing act. There had to be enough of the play present to make sense dramatically. The programme included synopses of each scene, because even for members of the audience familiar with Shakespeare's *Measure for Measure*, Gildon's version was different enough to be confusing. As in all of our productions using spoken excerpts from a play and extensive music, we took care not to make the evening too long. Richard Clifford devised the proposed script with my input and suggestions. For this piece, although we knew we wanted to use all of *Dido and Aeneas*, there were a number of musical gaps to fill and the director wanted underscores in several places as well as some transitional music.

Gildon presents Purcell's famous music drama as 'a Mask, in Four Musical Entertainments', corresponding to the three acts of the opera and finishing with the Prologue, which relates the descent to earth of Venus and Phoebus' glorious passage over the sea. No music survives for the Prologue to *Dido*. This has often been solved in performances of *Dido* by having the Prologue recited, or simply omitting it or substituting some other framing device for the opera.

Gildon uses *Dido and Aeneas* as a play-within-a-play: a series of court masques that Lord Escalus designs for Angelo, hoping that the music will prevent

Angelo from acting on his lust for Isabella. Dramatically, then, the music is very important, not least because it doesn't seem to work as intended – Angelo's illicit desire for Isabella is only inflamed. So it was important for us to perform all of *Dido and Aeneas* – interpolated into Gildon's text – along with some other music by Purcell to cover the scene transitions. For incidental music underscoring in a few speeches we used solo harpsichord, which is less overpowering for modern actors than, say, a muted string quartet.

AEW: *Let's move on to Folger Theatre's 2018 production of Davenant's* Macbeth, *for which you were musical director, while Richard Schoch and I led the scholarly team that was embedded in the rehearsal process. What were some of the first decisions made about what the production should 'sound' like?*

RE: It was clear from the first production meetings with Robert Richmond, the stage director, that he not only wanted to use Restoration music for the elaborate set pieces sung by the witches – that was a given, considering the production's research dimension – but he also wanted to use period music and various sound effects at other points in the play. Throughout the show there were underscores of various tunes, drones, and harmonics from the strings, often accompanied by an admittedly modern instrument, the eerie-sounding waterphone. These underscores were designed to respond to the action and were mostly improvised. We also used period bells and percussion, primarily tambourine and tabor, to round out the acoustic instruments used in various contexts. So, we effectively created a varied soundscape for the entire production. Which is a very Restoration thing to do!

The fact of Robert's meta-theatrical concept for the production – *Macbeth* was being performed in Bedlam asylum just after the Great Fire of 1666 – made the use of Restoration-era music all the more necessary. However, Robert's decision to emphasise the play's Scottish setting inspired other musical choices. In our initial discussion, he had very clear ideas about which sort of additional music he wanted to use, music that had a Scottish flavour but was not from the Restoration. So, the result was a hybrid approach, combining seventeenth-century theatre music (sometimes used in unconventional ways) with sound effects, sound design, and some eighteenth-century music, especially Scottish tunes.

AEW: *When it comes to Davenant's* Macbeth, *there are several period musical compositions that could be used. What decision did you make?*

RE: The early Restoration performances of the play may have had some music composed by Matthew Locke and probably relied on musical settings from before the Civil War, given that some of the song texts for Davenant's musical scenes are taken from the 1623 First Folio text of *Macbeth* and also from Thomas Middleton's *The Witch* (c. 1615). I decided to use most of the surviving music by John Eccles and not to include any of the surviving pieces by Richard Leveridge. Eccles's music is more interesting than Leveridge's and is a little closer in time to our setting of the play in 1666. We included Eccles's music for the four witches' songs: 'Speak, sister, speak', 'Let's have a dance', 'Hecate! Oh, come away', and 'Black spirits and white'. Apart from a couple of short instrumental symphonies, that is all that we have of Eccles's setting. Since I was interested in at least giving a sense of the original proportions between music and the spoken play, we needed to choose additional music, including a set of pieces to be played while the audience arrived and gradually apprehended the dramatic conceit of the Bedlam setting. Then, we wanted to include something in the way of the act tunes.

AEW: *What about using theatre music that was not composed for* Macbeth?

RE: In a way, the paucity of early Restoration musical sources for Davenant's *Macbeth* is an advantage for artists today. One can feel justified in drawing on some of the roughly contemporaneous theatre music not associated with this particular play. Such borrowing and reuse is entirely in the spirit of Restoration theatre. We began with a few movements by Matthew Locke and used the curtain tune from his music for *The Tempest*. We didn't restrict ourselves to music from the 1660s, although I myself was primarily interested in using music from the seventeenth and eighteenth centuries. This version of *Macbeth*, after all, was performed on the London stage well into the eighteenth century, which meant that we had a kind of historical license to include music by Purcell. In addition to instrumental music from his dramatick operas, we used his overture to *Dido and Aeneas*, his famous mad song for Bess of Bedlam ('From silent shades'), and the *Funeral March for Queen Mary*. The rest of the music, as I mentioned earlier, was drawn from the wonderful seventeenth-century repertoire of English and Scottish country dance and from various Scottish sources of fiddle and bagpipe music. Music with a very Scottish feel was used mainly in scenes set on the heath.

Although we used a great deal of period music, we used it in our own way, not in the way it would have been used in seventeenth-century productions at Lincoln's Inn Fields or Dorset Garden. For instance, we wanted to emphasise the prominence of Lady Macduff, one of the major and most

Figure 7.1 In this scene from Folger Theatre's 2018 production of Sir William Davenant's *Macbeth* (dir. Robert Richmond), the three witches (Emily Noël, Rachael Montgomery, Ethan Watermeier) sing 'Black spirits and white'. Set design by Tony Cisek and costume design by Mariah Hale. Photograph by Brittany Diliberto.

interesting differences between Davenant's version and Shakespeare's original play. So we gave Lady Macduff not exactly a Wagnerian leitmotif, but a consistent underscore tune, the wonderful melancholy Scottish tune 'Long cold nights', from *Apollo's Banquet* (1669). We also repeated other music in a similar leitmotivic fashion. After Duncan's murder we used Purcell's *Funeral March for Queen Mary* and repeated it at the end of the play after Macduff kills Macbeth.

In other sequences, we conformed more closely to a Restoration treatment of music. We kept Eccles's settings of the witches' songs where they originally appeared in Davenant's script. This is where we came closest to the Restoration idea of masque scenes, musical and visual entertainments interpolated into the drama action, and so offered our audiences an effect similar to that in the seventeenth-century productions [see Figure 7.1]. The first such instance occurs in the second act, with two songs, both for the witches with chorus, soloists, and the string band. These songs ('Speak, sister, speak' and 'Let's have a dance') are intentional and entertaining interruptions of the dramatic action. The other two songs by Eccles are sung just before Act 4, Scene 1, and constituted our most substantial musical interlude of the evening, occurring in our production right after the intermission. After soprano Emily Noël sang Purcell's 'From silent shades' in the character of a Bedlam inmate cast as one of the witches in *Macbeth*, we moved directly into 'Hecate! Oh come away' and 'Black spirits and white', both of which included choruses, solo witches, (an offstage) Hecate, and orchestra.

What was striking, I think, for our audiences was that the cheerful music of these set pieces and the delight of the witches in their mischief seemed to work on a number of different levels. The fact that the action of the play simply stops for the lively choruses and solos with active string parts makes a welcome musical moment in what is, after all, a tragedy. These musical scenes were perceived as comic interludes, but I think that many in our audience could also connect the witches' evil intent with the more serious surrounding text. I imagine it was much the same experience for Restoration audiences.

AEW: *The consistent and deliberate presence of music in Davenant's* Macbeth *makes particular demands on musicians and performers as they work together to create the world of the play. How did such demands manifest themselves in this production?*

RE: One of the most interesting and rewarding aspects of our ventures into Restoration Shakespeare has been the synergy which arises between actors and musicians. The question of who sang what in the original productions is an interesting one. Some actors seem to have been expected to sing on stage as required – like Henry Harris singing the 'Echo duet' as Ferdinand in *The Tempest* – but it's difficult to figure out how much musical training they brought to the stage. Other actors didn't sing at all; rather, they played characters who were sung to, like Thomas Betterton playing Angelo in Gildon's *Measure for Measure*, listening to Purcell's *Dido and Aeneas* performed for him.

And when we think about modern productions of Restoration dramatick opera, the issue of casting gets even more complicated. If we elect to include period music, then naturally we want to use singers who know the style and so can work easily within the same sound world as the instruments. But those same expert singers, even if they are comfortable moving around on stage, usually don't have the same acting skills as professional actors. And the opposite is also usually true: even classically trained actors don't have (with some exceptions) much experience with historically informed musical performance. Of course, many actors do have some musical training and most can sing, often well, in various contemporary styles. But overwhelmingly they lack knowledge of period music and period style.

Here's an example: Eccles's music for Davenant's *Macbeth* calls for several soloists, including the witches, and each of the four songs also calls for a chorus. One of our witches was a professional singer of early music. This casting choice was necessary because there are some passages for the witches that require considerable technical skill. Another singer lacked experience with this sort of period music but was a strong and flexible musician. The third was an actress with a very nice voice and a good ear, but not much musical training. By having performers with different but complementary skills, we could meet the play's musical and dramatic requirements, without neglecting or forsaking anything. It's also important to remember that the most important thing in these songs (like those for the witches in *Dido and Aeneas*) is characterisation, not beautiful vocal production.

We taught a few of the choruses to most of the remaining cast, regardless of which character they played. Fortunately, most of them were perfectly able to carry a tune and some could read music, which helped the learning process. A few actors really could not sing at all; and we so used a significant portion of music rehearsals to coach them in the appropriate singing style. In spite of the fact that some actors were initially dubious about doing this sort of specialised singing, we were all very pleased with the result. It turns out that learning a few Restoration songs isn't too difficult for most actors today. In fact, several actors brought really strong characterisations to their singing parts, and one (Louis Butelli, who played Duncan) even took on a solo, which became a really entertaining feature of the song.

Our casting decisions may be a good model to consider in future productions of Restoration Shakespeare and dramatick opera. Include at least one 'real' singer who enjoys acting and also enjoys coaching and helping actors. And make sure that a good proportion of the actors have some musical skill and, crucially, a willingness to try an unfamiliar vocal style.

AEW: *Beyond the important issue of casting, what advice do you have for a director today with respect to the musical components of Restoration Shakespeare? After all, one of the most difficult tasks for the artistic team is to figure out how to fit these lavish musical entertainments into an otherwise strongly dramatic narrative.*

RE: Restoration versions of Shakespeare do present stage directors with a unique set of problems, given the amount of music that is integral to the production. Of course, directors can decide that the music isn't actually integral, they can dispense with some, most, or all of the music, and then perform the piece as essentially a spoken drama. But this seems to me an impoverished choice. Because we know – from performing Davenant's *Macbeth* – that these plays, when performed with care, do appeal to audiences today. Other sorts of directors, especially those without much knowledge of Restoration music, will be drawn to creating sound design or using new compositions, either recorded or performed live. Such a production – which honours the place of music in Restoration Shakespeare but gives it a modern twist – can definitely succeed with the audience. And although it's an approach not very likely to be adopted by commercial theatres, an artistically successful production can use only period instruments and only seventeenth-century music. There's a range of approaches for a director or producer to take.

But it seems to me that pieces like Shadwell's *The Tempest*, Davenant's *Macbeth*, and all the other Restoration Shakespeare adaptations constitute a type of music-saturated drama that might be most successful with a hybrid style of period music and contemporary sound design, like the style we developed for our production of *Macbeth*. In this way, perhaps we can best reconcile historical performance genres with the need to create performance experiences that are meaningful to audiences today.

It's certainly possible to use period music, even primarily period music, within the context of contemporary sound design. The string band can be as small or large as space and the production budget allow. With electronic help, a combination of the acoustical instruments and period and/or modern sound effects can be integrated into a unified soundscape. This mixed approach can present audiences with an experience that is familiar and yet can also convey the delight that Restoration audiences took in stage performance, where the focus shifted easily from spoken drama to music and back again.

CHAPTER 8

Davenant's Lady Macduff and the Subversion of Normative Femininity in Twenty-First-Century Performance

Sara Reimers

Apart from its inclusion of singing and dancing witches, William Davenant's 1664 adaptation of *Macbeth* is most famous for expanding the role of Lady Macduff. Augmenting the mere forty-four lines afforded the character in Shakespeare's 1623 folio *Macbeth*, Davenant gives Lady Macduff an additional four scenes, in which she voices powerful political arguments and demonstrates considerable agency. Even so, many critics have dismissed the Restoration theatre's version of Lady Macduff as a hollow dramaturgical device, designed simply to act as a virtuous foil to a villainous Lady Macbeth. As Peter Dyson puts it: in Davenant's *Macbeth* '[m]oral abstractions, disguised as characters, are played off against each other'.[1] Dyson's damning appraisal might hold some truth on the page: the villainous Macbeths and the saintly Macduffs on first read can seem like pale imitations of Shakespeare's more ambiguously drawn protagonists. Yet on the stage, with all the interpretative opportunities of performance, the sophistication of Davenant's dramaturgy comes into its own. This chapter draws on practical explorations of Davenant's text to argue for the radical potential of Lady Macduff in performance.

Anne Greenfield has already made the case for a critical reassessment of Davenant's Lady Macduff, arguing that the character's outspoken criticism of her husband renders her a 'subversive tragic heroine'.[2] This chapter offers a *creative* reassessment of the role, taking Greenfield's assertion as a jumping-off point for feminist theatrical exploration. I begin by examining the depiction of Lady Macduff in twenty-first-century productions of Shakespeare's *Macbeth*. Outlining trends in the depiction of the character

---

[1] Peter Dyson, 'Changes in Dramatic Perspective: From Shakespeare's *Macbeth* to Davenant's', *Shakespeare Quarterly*, 30.3 (1979): 402–7 (405).
[2] Anne Greenfield, 'D'Avenant's Lady Macduff: Ideal Femininity and Subversive Politics', *Restoration: Studies in English Literary Culture, 1660–1700*, 37.1 (2013): 39–60 (40).

in anglophone performance contexts, I argue that concepts of the victim and the mother define the interpretation of Shakespeare's Lady Macduff in twenty-first-century performance. Utilising practice-as-research methodologies, I then offer a scene-by-scene analysis of Davenant's Lady Macduff, highlighting various ways in which the role was illuminated through practical exploration. This analysis focuses on two performance case studies in which I participated: the Folger Theatre's 2018 production of Davenant's *Macbeth* in Washington, DC, and scholar-practitioner workshops on the same play held in 2020 in London. Reflecting on these artistic experiences, I argue for the feminist potential of the role in performance, suggesting that Davenant's Lady Macduff makes a welcome addition to the twenty-first-century classical performance repertoire.

Shakespeare's Lady Macduff

In Shakespeare's *Macbeth*, Lady Macduff is a victim of what media studies scholars call 'fridging'. The term, coined by Gail Simone in 2000, responded to an incident in the comic book *The Green Lantern* when the eponymous hero returns home to find his girlfriend has been murdered and her body put in the refrigerator.[3] 'Fridging' has come to describe a broader literary and filmic trope in which female characters are wounded, raped, or murdered in order to reveal something about the male protagonist. Shakespeare's Lady Macduff appears in only one scene, at the end of which she is murdered. In keeping with the fridging trope, Lady Macduff's murder serves to 'put an exclamation point on the horrors wrought by Macbeth' and 'augments Macduff's motivation for vengeance'.[4]

While it may appear anachronistic to apply this term to an early modern play, the notion of 'fridging' provides a valuable lens through which to view a twenty-first-century performance trend which accentuates Lady Macduff's victimhood. Contemporary artists appear to delight in finding new and inventive ways to make Lady Macduff's murder particularly horrible, thereby emphasising Macbeth's villainy and the righteousness

---

[3] Hailey J. Austin, '"If She Be Worthy": Performance of Female Masculinity and Toxic Geek Masculinity in Jason Aaron's *Thor: The Goddess of Thunder*', in *Superheroes and Masculinity: Unmasking the Gender Performance of Heroism*, ed. Sean Parson and J. L. Schatz (Lanham, MD: Lexington Books, 2019), 29–46 (34–5).
[4] Ted H. Miller, 'The Two Deaths of Lady Macduff: Antimetaphysics, Violence, and William Davenant's Restoration Revision of *Macbeth*', *Political Theory*, 36.6 (2008): 856–82 (858, 859).

of Macduff's subsequent actions: the more horrible her death, the more noble the cause. A survey of some recent anglophone productions of Shakespeare's *Macbeth* reveals a trend in staging choices that emphasise the domestic context in which we see her, foreground her personal vulnerability, and render her murder particularly brutal.

A common approach in performance is to contrast the domesticity of the Macduffs' home with the formality of Macbeth's castle. For example, in the recording of his 2001 Royal Shakespeare Company (RSC) production, Gregory Doran's version of the scene takes place at bath time in the Macduff homestead.[5] Diane Beck's Lady Macduff speaks to Ross as she scrubs two of her young children in the tub, and later leaves them to tend to a crying baby in the next room.[6] Graeme Flynn's 'Young Macduff', recently bathed, is wrapped in a sheet, his bare shoulders accentuating the fragility of his small frame. Beck's Lady Macduff cuts a dowdy maternal figure, her shapeless thick, grey woollen jumper a stark contrast with the figure-hugging silken gowns worn by Harriet Walter's Lady Macbeth. Costume likewise played an important role in establishing both domesticity and vulnerability in the 2015 Tara Arts production directed by Jatinder Verma.[7] Shalini Peiris's Lady Macduff appeared to be ready for bed, wearing a fluffy white dressing gown for her urgent exchange with John Afzal's grey-suited Ross. Deven Modha, who was playing her son, also wore a costume that evoked a comfortable domesticity, with a white T-shirt with striped trousers reminiscent of pyjama bottoms. Presenting the Macduffs in a state of undress locates them in the domestic sphere and adds to the sense that they are ill-prepared to flee their home when news of approaching danger arrives. The staged violence in Verma's production worked alongside the scene's domesticity to make the action particularly brutal. Macbeth's henchman pulled Lady Macduff by the hair and hit her in the face, before breaking her son's arms and killing him with a blow to the neck.

---

[5] Gregory Doran (dir.), *Macbeth*. RSC, 2001. www.digitaltheatreplus.com/education/collections/illuminations/macbeth-illuminations-rsc. Performed by Antony Sher, Harriet Walter, Nigel Cooke, and Diane Beck.

[6] Rupert Goold's version of this scene in his Chichester Festival Theatre production, filmed in 2010, similarly evokes bath time, taking place in a shower block and beginning with Suzanne Burden's Lady Macduff drying Young Macduff's hair.

[7] Jatinder Verma (dir.), *Macbeth*. Tara Arts, 2015. www.digitaltheatreplus.com/education/collections/tara-arts/macbeth. Performed by Robert Mountford, Shaheen Khan, Umar Pasha, and Shalini Peiris.

Antoni Cimolino's 2016 production for the Stratford Festival, Ontario, also included a fight sequence, in which Sarah Afful's Lady Macduff was grabbed from behind, forced to watch as her son was stabbed, and then thrown to the ground, kicked in the stomach, and dragged off-stage.[8] The violence towards Afful's Lady Macduff was rendered particularly shocking as she was depicted as being pregnant, something that was also true of the Lady Macduffs in Aaron Posner and Teller's 2008 production at the Folger Theatre and Polly Findlay's 2018 RSC production. Donnellan's Cheek by Jowl production went even further in the cruelty exacted on Lady Macduff, as Peter Kirwan's description demonstrates:

> Lady Macduff, her hands bound behind her, screamed. She then threw herself over a box, spread her legs and jerked, and then her neck snapped to one side, all while Macduff sat silently between his wife and son.[9]

By interpolating sexual violence into the scene, albeit staged in an abstract way, Donnellan takes the fridging trope even further: it is not enough for Lady Macduff to witness her son's murder shortly before her own demise, but further cruelties must be inflicted upon her before her suffering is allowed to end.

It bears remembering that Shakespeare's text does not call for onstage acts of violence towards Lady Macduff. As Ann Blake points out, '[o]nly young Macduff is killed on stage, [whereas] the slaughter of Lady Macduff and her other children, "all my pretty chickens", is, like the murder of Duncan, left to the appalled imagination'.[10] Yet in the play's recent performance history violence and cruelty towards Lady Macduff is commonplace. No such violence occurs in Davenant's *Macbeth*, as classical convention dictated that violence should not be enacted on stage. Indeed, Davenant's version of the scene is abridged before the murderers arrive. Subsequent actor-managers went even further, with Kemble, Macready, Charles Kean, Irving, and Forbes-Robertson cutting Act 4, Scene 2 entirely. Phelps initially included it in his adaptation, but subsequently 'cut is as being too painful'.[11] Tormenting Lady Macduff is, it seems, a peculiarly recent phenomenon. Yet this framing of the character as mother and victim provides an influential interpretative lens for contemporary practitioners approaching Davenant's Lady Macduff.

---

[8] Antoni Cimolino (dir.), *Macbeth*. Stratford Festival, 2016. www.digitaltheatreplus.com/education/collections/stratford-festival/macbeth. Performed by Ian Lake, Krystin Pellerin, Michael Blake, and Sarah Afful.
[9] Peter Kirwan, *Shakespeare in the Theatre: Cheek by Jowl* (London: Arden Shakespeare, 2019), 61.
[10] Ann Blake, 'Children and Suffering in Shakespeare's Plays', *The Yearbook of English Studies*, 23 (1993): 293–304 (295).
[11] John Wilders, *Macbeth: Shakespeare in Production* (Cambridge: Cambridge University Press, 2004), 178.

Methodology

The following analysis draws on two recent creative engagements with Davenant's Lady Macduff. The first was Robert Richmond's 2018 production of Davenant's *Macbeth* at the Folger Theatre in Washington, DC. Staged as part of the Arts and Humanities Research Council (AHRC)-funded 'Performing Restoration Shakespeare' project, from which this edited collection emerges, this full Equity production was also part-funded by the Folger Theatre. The production was part of the project's practical exploration of the performance potential of Restoration adaptations of Shakespeare's plays, both then and now. In this production, the roles of Macbeth and Lady Macbeth were played by Ian Merrill Peakes and Kate Eastwood Norris respectively, while Macduff and Lady Macduff were played by Chris Genebach and Karen Peakes. Ian, Kate, and Karen had all played their corresponding roles in Shakespeare's *Macbeth* in the 2008 Folger Theatre production, directed by Aaron Posner and Teller. Alongside the company of actors and musicians, a team of nine scholars was embedded in the production, observing rehearsals and contributing to, as well as learning from, the creative work of the artists.[12] We each adopted a different method for engaging with rehearsals, based on our individual research specialisms. I utilised an ethnographic approach to documenting the activities and discussions that occurred during the rehearsal process.[13] In this model of rehearsal studies, the scholar is positioned not as a director or dramaturg, but as a participant-observer: one who is 'both vitally enmeshed in the daily experiences of the people being studied and, at the same time, sufficiently distanced to make observations, write notes about what is occurring and find time to write these up in more detail'.[14] The particular value of a rehearsal studies methodology is that it enables a researcher to see the progress of ideas from inception through to the final staging and I analyse both rehearsal and performance in my argument.[15]

---

[12] The team of scholars included the project's Principal Investigator Richard Schoch, Co-Investigator Amanda Eubanks Winkler, Research Fellow Claude Fretz, and Lisa Freeman, Sarah Ledwidge, Deborah Payne, Andrew Walkling, and Stephen Watkins. I would like to acknowledge the role played by the other members of the research team in shaping my thinking on this work, as well as the gratitude for the courage and creativity of the artists whose work has informed this chapter.

[13] I observed rehearsals from Monday 6 August to Saturday 18 August 2018.

[14] Gay McAuley, *Not Magic but Work: An Ethnographic Account of a Rehearsal Room Process* (Manchester: Manchester University Press, 2012), 9.

[15] My observations of performance are based on a recording of the production's dress rehearsal filmed on 2 September 2018. This recording is available in Folger Shakespeare Library's reading room, as part of its collection.

dynamics that this unlocked were eye-opening. When Lady Macduff used 'Alas!' dismissively, she drove the scene and forced Lady Macbeth to work harder at convincing Lady Macduff of her argument. By contrast, when Lady Macduff sought to persuade Lady Macbeth, the status reversed, and it was Lady Macduff who was working to convince a more resolute Lady Macbeth. Most interestingly, when Lady Macduff's intention was to provoke Lady Macbeth, the pair had a heated exchange, in which the wresting of ideology foreshadowed Lady Macduff's later exchanges with her husband. This interpretation provided a valuable insight into Davenant's dramaturgy, as it brought to the fore the ideological differences between the two formidable women and the character-driven expositional function of the scene.

Having established the power of presenting the women as equals, we went on to explore how the context of their exchange effects interpretation. Focusing on the difference between public and private spaces, we first played the scene as if it were set in a busy hall of the Macbeths' castle, emphasising Lady Macbeth's role as host. The public setting lent the scene a formality, as Lady Macbeth directed servants (obligingly played by other members of our workshop company) and sought to reassure her guest. In this context, reassuring Lady Macduff took on a political role; Lady Macbeth's praise of the glories gained in battle were spoken as the acting head of a household, galvanising her people while the menfolk were absent. With this inflection, Lady Macduff's insistence on the vaingloriousness of war was highly subversive and foreshadowed her discussions with her husband in later scenes in which she challenges conventional wisdom.

We then relocated the scene to a private location in the castle. In this more secluded context, the intimacy between the two women came to the fore and the attempts of Paula's Lady Macbeth to reassure Esther's Lady Macduff seemed to come from a place of genuine concern for her friend's welfare. Responding to this kindness, when Esther's Lady Macduff was advised to rest, she took Lady Macbeth's hand and curled up on the floor at her feet. By making Paula's Lady Macbeth remain with her while she dozed, Esther's Lady Macduff forced her friend to read Macbeth's letter over her sleeping form. This lent an urgency to Lady Macbeth's engagement with the letter, as she read it furtively, lowering her voice when Lady Macduff rolled over in her sleep. On the one hand, this interpretation rendered the scene comic, as the two women competed to achieve their objective in the scene. But on the other hand, it also hinted at a once close relationship between the women, replacing the previous antagonism with a comic tenderness and rendering them both more human.

Spells and Spectating: Act 2, Scene 5

Act 2, Scene 5, takes place upon the heath. Lady Macduff and her maid enter and discuss the desolation of the place. Macduff then joins them and moments later the three witches appear and begin their song 'Speak, sister, speak', in which they 'rejoyce when good Kings bleed' (2.5.40), alluding to Duncan's death earlier in the play. The Macduffs reflect on the strangeness of the spectacle before the witches begin a second song, 'Let's have a dance'. Macduff, who is frightened by the witches, comments approvingly on his wife's courage and questions the witches, who prophecy the death of Macduff's family. The witches disappear and Lady Macduff shuns their prophecy, suggesting that 'Their words are like / Their shape; nothing but fiction' (2.5.89–90). Amanda Eubanks Winkler foregrounds the historical importance of Lady Macduff's response to the witches, observing that '[f]or the discriminating lady, these witches are full of sound and fury, but ultimately signifying nothing – a significant departure from the powerful prognosticators in Shakespeare's original or even the entertaining and astonishing witches from the 1623 folio *Macbeth*'.[29] Thus, in this scene, Lady Macduff – unlike her husband – represents the voice of reason and dramaturgically functions to represent a virtuous response to the 'Messengers of Darkness' (2.5.85).

In twenty-first-century performance, Davenant's treatment of the witches poses some challenges. John Eccles's score draws on seventeenth-century liturgical and folk traditions, which in a Restoration context would have foregrounded the witches' transgressive behaviour; however, to an untrained modern ear, these connotations are lost.[30] The song and dance routines thus require careful dramatic framing in order to guide a twenty-first-century audience's interpretation of the action. Davenant helps contemporary directors address this challenge by positioning the Macduffs as spectators of the witches' performance, meaning that they can act as an interpretative conduit between the witches and the audience. Lady Macduff's contempt and Macduff's fear may help spectators to interpret the witches' behaviour as malign, despite the beauty of the music. However, staging the Macduff's spectatorship presents practical challenges. Firstly, the pair need to be seen, but must not upstage the witches. Thus, a suitable location from which to spectate must be found.

---

[29] Amanda Eubanks Winkler, *O Let us Howle Some Heavy Note: Music for Witches, the Melancholic, and the Mad on the Seventeenth-Century English Stage* (Bloomington: Indiana University Press, 2006), 42.

[30] See Eubanks Winkler, *O Let Us Howle*, 18–62.

Secondly, realist staging conventions often render on-stage spectatorship peculiarly challenging for contemporary performers. This was something raised by Chris Genebach: 'we have quite a big acting challenge ahead of us if we're going to be on the stage … how we watch it and how we take in the music'.[31] Karen Peakes also found the scene daunting: 'It was, for me, overwhelming, to say the least: to see it in context, the length of it and we're just trying to figure out our journey …'.[32] Chris expressed concerns that the Macduffs' presence on stage could prove 'distracting for an audience to wonder how we're taking it in' and suggested it might be preferable for them 'just to watch and listen to the words and the music …'.[33] Chris raises an interesting point: How do we envisage the function of this scene? Is it there for the spectacle or is it there to tell us about the Macduffs, or both?

Ultimately, Robert leaned towards the first interpretation, presenting the spectacle in a way that would be comprehensible to a contemporary audience while downplaying the significance of the Macduffs. In the final staging, the pair, having spoken their brief exchange, then exited before the witches appeared. After 'Speak, sister, speak', the pair spoke their brief exchange in the central aisle of the auditorium – 'What can this be?' (2.5.43) – before exiting and re-entering on stage to watch 'Let's have a dance'. For this act of spectatorship, the pair were positioned upstage and were dimly lit, so it was not easy to see their response to the witches' songs. The inspired incorporation of Louis Butelli's Duncan into the choreography rendered 'Speak, sister, speak' suitably grotesque and comically troubling. But because the Macduffs remained off stage, the audience did not see the couple responding to the spectacle of witchcraft. Such is the nature of staging a play: deciding what goes in the spotlight and what goes unseen is a fundamental part of a director's job, and Robert's staging powerfully conveyed the macabre nature of witchcraft. However, with the Macduffs somewhat removed, the staging left unanswered some important questions about Davenant's dramaturgy: What do we learn about the Macduffs from their opposite responses to the action? How might the couple act as a conduit between the musical action and the audience?

Exploring these questions was a focus of the London workshops. And although we couldn't fully stage such a complicated scene in a single workshop, we were able to do a rough blocking, which was sufficient for our

---

[31] Interview with the author, 17 August 2018.
[32] Interview with the author, 17 August 2018.
[33] Interview with the author, 17 August 2018.

research purposes. I invited the actors to improvise their response to the music, asking the Macduffs to focus on making their attitude towards the witches particularly clear. As the witches, Paula, Miranda, and Rob established their world of witchcraft by incorporating random items from the room into their 'spell' with a large fan, water bottles, and assorted coats and jackets forming the basis of their incantation. Christopher's Macduff was obviously captivated by the action, trying to get ever closer to the witches to see what they were doing. In contrast, Esther's Lady Macduff attempted to hold him back, demonstrating her scepticism and a desire to leave the perilous heath. When 'Speak, sister, speak' concluded, the brief exchange between the Macduffs attracted the attention of the witches and through the course of 'Let's have a dance' the witches gradually drew the Macduffs into the centre of the action, reluctant at first but ultimately compelled to participate in the witches' dance. There was something fascinating about this improvised response to the musical stimulus: it vividly demonstrated the Macduffs' differing responses to the witches and blurred the line between spectator and actor. Understandably, the improvised performance was somewhat chaotic, but it provided valuable dramaturgical insights. In this staging we *saw* Lady Macduff's rejection of the witches as well as hearing about it. This visual proof of Lady Macduff's mettle seems fundamental to her positioning as the play's virtuous heroine. Furthermore, this staging powerfully established her strength of character ahead of her confrontation with Macduff in Act 3, Scene 2.

Politics and Persuasion: Act 3, Scene 2

Act 3, Scene 2 forms the basis of Anne Greenfield's argument that Lady Macduff is a subversive tragic heroine. In this scene, Lady Macduff questions her husband's desire to challenge Macbeth and the couple debate the legitimacy of regicide. The scene is rhetorically formal, written in rhyming couplets which drive the Macduffs' debate. It is remarkable for being such an evenly weighted discussion. As Greenfield observes, '[t]his conversation acts as a rare moment, in an otherwise morally reductive play, in which the ethical and political complexities of loyalism are genuinely engaged with' and remarkably 'Lady Macduff of all people is the one character who is allowed to raise these questions'.[34] For the Folger production Robert made a significant dramaturgical intervention, merging this scene with Act 3, Scene 6, and thereby combining the Macduffs' two relatively short scenes

[34] Greenfield, 'D'Avenant's Lady Macduff', 54.

in Act 3 – they are sixty-five and thirty-six lines long respectively – to create one longer scene. Robert's stage directions emphasise the context of the Macduffs' homestead, with sound effects – 'a fire crackles, a baby cries, and the sound of cattle in the distance'[35] – and stage directions – '*Lady Macduff with a baby in arms*'[36] – evoking the domestic setting.

From the first stagger through on 10 August, Macduff's impending departure drove the scene, with Robert asking stage management to source a bag for the rehearsal which would signify Macduff's intended departure from the outset. Robert established the given circumstances of the scene for the actors: Macduff is ready to go and seeks a parting kiss or a blessing from his wife, a 'prize' that she withholds. While this instruction to the actors provided a clear, playable objective for the scene, it positioned Lady Macduff as reactive rather than proactive, responding to her husband's actions rather than initiating any herself. Robert's decision to emphasise the domesticity of the scene by giving Karen and Chris the point of concentration 'don't wake the baby' positioned Lady Macduff primarily as a wife and a mother, rather than also as a political agent. Robert's approach was informed by a concern that the political and philosophical debates with which Davenant engages in this scene, which responded to the particular preoccupations of his Restoration audience, would have lost their potency for a twenty-first-century audience. Furthermore, the rhetorical style of the exchange, which is written in heroic couplets, defies the conventions of naturalism and some of the artistic team were concerned that the exchange would sound stilted and alienate the audience. By focusing on the action rather than the rhetoric, Robert successfully evaded these challenges, but at the cost of oversimplifying the role of Lady Macduff: her arguments in the scene were defined exclusively by her role as a wife and mother – not wanting her husband to leave, not wanting to wake their sleeping child – rather than by her strong and well-expressed political convictions.

Returning to Davenant's full text for Act 3, Scene 2 in the London workshops, our key aim was to explore Lady Macduff's agency in the scene. We wanted to examine a range of methods for presenting the rhetorically challenging text that would be engaging for a contemporary audience, whilst honouring the powerful equality evoked by Davenant's rendering of the pair's exchange. We began by adopting an abstract approach to the staging, taking the scene's rhetorical quality to an extreme by having Rob

[35] Richmond, '*Macbeth* By William Shakespeare', 44.
[36] Richmond, '*Macbeth* By William Shakespeare', 44.

and Esther deliver the text to the audience, rather than to each other, and asking them to focus on convincing their 'jury' on the legitimacy of their argument rather than on persuading the other. The result was unconvincing, lacking the charge of emotional connection. However, it did create a remarkably balanced dynamic between the pair and highlighted the importance of weaving together the personal and political in this scene. Another exercise we utilised to explore the power dynamic between the couple was to stage the scene as a tennis match, with the pair hitting the dialogue back and forth to each other over an imagined net. The exercise highlighted the significance of the scene's shared lines and added a passion and a force to the Macduffs' communication. Again, these were abstract workshop exercises rather than potential staging choices; but they provided an important context for the rest of the exchange: this was not a wife nagging her husband but two intellectual equals challenging each other on a difficult subject.

One of the challenges of this scene for contemporary practitioners is that it is driven by rhetoric rather than action. Thus, it is vital to keep the scene pushing forward in performance. The couplets and shared lines give the dialogue momentum but need a varied delivery to keep the exchange engaging for an audience unaccustomed to rhetorical drama. We experimented with actioning to explore the variety of tactics that could be employed by the pair – including cajoling, flattering, accusing, seducing – to persuade the other. Another element which added dynamism to the scene was to present the discussion as having real-world consequences. We experimented with the scene's given circumstances and considered the potential impact of Macduff naming what he plans to do at the top of the scene. Adding in two lines – Macduff: 'I'm going to kill Macbeth.' Lady Macduff: 'No.' – before Macduff began 'It must be so' (3.2.1) helped the actors to focus on the scene's stakes – will Macbeth live or die? – adding urgency to the exchange and grounding it in the concrete reality of the play's action. These activities increased the scene's tension, whilst keeping its political focus and providing a glimpse into the couple's relationship through the variety of tactics they employed to convince the other. Furthermore, in emphasising the political nature of the debate, it embraced the concept of Lady Macduff as a subversive tragic heroine. Greenfield argues that: 'By keeping her discussion centered on her husband's private intentions she gives the illusion of speaking on domestic, rather than political matters.'[37] However, by making Lady Macduff's desire to influence

---

[37] Greenfield, 'D'Avenant's Lady Macduff', 53.

real-world political outcomes her motivation in the scene, we rendered Davenant's dramaturgy even more radical.

Fight and Flight: Act 3, Scene 6

Act 3, Scene 6 sees Macduff and his wife debate the logic of his departure to England. Lady Macduff warns him that they are in danger and tries to persuade him that they should flee as a family. Macduff rebuffs the suggestion, stating 'Your Sex which here is your security, / Will by the toyls of flight your Danger be' (3.6.23–4). A messenger enters and notifies the couple of Banquo's death, prompting Macduff to make a hurried departure, spurred on by his wife. Lady Macduff then speaks a brief soliloquy, shedding a tear at her husband's departure – 'So falls the Dew when the bright Sun withdraws' (3.6.36). The amalgamated scenes in the Folger edit saw the 3.2 debate between the Macduffs reach a crescendo on the line 'In hopes to have the common Ills redrest, / Who wou'd not venture single interest' (3.2.57–8) and immediately segued into the text of Act 3, Scene 6, with Lady Macduff's line 'Are you resolv'd then to be gone?' (3.6.1). In Robert's staging, Macduff's affirmative prompted Lady Macduff to exit the stage to tend to their crying baby, returning nursing the child. Thus, the messenger's interruption to Act 3, Scene 2 was cut and this external influence on the action was lost. This choice kept the focus on the Macduffs' relationship rather than on their relationship with the outside world. It also meant that, in performance, the actors had to find a different motivation for Macduff's departure and for Lady Macduff's change of heart. In the final performance, Chris's decision as Macduff to go – 'Farewell; our safety, Us, a while must sever' (3.6.27) – met with coldness from Karen's Lady Macduff, who turned her back on her husband as she said 'Fly, fly, or we may bid farewell for ever' (3.6.28). As he reached the upstage exit, Chris's Macduff halted and said 'Flying from Death, I am to Life unkind, / For leaving you, I leave my Life behind' (3.6.29–30), before rushing back across the stage to kiss Lady Macduff. He then left in silence, before Karen's Lady Macduff spoke her tearful soliloquy. While these choices made good sense of Robert's edit, they had the unintended consequences of rendering Lady Macduff's response to her husband somewhat passive-aggressive and his departure the outcome of his strong will, rather than the result of urgent demands imposed by a malignant external force.

Thus, the Folger production raised questions about characters' intentions and narrative arcs – elements we explored further in the London workshops. Taking as our guide the strength and resolve that we had discovered in Lady Macduff in Act 3, Scene 2, we explored the dramatic potential of keeping the various possible outcomes of the scene in play: that is, if there is real doubt as to whether Lady Macduff and her children will flee with Macduff. By making 'But why so far as England must you fly?' (3.6.5) a genuine question, Esther's Lady Macduff sought a rationale for her husband's behaviour rather than censuring him with a rhetorical question. Rob's Macduff's poetically vague response – 'The farthest part of Scotland is too nigh' (3.6.6) – then prompted an outburst of anger from a Lady Macduff frustrated by her husband's unwillingness to talk to her as an equal. Forced to address his wife's concerns, Rob's Macduff then argued that Macbeth poses no threat to anyone but him. On the line 'If to be gone seems misery to you, / Good Sir, let us be miserable too' (3.6.21–2), Esther's Lady Macduff began to gather her coat and bags and made to follow Rob's Macduff out of the room. Rob gently put her belongings down, assuring her 'Your Sex which here is your security, / Will by the toyls of flight your Danger be' (3.6.23–4). Interrupted from their brief exchange by the messenger's appearance, the news of Banquo's death instigated a shift in pace and prompted Lady Macduff's change of heart on 'Fly, fly, or we may bid farewell for ever' (3.6.28). This interpretation of the scene further emphasised the Macduffs' equal relationship and also hinted at what was to come: Lady Macduff's change of heart and the courage she showed in bidding her husband depart foreshadowed the courage she would later show in the face of certain death.

Morality and Murder: Act 4, Scene 2

Act 4, Scene 2 of Davenant's *Macbeth* draws on the action of Shakespeare's version but alters it significantly. At the start of the scene, Davenant's Lady Macduff voices regret at her decision to encourage her husband to leave, suggesting that it was made on the spur of the moment and prompted by news of Banquo's death. Lennox advises her to have patience, but she rebuffs him, stating that her husband's 'flight was madness' (4.2.7). Lennox speaks well of Macduff before bidding Lady Macduff a hasty farewell. Immediately after Lennox's departure a Woman enters and announces the arrival of Seyton, who urges Lady Macduff to 'Fly with your little ones' (4.2.33) before swiftly departing. Lady Macduff then speaks a brief soliloquy asking 'Where shall I go, and whither shall I fly?' (4.2.45) before declaring 'I'le boldly in, and dare this new Alarm: / What need they fear whom Innocense doth arm?' (4.2.41–2).

In rehearsals for the Folger production, Robert worked with Karen to determine Lady Macduff's state of mind at this point in the play. The pair discussed the nature of Lady Macduff's distress and concluded that it is more interesting if she does not 'catch the panic' from Lennox and Seyton.[38] Instead, Robert chose to focus on Lady Macduff's anger at her husband, asking Karen to play the scene with the acting note 'you want a divorce'. This direction added fire to Lady Macduff's exchange with Lennox, but it also ensured that she viewed her predicament through the lens of her marriage, in the same way that Act 3, Scene 2 was played as a marital, rather than political, dispute. It is highly unlikely that such a specific note would be evident to audiences in performance, but it was accompanied by staging choices that further emphasised Lady Macduff's role as a wife and mother. For example, throughout the scene Karen's Lady Macduff was holding a bundle representing a baby and, in the act of rocking the baby, she was constantly moving, giving her a physical instability even in her principled resolve. Lady Macduff's resolve was further undermined when, after declaring 'I'le boldly in, and dare this new Alarm' (4.2.41), she remained on stage, looking out front as Chris's Macduff entered from upstage right and briefly seemed to see his wife before she stepped backwards and exited the stage. This staging choice put the emphasis back on Macduff, denying Lady Macduff the opportunity to exit on her own terms, in the manner suggested by Davenant's text. It afforded a powerful segue into the following scene but came at the cost of undermining Lady Macduff's agency. This decision was arguably influenced by Shakespeare's *Macbeth*, in which Lady Macduff's death is significant primarily because of its effect on Macduff.

One of the elements that the Folger staging brought home was the power of seeing Seyton with Macbeth in Act 4, Scene 1 and then with Lady Macduff in the following scene. Seyton's appearance in both scenes located Lady Macduff within the same world as Macbeth and thus positioned her more closely to the action of the wider play. Furthermore, the comings and goings in Davenant's adaptation of Act 4, Scene 2 – with Lennox, a Woman, and Seyton all speaking with Lady Macduff within just thirty-five lines of text – place Lady Macduff at the centre of a household. Drawing on these observations from the performance, in the London workshops we sought to emphasise Lady Macduff's status as the acting head of the household, who must make a decision that will have consequences for people beyond her immediate family.

[38] 11 August 2018.

Of particular importance in our exploration was Lady Macduff's tone in her final soliloquy and the interpretation of her final line, 'What need they fear whom Innocense doth arm?' (4.2.42). Scholars have debated the degree to which Lady Macduff relies on Providence. Ted Miller suggests that Lady Macduff maintains her faith in Providence until the end, arguing that her unwavering belief 'is the cause of her undoing'[39] and that Davenant uses it to critique the conservative Anglicans who believed Providence 'trump[ed] the plea for a pragmatic means to a restoration'.[40] Countering this assertion, Greenfield argues that Davenant uses Lady Macduff's belief in Providence 'to emphasise her virtue'.[41] Greenfield continues that Lady Macduff's disavowal of Providence – 'But I remember now / I am in a vicious world, where to do harm / Is often prosperous, and to do good / Accounted dangerous folly' (4.2.37–9) – serves 'as a means of emphasizing the injustice of her death' and 'heightening the dramatic pathos of the event'.[42] Using this scholarship to explore how the scene could be played, we tried three approaches to Lady Macduff's final couplet, 'I'le boldly in, and dare this new Alarm: / What need they fear whom Innocence doth arm?' (4.2.41–2). The first time Miranda played the couplet as offering succour to Lady Macduff; a reassertion of her unshaking belief in Providence that she first voices in Act 2, Scene 5. The second time we explored what would happen if there were a note of uncertainty, as if she were trying – but failing – to convince herself of divine justice. The third and final time, Miranda spoke the soliloquy bitterly. Having resolved to face her assailants bravely, Lady Macduff was fully aware that she faced certain death and sarcastically mocked her earlier naivety. In the workshop, Miranda's performance of this final version was particularly striking because she engaged closely with the audience, asking us the questions directly before deciding courageously to face her foes, no longer protected by her faith. While I would not ascribe authorial intent to this final interpretation, it is nonetheless a choice that is available to a contemporary director and has significant consequences for the character of Lady Macduff. In losing her faith in Providence, Lady Macduff changes: she becomes a character who is altered by the events of the play. While losing her faith might render her less virtuous, it might, for a twenty-first-century audience, render her more human.

[39] Miller, 'The Two Deaths of Lady Macduff', 872.
[40] Miller, 'The Two Deaths of Lady Macduff', 870.
[41] Greenfield, 'D'Avenant's Lady Macduff', 55, n.11.
[42] Greenfield, 'D'Avenant's Lady Macduff', 55, n.11 (emphasis original).

Conclusion

Having spent so much time in the company of Davenant's Lady Macduff, first at the Folger and then at the London workshops, it strikes me as remarkable that scholars have dismissed her as 'submissive, unobtrusive, and weak'.[43] In every scene in which she appears Lady Macduff speaks her mind, not afraid to contradict or challenge her host, her husband, or a Scottish thane when she disagrees with them. She speaks passionately and articulately about complex subjects. While Davenant may have written her as a virtuous foil to Lady Macbeth, in the three-dimensional context of performance she emerges as a rich and compelling character. Indeed, a reappraisal is needed of the notion that Davenant's dramaturgical rationale for developing Lady Macduff inevitably renders her a walking literary device, because the more compelling her character, the more vividly she serves as a contrast to Lady Macbeth. For too long, scholarship focused on *why* Davenant expanded the role of Lady Macduff without giving due attention to *how* he developed the role. Read through the lens of dramaturgical pragmatism, a role is always liable to be seen as lacking. But read through Greenfield's revisionist lens, a subversive heroine materialises and, with this approach informing theatrical practice, a remarkably powerful character emerges.

I am not alone in my admiration for the character in performance: speaking during the Folger rehearsals, Karen remarked 'I love her. And the more we're working on it, the more I do love her, and I just appreciate Davenant's ability to write a female character like this. I just feel like she's so of this Me Too Movement age …'[44] This sentiment was echoed by members of the London cast, who reflected that Davenant's Lady Macduff offers the contemporary actress a 'more well-rounded and interesting female role without having to cast gender-blind'.[45] Here, Paula hints at the contemporary significance of Davenant's Lady Macduff: for the twenty-first-century actress, being offered the role of Shakespeare's Lady Macduff means appearing in one scene and most likely involves a lot of screaming,[46] whereas being offered the role of Davenant's Lady Macduff means

---

[43] Elizabeth Howe, *The First English Actresses: Women and Drama 1660–1700* (Cambridge: Cambridge University Press, 1992), 152.
[44] Interview with the author, 17 August 2018.
[45] Paula James, email to the author, 20 February 2020.
[46] It is noteworthy that directors are starting to reimagine Lady Macduff's role in Shakespeare's play: Yaël Farber's 2021 production for the Almeida Theatre in London augmented the role significantly and Akiya Henry, who played Lady Macduff, received an Olivier Award nomination for her performance.

challenging Lady Macbeth, watching witchcraft, and debating politics. I am not suggesting that the role is a feminist icon; indeed, sustained effort is needed from the director and the performers to actively empower the character and resist the familiar tropes of mother, wife, and victim that ghost the role. But unlike the 'fridged' victim in Shakespeare's play, Davenant's Lady Macduff lives before she dies. And in doing so, she opens up a host of possibilities for feminist artists in the twenty-first century.

CHAPTER 9

Facts as Ideas: The Theatricalisation of Scholarship

Kate Eastwood Norris

The harpsichord finished its final notes of peppy pastoral preshow music, and the backstage chatter came to a hush. Offstage left, I listened for the clanking of a heavy set of metal keys and the screech and bang of an iron door to come from the inner above. When the sound of exactly three footsteps from a man's heeled shoe had echoed down the worn wooden stairs, I tugged on my bedraggled wig one more time, made sure the ripped part of my stocking was showing, took a deep breath, and entered. Slowly and constantly rubbing my artificially dirtied hands to show that I was the scheming sort, I paced the upstage hallway separated from the rest of the playing area by barred metal gates held closed by a lock until the man with the keys would let me out. Not your typical entrance for Lady Macbeth; but then nothing about this production was ordinary.

The concept for Folger Theatre's 2018 production of Sir William Davenant's *Macbeth* was this: in 1666, the inmates of Bedlam, that famous asylum of yore still operating in Restoration London, were putting on *Macbeth* (Davenant's 1664 adaptation, not Shakespeare's First Folio text) for an audience of well-heeled and curious patrons to raise money after the recent fire that devastated the city (the calamity now known as the Great Fire of London). Judging from the ripped curtains hanging from rusty bars, the filthiness of the inmate's clothes, and their own disordered mental states, it was clear this place could use some help. But underneath that innocent plea for alms was a more sinister intent: to replace the prop knives with real ones in the scene of Duncan's murder, thus taking advantage of the performance to actually murder Bedlam's tyrannical Warden, who had been cast in the role of Duncan. Although this inventive conceit served the vision of the play's director, the Folger's initial decision to stage a Restoration version of a famous Shakespeare play originated within the vision of an entirely different group of people. A group of scholars in an effort to reinvigorate Restoration theatre for today's audiences wanted to collaborate with artists, not to reproduce what might have been seen and heard in a Restoration theatre but to discover what the impact of historical knowledge on a contemporary rendering of the play might be.

To know what happened, in one sense, you had to be there. Anything written about this production, whether reviews printed during the run or a chapter like this one published several years after the fact, is inevitably dealing with a product of the past. Capturing the moment-by-moment experience of a theatrical event is doomed to a certain subjectivity, not only because all participants had their own individual experience but also because everything that can be discussed is no more than a memory. Even if it is, however, difficult to fully remember everything that happens during the few immersive hours of performance, the longer and exploratory nature of the rehearsal process inherently allows more opportunity to document and consider events. In other words, when considering a theatrical event, although there is value in describing what the product was like, there is much to be gained from analysing how it was made.

Enter on cue 'Performing Restoration Shakespeare': a three-year research project that included a production of Davenant's *Macbeth* complete with script changes and period music in August and September 2018 at Folger Theatre in Washington, DC. Nine scholars, primarily from the United Kingdom and the United States, travelled to the Folger to explore their specific areas of concentration (Shakespeare, theatre history, music) by participating in the rehearsal process for a Restoration version of Shakespeare. As an artist hired to participate in this project – and also a student in the MFA in Shakespeare and Performance program at Mary Baldwin University in Staunton, Virginia – I leapt at the chance to experience the artistic and scholarly perspectives at the same time. I got to play Lady Macbeth (see Figure 9.1), a notch in the belt for any actress, and was allowed by my university to make the play count as an independent study class, with an earlier version of this chapter as the outcome.

On its website, 'Performing Restoration Shakespeare' states that a primary goal for the project was to propose 'a dynamic historicist alternative to performance practices aimed at reviving "original styles" or conventions'.[1] Because the project's methodology was to foster collaboration between scholars and artists to create fresh theatrical experiences, documenting that process from an actor's point of view seems a worthy goal for this chapter. Current theatre studies practitioners champion the idea that research by theatre makers is inherently different to that of traditional academics. Marco De Marinis and Marie Pecorari explain: 'in the field of theatre,

---

[1] The project's website is www.restorationshakespeare.org.

Facts as Ideas: The Theatricalisation of Scholarship

Figure 9.1 Kate Eastwood Norris as Lady Macbeth in Folger Theatre's 2018 production of Sir William Davenant's *Macbeth* (dir. Robert Richmond). Set design by Tony Cisek and costume design by Mariah Hale. Photograph by Brittany Diliberto.

various types of theatrical experience involving and mixing together theory and practice, seeing and making, knowing and knowing-how-to-do, are at play'.[2] By relating from an actor's standpoint the various types of experiences at play in our particular production, I hope to offer in this chapter a perspective that complements that of the scholars involved in the project.

First, I explain the institutional parameters for the production (jointly established by 'Performing Restoration Shakespeare' and the Folger Shakespeare Library and Theatre) and the creative parameters – or concept – of the eventual production itself. Second, I then offer a first-hand account of the production that describes both the challenges and benefits of interaction between artists and scholars. I include excerpts from interviews with actors and scholars involved in the project to add additional

---

[2] Marco De Marinis and Marie Pecorari, 'New Theatrology and Performance Studies: Starting Points towards a Dialogue', *The Drama Review*, 55.4 (2011): 64–74 (68).

perspectives. Using this information, I postulate that sensitivity towards how scholarship is shared with an artistic team and allowing that process sufficient time to unfold are both essential for scholarship to enrich a theatrical production. If scholarship is treated merely (and unhelpfully) as a rule to be applied, then it functions as an unyielding force in rehearsal, such that the best possible outcome is compromise or concessions between scholars and actors. But if scholarship is considered as an idea or an invitation to new possibilities, then actors and scholars can collaborate and work together to create something new.

Because I have appeared in thirteen productions at Folger Theatre, I had become accustomed to seeing people with furrowed brows and a faraway look in their eyes clutch towering stacks of books as they scurried about the property. This constant scholarly presence, I have to admit, sometimes made me feel defensive about my own performance-based approach to Shakespeare. First of all, my pursuit of Shakespearean truths is necessarily loud and involves large numbers of people while theirs follows the typical library etiquette of silence and is achieved mainly in solitary concentration. While scholars write books that may well be read for decades to come, I create performances that disappear as soon as they are over. It seemed to me a Shakespeare scholar's authority – expressed with at least outward decorum and manifested in the powerful written word – was totally unlike my authority as an actor. As if to make that very point, the entrance to Folger Theatre and the entrance to the reading room itself are at opposite ends of the Folger Shakespeare Library's main building on East Capitol Street in Washington, DC. Quite literally, Folger actors use one door and Folger scholars use another door, as if we were entering different worlds. If scholars ever came to the theatre, it was usually as audience members. But they rarely engaged in conversation with the actors afterward, much less offered an opinion about anyone's performance. To my insecure self, and to many other actors, such restraint on the part of the academics indicated only one thing: they must have hated the show.

Even though I know and work with Shakespeare scholars on many university campuses, I still tend to revert to an 'us' and 'them' mentality in rehearsals. But I was eager to overcome this false binary between scholars and performing artists.

Folger Theatre staff and the academics involved in 'Performing Restoration Shakespeare' made this possible by including the team of nine scholars in every rehearsal for the first two weeks, with the two principal scholars (Amanda Eubanks Winkler and Richard Schoch) remaining with us through opening night. The set was mostly built before rehearsals began, allowing us all to work in the theatre instead of inside the usual small rehearsal room. Scholars sat in the audience seats while the artists ran around the stage. A video crew from Blue Land Media, responsible for producing a 'behind-the-scenes' documentary on the production, recorded the entire first read-through and many rehearsal sessions over the next few weeks. For me this was initially a discomforting experience, having an audience present (and sometimes recording) right from the start. I felt that I had to 'perform' for them, even though rehearsals had barely started. Yet as the novelty of their presence wore off, so did the pressure to treat them as an audience. Knowing why the scholars were there in the first place helped me to reframe my understanding of the collaborative project in which we were all engaged.

Our first week of rehearsal consisted of the usual first read-through, small amounts of table work, then the beginning of staging. We also heard from Richard Schoch and Amanda Eubanks Winkler, the lead scholars for 'Performing Restoration Shakespeare', about their excitement and hopes for the project. I learned that the cast was not hired to recreate a period-specific acting style but rather to participate in something like a theatrical experiment conducted in a living laboratory. This knowledge inspired a sense of discovery among the participants and furthered the project's goal of combining historical knowledge with the demands of creating a contemporary performance of Restoration Shakespeare.

Part of one day in that first week was set aside for ten-minute presentations by roughly half of the scholars about their specific areas of focus, most of them concerning the Restoration theatre, acting, and rehearsal processes. The second week, when Folger Consort musicians arrived for rehearsals, we heard from the music scholars. These presentations were useful in terms of revealing why the scholars were scribbling so furiously in their notebooks during rehearsals – they were just as much engaged in the creative process as we were. The fact that several scholars needed to be cut off at the ten-minute mark showed their own enthusiasm for Restoration Shakespeare. At the end of these illuminating sessions, I had a better idea of who might be able to help me and, more importantly, whom I might be able to help. The notion that I could contribute anything to scholarly work was, while not a revelation, an exciting prospect that began to relieve me of an admittedly defensive attitude about who would claim authority in the room. Some scholars seemed eager to test their theories and previous research by wanting their information embodied or acted upon by a performer, sometimes right away. Others wanted to observe, more or less neutrally, how we chose to respond in rehearsal to the information they supplied. What I did not expect, again revealing my biased preconceptions about scholars and their process, was that many of them wanted to learn from how the actors worked. The idea that scholarship was a two-way street, that actors could help scholars – and not just the other way around – was for me a new experience.

We were all able to further our respective interests during half-hour interviews scheduled by the scholars with various cast members. Inevitably, these meetings turned out to be challenging to implement because the demands of the rehearsals required every actor to be present and on call nearly all of the time. When I was not working on stage, I was watching from the wings, trying figure out what kind of world we were trying to make. The individual goals of the scholars became lost to my consciousness in pursuit of the goals dictated by the show.

Although the director and a few actors called on the scholars during rehearsal to provide information as though they were a many-headed dramaturg, most interaction between scholars and artists occurred during the formal presentations at the start of rehearsals and the informal interviews that took place throughout rehearsals. It became immediately clear that this was not enough time for the scholars or for some of the more interested artists. The only other time during rehearsal available for conversation was on the rare occasion when both the scholar and the actor happened to be free, or during the Actors' Equity-required ten-minute breaks. The scholars were given clear instructions that they were not to 'bother' the actors during these breaks, but when someone so obviously excited about what you are both working on comes up to you to say something then stops because they are not supposed to, it is hard to turn them away.

As a result, many awkward and hurried conversations took place on the steps outside the theatre under the guise of casual conversation. Some were illuminating and inspiring, others initially produced frustration. During one break, a scholar asked me if I found it interesting that the reason Restoration audiences thought Lady Macbeth went insane was because she willingly relinquished her womanhood in the 'unsex me here' speech. For me, that was an idea about Restoration morality and social history, not something that I could psychologically play as an actor. So, when the break came to its quick end, I could say only that the idea was certainly intriguing. I then had to go inside and rehearse that very speech, firmly believing Lady Macbeth went mad for many other reasons than a social transgression, but also feeling rude for having ignored what the scholar had said.

The parameters of scholar–artist interactions were clearly restricted, but this does not at all imply that nothing came of it. Many were the moments of fruitful collaboration where the results became evident in the performance. Later in this chapter, I explain how even that brief conversation about Lady Macbeth's womanhood became vital to my portrayal of her character, something I did not anticipate at the time. Even frustrating interactions became lessons in how we could speak more effectively to each other. Yet because the play's director was the final authority in the room, many ideas that were floated during official and unofficial exchanges between actors and scholars inevitably remained just ideas. They were not acted upon because they didn't conform to the director's vision for the production.

One would think that for a production of *Macbeth* set in an insane asylum, any idea could be made to work. Restoration theatre architecture and staging practices could still be given a nod despite the Folger Theatre being a mixture of Elizabethan and Jacobean architecture. A proscenium Restoration theatre like Dorset Garden would have traps on the stage floor and a large substage area for the machinery needed to operate the traps.[3] Folger Theatre has about a four-feet-high stage (no space for machinery or people) with no traps whatsoever. Nor can there be a Restoration-style music room above the proscenium arch because there is no proscenium and no fly space. (In our production of Davenant's *Macbeth*, the musicians were placed in the theatre's Elizabethan-style 'inner above', where they were visible to the audience.) In his programme notes, director Robert Richmond observed that the Bedlam setting 'has the elements of a makeshift, openhanded theatre set up in the public space and the settings and props are from things that can be found inside the hospital'.[4] Because Bedlam had been transformed into a 'makeshift theatre', the production's design team made the resourceful decision to create Bedlam's version of a Restoration stage rather than to recreate an actual Restoration stage.

While period-style footlights and candelabras were used, creative solutions for the lack of fly spaces and traps came into play. Lights placed behind tattered curtains made for creepy gravity-defying shadow effects. Set designer Tony Cisek ingeniously capitalised on the fact that the original Bedlam was built over a sewer to create our version of a Restoration trap and substage. He placed a grated hole at the downstage edge of the extended thrust stage, out of which the sewer's noxious fumes (in reality, dry ice) emerged. Lit from below, this part of the stage served as

---

[3] See Mark A. Radice, 'Theater Architecture at the Time of Purcell and Its Influence on His "Dramatick Operas"', *The Musical Quarterly*, 74.1 (1990): 98–130.
[4] Robert Richmond, *Macbeth* programme notes, Folger Theatre, 2018.

the witches' cauldron when they summoned Hecate and also gave Lady Macbeth a place to perform her own conjuring of dark spirits. Despite these creative solutions, one scholar, clearly excited by the importance of the substage in Restoration theatre practice, could not seem to let the topic go. For instance, when we were struggling to figure out how to make Banquo suddenly appear during the banquet scene, it was frustrating to hear repeatedly that some Restoration theatres had trapdoors. True, but the Folger Theatre didn't; and so that was simply not an option for us.

Eventually a creative solution was found that involved Banquo appearing from behind curtains. But some of the actors (including me) found it irksome that this particular scholarly insight was offered so insistently, despite being so unhelpful. There wasn't a trap on the stage floor; and even if the set designer added one at the last minute, there still wasn't enough room for someone to enter from beneath the stage. It was a non-starter. In the theatre, if an idea does not or cannot work, you try something else and move on; or at the very least, you put the idea into your toolbox for a future production. In this case, the repeated reminder of what we simply could not do made scholarship about Restoration trapdoors operate as an imperative that the production failed to act on rather than an idea to explore. As a result, there was neither a sense of collaboration nor compromise.

Acting in a Restoration style was a possibility we addressed, but (at least for me) not adequately. In this case, what could have been a collaboration ended up feeling more like a compromise. Beyond the blending of historical knowledge and set design, Richmond's decision to set the play in Bedlam served as a possible bridge between Restoration and contemporary acting styles. As Richmond observed in his programme note: 'The history of Bedlam as a hospital is rich. The name has entered our language as a description of inhumanity and chaos. This allows the acting approach of the play within the play to be demonstrative and closer to a Restoration style.' After the inmates-turned-actors murder the Warden/Duncan, things become worse and 'from this point on, the acting is rooted in realism and more akin to twenty-first-century performances of this play'.[5] Richmond's language here is telling. Restoration style is considered an historical artefact to be contained within the Bedlam setting while contemporary performance is considered to be realistic and thus needing no aesthetic container. Yet the idea that Restoration-style acting must be couched in the behaviour of the insane in order to be palatable to today's audience sets up that style as artificial and distanced from our modern

[5] Richmond, *Macbeth* programme notes.

sensibility, thus making it difficult for the audience to empathise with such characters and difficult for the actors to plausibly portray them.

In a Restoration comedy of manners, formality and artificial or indicative gesture are welcome, precisely because such manners are integral to the comedy itself. In a tragedy, however, the idea of 'bows and curtseys and formalised gestures of deference, deprecation, flattery, or mock-modesty' becomes more problematic when what is called for is terror, hatred, fear, and madness.[6] In addition, the actors in our production were shown renderings of period gestures – for example, from John Bulwer's *Chirologia* (1644) – but the director offered little instruction on how, when, or why to use them. Though I felt like we had missed an opportunity for meaningful collaboration with scholars on this topic, it is true that the demands of putting the show on its feet became more urgent than taking the time to learn how to act in a certain physical style or how to blend period style with modern realism to create a new one, which was, after all, the director's original idea. Nonetheless, an informal blending of sorts between scholarship and acting took place, though late in the rehearsal process. Any formalised gestures began as the individual 'tics' of the various Bedlam inmates, which were then subtly incorporated into their roles in Bedlam's production of *Macbeth*.

This outcome felt more like a compromise than a collaboration. It was clear that the production aimed from the beginning to find a reason for Restoration-style acting rather than simply to accept it as integral to the process. This choice did end up proving to be a practical one due to the cast's lack of familiarity with Restoration style and the lack of sufficient time to learn it. Also, how we might have learned it was restricted to the perusal of static images, making it difficult to translate the idea into action. Copying a gesture for no other reason than people in the past may have used it presents a challenge to today's actor, who throws around phrases like 'organic movement' and prizes subtlety.

Yet in an 'unsanctioned' moment I instigated with scholar Richard Schoch, I learned that Restoration gesture was not just an added decorative layer but originated from an emotional state and not the need to describe an object or place, which is how most actors use gestures today. Richard also translated the Latin captions under the drawings of hand gestures in *Chirologia* (literally, 'the language of gesture'), after which I came to see that even small changes in gestures could indicate entirely different meanings.

---

[6] George R. Kernodle, 'Style, Stylization, and Styles of Acting', *Educational Theatre Journal*, 12.4 (1960): 251–61 (258).

My eyes opened to these facts, I then watched rehearsals and saw that a few of us were exploring how to use period gestures in our performance. Some used broad gestures to indicate emotion, some to describe a noun, and others, including myself at times, just waved our arms around in a vague but determined manner. It looked artificial because it was artificial; and because we were all moving in different ways, there was no cohesive style. Had I been given the time or the power to share Richard's scholarly insights, perhaps a collaboration could have begun to take place and we could have created a whole new form of movement that combined elements of Restoration and contemporary acting style. Judging from how often this topic was raised during our breaks, I am certain that many scholars were itching to find a way to accomplish just that. But the director had other priorities and so did the demands of the production. There were fights to practice, scenes to block, blood to apply, and this particular *Macbeth* also happened to contain a number of songs to rehearse. So, we compromised.

Obstacles, frustrations, and compromises are worth considering when examining and learning from an event, but so are moments of success. Though I myself had many of the latter from which to choose, there is one moment that most readily demonstrates my point about how and when scholarly information is used by actors. This particular experience both illustrates the tensions between theory and practice and offers a way to resolve them. Surprisingly, this experience was the hurried and initially frustrating conversation about Lady Macbeth going insane because she had relinquished her femininity to achieve her goals.

Fortunately for me, most of what the scholars had to impart about Lady Macbeth had less to do with subjective opinions about her personality and more to do with the era in which the play was written. Through their guidance, I was able to understand the possible origins for some of the changes Davenant had made to the script, and thus understand more about this particular Lady Macbeth. Because women were finally allowed onstage during the Restoration, Davenant purposefully enlarged the female roles in *Macbeth*. Lady Macduff in particular had a lot more to do and say and Lady Macbeth had an extra scene of madness before her handwashing scene. Both characters even had a new scene of their own – in Shakespeare's version, they never meet. These additions were pointed out to me by some of the scholars with such excitement that I felt myself looking for traces of feminist ideals within my script wherever I could. Alas, in the scene between the two women, they argued about their husbands and the ramifications of their actions, while Lady Macbeth's extra mad scene (4.4) involved deflecting blame for her deeds by telling Macbeth that it was all his fault.

Having played Shakespeare's Lady Macbeth a few years before, I began mining Davenant's new scenes for evidence that might bolster my original idea of her character as well as indicate how the adapted Lady Macbeth might be different from the original version. While it is comforting to be reassured that one is on the right track rather than admit a change in course, it became clear that comfort would prove elusive. I have always thought of Lady Macbeth as an incredibly strong woman who played her role in patriarchy's game only to achieve her own ends. Thus, I was disappointed that Davenant's adaptation contained nothing to confirm or reinforce my previous opinion. In a sense, his version even refuted it. I initially perceived this new Lady Macbeth to be so weak (she blames her husband for their downfall) that she considered herself a victim rather than strong enough to admit she had a hand in creating her own tragedy. In Davenant's Act 4, Scene 4 – a scene that has no parallel in Shakespeare's text – she enters pursued by the ghost of Duncan and begs Macbeth to relinquish his crown. When he responds by retorting that she was the one who told him to get the crown in the first place, she tells him 'You were a man, and by the charter of your sex, you should have governed me', and that 'There was more crime in you when you obeyed my Councels than I contracted by my giving it.' All the guilt is on his head, not hers. My modern mind, not considering that a Restoration audience might have found Lady Macbeth to be making a valid point, immediately concluded that Davenant believed she was not worthy of her own tragedy, or, at the very least, not willing to accept her share of responsibility for their own doom.

I did not want to allow Lady Macbeth a weakness Shakespeare did not give her as pointedly as Davenant did, but that was my job. The lines just referenced always produced a scoff from the audience, and for the longest time I could not get rid of my own inward cringe. I looked hard for a way to maintain my ideas about her strength and self-awareness, yet still say the lines. Was she saying them because she was going insane and not thinking properly? Perhaps, but how do you play that without a general wash of madness? Did she say them only because she was panicking because a ghost was pursuing her wherever she went? Maybe. But it's clear in Lady Macbeth's mind that her husband is guiltier than she. In my struggle to maintain my original idea of the character while also having to speak the lines in a plausible way, that quick conversation on the stairs about Restoration Lady Macbeth's obsession with her womanhood kept popping into my mind.

What if the scholar was correct, and this Lady Macbeth was a product of her time when men and women inhabited clearly defined roles and paid a price for deviating from them? I am fully aware that patriarchy was alive and well long before Shakespeare wrote *Macbeth*, and it could easily be argued that Lady Macbeth had always been courting danger as soon as she exchanged milk for gall. There was already plenty of language, furthermore, about her preoccupation with traditional gender roles in the original version. But I always took her primary issue to be not how she relinquished her own gender but rather how Macbeth did not embrace his own gender more fully.

Davenant's new scene in Act 4, precisely because it indicates Restoration gender norms, provides a way to understand Lady Macbeth's journey into madness. The specificity of this scene coloured everything around it. By taking information about the past and turning it into Lady Macbeth's present, I concluded that Lady Macbeth really does mean what she says, often a helpful choice for an actor to make. This may seem an obvious interpretation, but Davenant's Lady Macbeth says many things she does not believe. Her tendency to veil statements of truth or to lie outright are strategies she continually employs to manipulate those around her. To take her words in Act 4, Scene 4 as a moment of unabashed honesty would still allow me to attribute her words to panic and the onset of madness, while also grounding those words in something real and solid. She could feel both guilty and victimised; she could be both strong and weak. If this collaboration between a scholar and an actor changed the audience's reception of those lines to anything other than an experience of the ridiculous, I will never know. (The audience's repeated scoffs suggest it didn't.) But at least I was able to find a logic that worked for me. By situating Davenant's Lady Macbeth in her own time period, I introduced the audience to a different version of the iconic character: a woman they could still recognise, but one more complex and specific.

Most importantly, this reasoning also makes Davenant's new scene something other than merely an extra mad scene. The reason why I thought Lady Macbeth's new scene was just an extension of her last one, and that nothing had changed for her between them, is worth consideration. Certainly, this assumption stemmed from my entirely biased opinion that Davenant was no Shakespeare, which proved to be a highly problematic view until I began to treat our play as its own story, complete in and of itself and not a curious derivative. I think my main struggle, however, points to my premise about the importance of how scholarship is both presented to and received by actors. Because scholarship carries authority that is often bolstered by evidence, time, and discourse, and especially because this particular bit of scholarship dealt with the perspective of an entire society, I initially felt a self-imposed pressure to apply this single scholarly insight to absolutely everything I thought about Lady Macbeth and her journey in the play. As rehearsals continued, however, I became aware that historical scholarship is itself a creative act, in that historical evidence needs to be interpreted just like a dramatic text is interpreted. The director was not involved in the discussion so there was no sense that this production wanted to highlight problematic gender roles in any way. In fact, there was barely a discussion at all. I alone was responsible for deciding whether to treat the information I was given as a fact to be comprehended or an idea to be acted upon, just as I was responsible for where and when I chose to implement it.

Other than wanting to indulge in misgivings about my own authority in the creative process, there was no reason I could not use information about Restoration gender roles to help me play Lady Macbeth's guilt and responsibility for her doom in the final handwashing scene. Besides, what actress wouldn't want to appear mad and then come back in even worse shape, and, moreover, with a solid reason for doing so? Scholarship about a historical issue thus allowed me consistency of character, even as it changed my understanding of the character. If I had started by treating this knowledge not as a hard-and-fast rule but as a way to add complexity to my character, then I could have come to this conclusion a lot sooner.

How this particular scholarly information was presented to me is another worthwhile area of investigation. On the one hand, I wish I had been able to have had more than a brief conversation with this scholar, not only because it might have helped me but primarily because it was so fast and random an event, I can't remember which scholar it was. I don't know if the scholar in question realises how much they helped shape my performance. I find this situation frustrating and wonder what we could have come up with together if only we had been given more time to collaborate.

On the other hand, the fleeting nature of our exchange matched an aspect of the theatrical process that is useful to understand. Ideas in theatre often occur suddenly and at random. A large part of rehearsal consists of grabbing one of the many ideas popping up in the room, applying it right away, trying five different ways to implement it, letting it marinate for a few days, or just letting it go and moving on because previews are a week from Tuesday. It may well be that if more time had been set aside to focus on an in-depth discussion of the scholar's information, I would not have been able to allow it to function with the mercurial and experimental qualities of an idea. I have discovered over the years that it is possible to talk an idea to death. When an idea becomes deeply established in my mind through sustained discussion, I find it harder to translate that idea into embodied action. It can feel like an intellectual, not an organically creative, exercise. Ironically, then, the lack of time to discuss the information was frustrating in the moment but beneficial for achieving a good outcome in my performance.

Also, because the information was casually presented to me as 'interesting' and not freighted with the solemnity of a lecture, it was well suited to my actor brain that operates better when asked the question 'what if' instead of being told 'it is' or 'it was'. Although there are many parts of our psyche other than our imaginations, actors do rely heavily on that frequently maligned maker of meaning. My experience as a scholar is limited, but I do not think that asking 'what if' is an unusual event in scholarship either. Is that not what a scholar does when formulating a starting hypothesis? As part of the 'Performing Restoration Shakespeare' research project, the production itself was designed to answer the larger question 'what happens when scholars and actors work together'? I offer the suggestion that if we all come knowingly and purposefully from the place we have in common, which is a place of questioning more than a place of definitively knowing, and that entertains ideas rather than adheres to facts, then we will have a greater chance at finding the answer.

Were any of my conclusions shared by my fellow participants? Though I cannot fully answer that question, what follows are excerpts from a short questionnaire that I emailed to both the cast and the scholars after our production of *Macbeth* had closed. Though not everyone involved in the production responded, many did, and with enthusiasm. I present some anonymised extracts from the questionnaire (with the permission of the respondents) to illustrate both the similarities between actors and scholars and the misconceptions we continue to have about each other.

> Question 1: From your point of view, what do you want actors/scholars to know about what it is like to be an actor/scholar?
> 'We cannot claim "truth".'
> 'We are always going on voyages of discovery and creativity.'
> 'We are passionate and excited about what we do.'
> 'It is a creative endeavour … it's a process.'
> 'We are ultimately limited in the extent to which we can reconstruct what happened.'

Surprise! Every response listed above was from a scholar. Actor's answers included 'we can't be trapped by the past', 'every actor's process is different', 'we cannot try for an objective assessment', 'we can't replicate a hard and fast truth', and all sorts of other things we cannot do that the scholars were never interested in having us do in the first place. The defensive nature of some answers from the actors is in sharp contrast to the often emotionally centred responses from the scholars. This reiterates my own struggle with reflecting on the scholarship about Davenant's Lady Macbeth. At first the scholarship felt like a direct challenge to my process as an actor. And I wasn't the only member of the cast who erected imaginary barriers between themselves and the scholars. I would like to stress that, at least for me, my insecurities have less to do with stereotypical notions about neurotic actors and more to do with my deep respect for scholars and their work. It is clear, nonetheless, that using information as an idea instead of as a fact, and that posing a question is more useful to the process than rushing to an answer, would be a large part of a preferred methodology for all of us.

> Question 2: In terms of your interaction with actors/scholars, what constituted for you the most surprising or valuable experience?
> Actors:
> 'Learning about the Restoration period helped me better inform my acting choices.'
> 'I learned about more tools to put in my toolbox.'
> 'As I learned from the musicologists about the technique and oddities of Baroque music, I better understood that the music was the key to the witches' magic in this production.'
> 'Their knowledge of the time period during which the play was written, made my own sense of the play and character feel more tangible.'
>
> Scholars:
> 'Seeing how the cast approached the play.'
> 'It was fascinating to watch you and Ian work your way into these new versions of Macbeth and Lady Macbeth.'
> 'It was fascinating to watch the ways in which you each worked to make your part playable within the constraints of the Bedlam context.'
> 'I found the process of observing rehearsal and then discussing this with actors to be incredibly rewarding.'

These selected responses reveal an overall theme. For the most part, the actors referenced something they had learned whereas the scholars focused on something they had observed. This is not surprising, because the journey for the actors ended with the production's closing night while the journey for the scholars would continue for months and even years, as they reflected on the production in conference papers and eventually in published books and articles. A few scholars mentioned one-on-one collaborative moments in which they were able to be active participants alongside the actors, but the idea that actors had anything to teach scholars appeared infrequently in their own responses to my questionnaire. Again, actors cannot immediately know what contributions they made to the eventual scholarship on our production of Davenant's *Macbeth* because scholarship and academic publishing take time. Even so, the responses to the questionnaire imply that, at least in rehearsal, one camp provided the knowledge while the other was responsible for using it. This is still collaboration, but not quite the dream of Richard Schoch, who wrote in his answer to a question about similar future endeavours: 'We want to be partners in the artistic process – we are co-creating the production – and not just an optional resource that can be consulted as needed in the rehearsal room.'

> Question 3: What would you recommend that might help facilitate this process in the future?
> Scholars:
> 'The scholars and creatives need to be on the same page from the beginning.'
> 'Scholars should work together a few days before hand to make sure everyone is on the same page.'
> 'The scholars need to be involved more fully in the pre-production process ... because we need to ensure that the artistic company understands what the undertaking is.'
> 'A stronger shared understanding of the goal of the project—performance as research, as much as performance as entertainment.'
> Actors:
> 'The main thing I would want is more time with them. More time equals more opportunity to play with the info.'
> 'I think what is needed to make the process stronger is more time ... the lectures the scholars gave were very interesting and informative, but also ended up feeling slightly rushed and at times disconnected from rehearsal.'
> 'If I had one recommendation it would be that there be more time allotted for the collaboration. One would crave an entire week of table work – director, scholars, actors, and designers spending time together.'
> 'Arrange a meet-and-greet before rehearsal ... it would have been SO wonderful to have had some time to process their scholarship before jumping into the table read.'

The consensus was clear. Everyone wanted more time, and primarily on the front end. It is interesting that the actors did not mention the need to 'be on the same page' from the beginning as much as the scholars did. Perhaps because that is exactly what actors use rehearsal for. We start from scratch to create a complete human being in a complete world in a mere three-and-a-half weeks. We use every single second of that time, and already think there is never enough of it. Thus, the addition of nine more people with their own needs and agendas beyond the shared one of putting on a production demands extra time in order to adequately include them. In a very real sense, however, 'Performing Restoration Shakespeare' was including us, not the other way around: the research project, funded by the British government, was footing the bill for most of everyone's salary, from the director to the understudies. I can't blame them for wanting to feel more integrated into the collaborative and creative process.

The scholars wanted a cohesive strategy and I believe that a better understanding of the project by the artists was also necessary to help them achieve this. If scholars and artists are indeed collaborating, then the nature and goal of our collaboration need to be made clear at the outset and then stressed throughout the process. A professional theatre production was certainly one of the project's goals, but so was developing a method for how scholars and artists can work together on historical performance genres like Restoration Shakespeare. Again, differing worlds of time come into play. More time at the beginning of the process to find out what the scholars were excited to discover and more time near the end of process to find out what the scholars did discover by collaborating with us would do wonders to create a true collegial atmosphere of collaboration and a better sense of the project as a whole.

It's difficult to conclude with a description of the methodology we all discovered, because during much of rehearsal the project took a back seat to the immediate demands of the production itself. Indeed, many actors did not even know that shaping a methodology was one of the project's primary goals. In terms of my own experience, I discovered a valuable approach to scholar–artist collaboration more than a complete system in itself. Beyond recognising and dealing with the different ways that time works for each group, it's also essential to recognise and embrace what we have in common. We all experiment, we all imagine, and we all ask, 'what if'. None of us knows anything for certain, and we are all researching in our own distinctive ways. Just as there can be no definitive performance of Davenant's *Macbeth*, there can be no essay on Davenant's *Macbeth* that ends all other arguments about it. What if we embraced the experimentation that is inherent to both theatre and theatre scholarship? What if an actor could greet each bit of historical information as an invitation to explore? What if a scholar could present their information as that very invitation? To accomplish that we each need to examine any preconceptions we may have about the other group and to remain sensitive to each other's process. If we try to discover something new rather than merely to prove what we already know, and if we keep reminding ourselves of that imperative, then we can create an endeavour not of compromise but of creativity.

CHAPTER 10

Syncopated Time: Staging the Restoration Tempest

Amanda Eubanks Winkler and Richard Schoch

When performance historians today analyse musical scores and dramatic texts from the early modern period, we face the challenge of interpreting notes first sung and words first spoken more than three centuries ago. In trying to understand historical performances *as* performances – as embodied events, not lifeless documents – we might conjure up the legendary ghosts of theatre history, just as Colley Cibber's *Apology* (1740) tried to conjure in words the flesh-and-blood acting of the deceased Thomas Betterton. But as Cibber himself reluctantly admitted, it was easier to know 'what' Betterton spoke than to know '*how Betterton spoke*'.[1] Cibber understood that the theatrical past can never fully escape the past; it must always remain somewhat mysterious to the present.

Instead of recalling the absent past, perhaps we are wiser to look for how the past survives in the present. What insights might emerge if we studied historical performances not through archival fantasies but through the embodied and material realities of performance practice? In such study, our goal would be not to abandon performance history but rather to put it in creative tension with the present moment. As Rebecca Schneider has explained, a temporal telescoping occurs in every performed instance of 'replaying' and 'reenactment'. Schneider argues that such moments invoke what Gertrude Stein called *syncopated time* – the instantaneous collision of past and present, that moment of temporal disruption when 'then and now punctuate each other' as the 'prior moment' touches the 'very fingertips of the present'.[2] For us, cultivating a syncopated time in which the past and the present would be simultaneously 'in play' gave us a new scholarly paradigm for investigating the rich and complex (yet still underappreciated) historical performance genre of Restoration Shakespeare.

[1] Colley Cibber, *An Apology for the Life of Mr. Colley Cibber, Comedian …*, 2nd ed. (London: Printed by John Watts for the Author, 1740), 83.
[2] Rebecca Schneider, *Performing Remains: Art and War in Times of Theatrical Reenactment* (Abingdon: Routledge, 2011), 2.

Despite having been popular in the theatre, Restoration adaptations of Shakespeare have been long maligned by literary and theatre historians, going all the way back to F. J. Furnivall's 1895 variorum edition of Shakespeare's *The Tempest*. Generations of scholars have objected to what they regarded as the mutilation of Shakespeare's sacred texts by Restoration adapters, the unfortunate reliance in the adaptations on the strict dualism of Manichean morality, the illicit addition of new scenes and even new characters, and, perhaps most destructively of all, the brazen interpolation of scenes rich in music, dance, and visual splendour. Much more recent scholars like Barbara Murray have been willing to study Restoration versions of Shakespeare as dramatic works in their own right.[3] But even scholars more sympathetic to the value of these play texts have tended to overlook or to play down the essential fact that those texts were the basis for intermedial performance events that appealed to audiences for decades and even centuries. By deliberate contrast, a fundamental principle of our research has been that Restoration Shakespeare cannot be properly understood apart from its life in performance. Indeed, Restoration Shakespeare as a performance phenomenon reveals meanings that elude any purely textual or musicological analysis. In this way, performance can make manifest to contemporary observers the reasons why Restoration Shakespeare appealed to its original audiences.

Our first opportunity to test this thesis with professional artists and the general public occurred in the summer of 2017, when we collaborated with Shakespeare's Globe to perform scenes and songs from Thomas Shadwell's 1674 operatic version of *The Tempest* at the Sam Wanamaker Playhouse, the indoor Jacobean-style theatre within the Globe complex. The public workshops, which were preceded by scholar–artist developmental rehearsals, were the first major event in our research project 'Performing Restoration Shakespeare' (2017–2020), generously funded by the UK's Arts and Humanities Research Council (AHRC).[4] The entire week-long event involved a team of fifteen international scholars chosen for their collective expertise in theatre history, Shakespeare studies, and historical musicology; Globe research staff, led by Will Tosh; an ensemble of five singers and five instrumentalists; a company of five actors, all with experience of performing at the Globe; and a ticket-buying audience who

---

[3] See Murray's *Restoration Shakespeare: Viewing the Voice* (Madison, NJ: Farleigh-Dickinson University Press, 2001).

[4] For further information, please see the project's website (www.restorationshakespeare.org). Richard was the project's Principal Investigator and Amanda was the Co-Investigator.

attended our performances over two days. For this week-long event that progressed from scholar–artist collaborative rehearsal to public workshops in which we presented selected scenes, Amanda served as musical director and choreographer and Richard served as stage director.

Before discussing the research findings that arose from the rehearsals and public workshops, we want to provide some theatre history background. In 1667, a year before his death, Sir William Davenant, founder and manager of the Duke's Company, joined forces with the young playwright John Dryden to adapt Shakespeare's *The Tempest*, one of just nine Shakespeare plays for which the Duke's Company possessed the performance rights. In revising Shakespeare's play, Davenant and Dryden expanded its musical elements. They retained the ballads sung by Caliban and others and Ariel's songs but then added two different types of musical performances: a duet between the characters Ferdinand and Ariel ('Go thy way') and an elaborate Masque of Devils that is performed before the frightened audience of Alonzo, Antonio, and Gonzalo. It is erroneous to think of the Restoration *Tempest* as a static or bounded work; indeed, new productions during the period adapted this adaptation, adding spectacle, new dances, and new settings of the songs by popular composers of the day.[5] Such an adaptation was made by Shadwell in 1674, when he transformed Davenant and Dryden's *Tempest* from a highly musical play into an opera. He added machine effects, expanded and rewrote the Masque of Devils, and inserted a new Masque of Neptune.[6]

Today, we think of opera as a dramatic work set entirely to music and performed by singers and instrumentalists. But Restoration audiences and performing artists had a more capacious understanding of opera. For them, 'opera' meant primarily a play with significant musical sequences and spectacular effects, such as *The Tempest*, Thomas Shadwell and Matthew Locke's *Psyche*, or John Dryden and Henry Purcell's *King Arthur*. Less frequently, the term also referred to a fully sung dramatic work, such as Nahum Tate and Henry Purcell's *Dido and Aeneas*. Thus, in the Restoration theatre,

---

[5] David Lindley discusses this desire for musical newness, although he overstates the persistence of the Restoration settings of *The Tempest* music in the eighteenth and nineteenth centuries; most of the 1674 music was jettisoned by then. However, an early eighteenth-century score, probably by John Weldon, but commonly misattributed to Purcell – an error repeated by Lindley – was performed throughout the eighteenth and nineteenth centuries, even as new songs were added by Linley and Arne; see David Lindley, '"Sounds and Sweet Airs": Music in Shakespearean Performance History', *Shakespeare Survey*, 64 (2011): 59–73 (64–7).

[6] For a concise summary of the musical changes between the Dryden–Davenant and Shadwell versions of *The Tempest*, see Andrew R. Walkling, *English Dramatick Opera, 1661–1706* (Abingdon: Routledge, 2019), 122, 138–9.

a work called an 'opera' usually was a work that combined speech, song, dance, and spectacle in a mutually constitutive way.[7]

This chapter focuses on how our experience of staging two scenes from Shadwell's operatic version of *The Tempest* – the Masque of Devils and the Masque of Neptune – illuminates both the aesthetic appeal of Restoration Shakespeare as a distinctive genre of historical performance and the tensions that inevitably arise when performing Restoration Shakespeare, tensions between historical knowledge, the practical realities of theatre-making, and the expectations of artists and audiences. Performing Shadwell's *The Tempest* conjured an often-challenging instance of syncopated time, when the past punctuates the present. Yet that experience of temporal dislocation was also productive, identifying parallels in how Restoration and contemporary audiences responded to particular scenes and, more broadly, revealing staging solutions that respected the original work's dramaturgy while also making the work appealing to an audience today.

The Implications of Space

As with any type of theatrical performance, the space where we worked framed and affected the reactions of both artists and audiences. The Sam Wanamaker Playhouse is a radically different space than Dorset Garden, the theatre for which Shadwell's version of *The Tempest* was written and where it was first performed. Opened in 1671 as the new home for the Duke's Company, Dorset Garden featured a proscenium stage with a large forestage, the customary shutter-and-groove system that allowed for perspectival scenery and quick scene changes, enough harnesses and wires to allow four separate performers to fly across the stage simultaneously, machines for special effects, multiple trapdoors, and a substage area large enough to accommodate actors and musicians.[8] In every respect Dorset Garden was a marked improvement on the smaller theatre at Lincoln's

---

[7] Amanda Eubanks Winkler, 'Opera in England', in *The Cambridge Companion to Seventeenth-Century Opera*, ed. Jacqueline Waeber (Cambridge: Cambridge University Press, 2022), 224–47; and Amanda Eubanks Winkler, 'The Intermedial Dramaturgy of Dramatick Opera: Understanding Genre through Performance', *Restoration: Studies in English Literary Culture, 1660–1700*, 42.2 (2018): 13–38.

[8] On the Dorset Garden Theatre see Robert D. Hume, 'The Dorset Garden Theatre: A Review of Facts and Problems', *Theatre Notebook*, 33.2 (1979): 4–17. For the ways music was staged in the theatre, see Mark A. Radice, 'Sites for Music in Purcell's Dorset Garden Theatre', *The Musical Quarterly*, 81.3 (1997): 430–48; Frans and Julie Muller, 'Purcell's *Dioclesian* on the Dorset Garden Stage', in *Performing the Music of Henry Purcell*, ed. Michael Burden (Oxford: Clarendon Press, 1996), 232–42 and Frans and Julie Muller, 'Completing the Picture: The Importance of Reconstructing Early Opera', *Early Music*, 33.4 (2005): 667–81.

Inn Fields (itself a converted tennis court) where the Duke's Company had been performing since 1661. Indeed, at the time of its opening, Dorset Garden was the largest and most technologically sophisticated theatre that had ever been built in England. Though it would be surpassed by even more elaborate successors, Dorset Garden set the standard for the next 200 years of what a major London theatre should look like.

As is well known, the San Wanamaker Playhouse, which opened in 2014 and is named after the Globe's founder, intentionally recalls the scale and architectural style of a Jacobean indoor theatre like the Blackfriars, the winter home of the King's Men (Shakespeare's company) from 1608 to 1642. It was never intended to reconstruct the Blackfriars, let alone to incorporate features of a Restoration playhouse like Lincoln's Inn Fields or Dorset Garden. The sketches used to construct the Wanamaker date from 1660 and are the work of John Webb, who designed the changeable scenery for Sir William Davenant's private production of *The Siege of Rhodes* (1656) at Rutland House.[9] Despite Webb's close association with one of the lions of Restoration theatre, the 1660 drawings are wholly nostalgic, recalling pre-Civil War theatrical architecture. In short, Webb's sketches look like an early seventeenth-century indoor theatre.

But as Richard told the Wanamaker audience on the first day of our public workshops, several features of the space they occupied would have been familiar to a Restoration playgoer like Samuel Pepys: a totally indoor theatre lit by candles; tiered seating for the audience on three sides, including private boxes on the sides of the stage; an upstage gallery for musicians; a trapdoor leading to a substage area; and above all, a strong feeling of intimacy between performers and spectators. When we staged the Masque of Devils, having room beneath the stage where unseen performers could be heard and having a trapdoor for stage entrances from below proved advantageous.[10] After all, devils lurk down in hell, not up in heaven. For our practice-based research purposes, the Wanamaker was ideal for exploring Restoration Shakespeare because it was a performance space that acknowledged theatre history but did not seek to recreate it. In a precise parallel, our goal throughout the entire project was never to recreate Restoration theatrical spaces or performance styles but rather to

---

[9] Gordon Higgott, 'Reassessing the Drawings for the Inigo Jones Theatre: A Restoration Project by John Webb?', *The Chamber of Demonstrations: Reconstructing the Jacobean Indoor Playhouse*, www.bristol.ac.uk/drama/jacobean/research4.html.

[10] On the Wanamaker as a venue for scholarly exploration, see Will Tosh, *Playing Indoors: Staging Early Modern Drama in the Sam Wanamaker Playhouse* (London: Bloomsbury Arden Shakespeare, 2018), particularly chapter 8, 'Music and Lighting in the Sam Wanamaker Playhouse'.

use our knowledge of theatre and music history to create performances of Restoration Shakespeare that are compelling and meaningful to audiences today. Keeping with this ethos, the Wanamaker was a place where theatre's syncopated time manifested itself strongly.

Archive and Performance

Although we were fortunate to collaborate with the Globe, our project deliberately presented an alternative to original practices, the widely influential scholar–artist research method that began at the Globe in the late 1990s and which sought to reconstitute in contemporary performance the style and conventions of early modern drama.[11] Adopting a different (though not oppositional) approach, we regarded the early modern performance archive not as a point of return but as a point of departure: the basis for experiments that result in fresh performances rather than a normative set of instructions for resurrecting past performance styles.

Indeed, we struggle to see how any conjectured period style for Restoration Shakespeare can be recreated in a contemporary performance. For example, the musical aspects of Shadwell's version of *The Tempest* – the version we selected for our workshop and performances at the Sam Wanamaker Playhouse – are richly documented in quarto play texts, printed song lyrics, and musical scores in both print and manuscript.[12] There is much primary material to study. Yet this archival plenitude reveals that the original 1674 production mounted by the Duke's Company at Dorset Garden, far from being a static (and therefore knowable) entity, was in truth a protean event characterised more by multiplicity than singularity.

---

[11] Some audience members who were Globe 'regulars' came to the performances with the expectation that our work would be in harmony with the Globe's influential and pioneering efforts in original practices, an approach collaboratively developed in the Globe's early years by the inaugural artistic director Mark Rylance, composer Claire van Kampen, and designer Jenny Tiramani. Through careful historical research, the triumvirate attempted to stage Shakespeare's plays as they were 'originally intended'. Audience members who identified with the Globe's founding ethos of performance reconstitution initially found our more dialectical approach to Restoration Shakespeare a bit elusive. For Rylance's explanation of original practices and its aims, see 'Playing the Globe: Artistic Policy and Practice', in *Shakespeare's Globe Rebuilt*, ed. J. R. Mulryne and Margaret Shewring (Cambridge: Cambridge University Press, 1997), 169–76. See also the section on original practices in Christie Carson and Farah Karim-Cooper, eds., *Shakespeare's Globe: A Theatrical Experiment* (Cambridge: Cambridge University Press, 2008), 29–126, which includes contributions by Rylance, van Kampen, and Tiramani. Although much ink has been spilled critiquing the original practices project, its promises are seductive – that by following a knowable set of historically informed practices, something of the past might be reconstituted through performance.

[12] [Thomas Shadwell], *The Tempest, Or the Enchanted Island* (London: Printed by T. N. for Henry Herringman, 1674); *Songs and Masques in the Tempest* (London, 1674).

It bears going into some detail on how the surviving documentary evidence raises more questions about performance history than it answers. Shadwell's *The Tempest* quarto, published in 1674, famously includes detailed and lengthy stage directions and descriptions of the scenery used in the original production. But because there is no corroborating visual evidence, we cannot be sure that what Shadwell describes is what the Dorset Garden audience saw and heard. It may well be the case that when Shadwell, in his famous opening stage direction, described a sinking ship, 'many dreadful Objects' flying across the stage, and a descending 'shower of Fire', he was offering an idealised account of how *The Tempest* might one day be staged, not how it was actually staged.[13] In addition to the play text, the lyrics to the sung portions of *The Tempest* were printed separately around the same time as the play was being performed.[14] Just as the focus of modern opera audiences moves back and forth between supertitles and the stage performance, so did Restoration audiences consult song texts or libretti during performances to understand words obscured through singing. Audiences could also purchase the sheet music to Ariel's songs, which allowed them to perform excerpts from *The Tempest* in their own domestic spaces.[15] But much like the publication today of songs from hit Broadway musicals, these arrangements of Ariel's songs do not necessarily reflect how they were performed in the theatre.

When we consider related manuscript sources, any presumption that there was ever a fixed performance of the Restoration *Tempest* quickly unravels. In addition to their printed version, Ariel's songs also exist in a concordant manuscript source dating from the same period. Copied by Edward Lowe, this manuscript contains vocal ornamentation not found in the printed version and may be associated with student performances at Oxford, where Lowe was Heather Professor of Music.[16] It bears remembering that Oxford was one of the places where the London patent companies performed during their annual summer tour of the provinces. It is thoroughly plausible that the Duke's Company performed *The Tempest* at Oxford University, on which occasion the singer playing Ariel added ornamentation to her songs. Such ornamentation may have been captured in Lowe's manuscript, which then becomes documentary evidence for an evolving performance event, the fullness of which remains elusive.

---

[13] [Shadwell], *The Tempest*, 1.
[14] *Songs and Masques in the Tempest*.
[15] *The Ariels Songs in the Play call'd the Tempest* (London, [1675]).
[16] On this source, see Amanda Eubanks Winkler, 'A Thousand Voices: Performing Ariel', in *The Feminist Companion to Shakespeare*, 2nd ed., ed. Dympna Callaghan (Malden, MA: Blackwell Publishers, 2016), 520–538 (534–5).

Other musical aspects of Shadwell's *The Tempest* survive in conflicting manuscript versions. Pelham Humfrey's 1674 music for the Masque of Devils and Masque of Neptune survives in a manuscript now at the Bibliothèque Nationale in Paris. Arranged for a smaller number of singers than was used in the theatre, the music was likely adapted for domestic private performances, yet further evidence of the production's popularity.[17] One of the songs in the Masque of Devils, 'Arise ye subterranean winds', was actually by the Italian composer and singer Pietro Reggio. An alternate version of this particular piece survives in a manuscript copied by Daniel Henstridge that appears to record the composer's virtuosic performance of his own song, even transcribing into phonetic spelling Reggio's heavily accented English.[18] Notably, the 1680 printed version of 'Arise ye subterranean winds' does not include the lavish ornamentation found in Henstridge's transcription, a further example of how a printed document can fail to fully capture the idiosyncrasy of a performance event.[19]

In our workshops and performances, we grappled with these and other inconsistencies in the evidentiary record. As scholars, we wanted to be in command of the relevant documentary sources, especially when they were contradictory, partial, or inconclusive. The epistemological gap between historical document and historical event was something to explore, not something to overcome. Yet as musical director and stage director, we had to decide in advance which scenes and which versions of which songs from Shadwell's *The Tempest* we were going to stage. Moreover, we knew that at some point in the rehearsal process the artistic company and scholarly team would have to commit to certain singing, acting, and staging choices. After three days of rehearsal we would present scenes before a paying audience. In the great tradition of the theatre, the unalterable fact of opening night does tend to focus everyone's efforts.

As musical director, Amanda's first tasks were to select the precise musical texts for the Masque of Devils and Masque of Neptune and to decide what type of singers and instrumentalists we would use. Although the 1674 quarto of Shadwell's *The Tempest* suggests that a lavish instrumental

---

[17] See Michael Tilmouth's discussion of the sources in Matthew Locke, *Dramatic Music*, ed. Michael Tilmouth, Musica Britannica, 50 (London: Stainer and Bell, 1986), 27–8.
[18] On Daniel Henstridge's manuscript transcription of Reggio's possible performance of 'Arise ye subterranean winds', see Rebecca Herissone, *Musical Creativity in Seventeenth-Century England* (Cambridge: Cambridge University Press, 2013), 377–84 and Herissone, 'Daniel Henstridge and the Aural Transmission of Music in Restoration England', in *Beyond Boundaries: Rethinking Music Circulation in Early Modern England*, ed. Linda Austern, Candace Bailey, and Amanda Eubanks Winkler (Bloomington: Indiana University Press, 2017), 165–86.
[19] *Songs Set by Signior Pietro Reggio* (London, 1680), 12.

ensemble was used in the original production, Amanda chose a much simpler grouping: four-part strings and a lutenist. Her decision was partly due to financial constraints but also partly due to the project's research methodology: because we were not recreating the Dorset Garden production, we had no need for a large number of musicians. A simple band would enable us to investigate the synthesis of music and acting in Restoration Shakespeare. In a similar way, Amanda opted to use just five singers – two sopranos, a male alto, a tenor, and a bass – for all the musical roles.[20] As a consequence, our tenor (Ben Inman) had to sing the parts of both Aeolus and Oceanus in the Masque of Neptune. Departing from historical precedent, which suggests that boys from the Chapel Royal took some of the high-voiced roles in the Masque of Devils and possibly also in the Masque of Neptune, Amanda decided that we should cast only adult singers.[21] Finally, the pressure of time stopped us from preparing an edition of the two masques that incorporated Reggio's ornaments, something we wanted to do. In the end, pragmatism dictated that we use a modified version of Michael Tilmouth's modern edition of *The Tempest* music. While Tilmouth's edition does not correspond to early twenty-first-century editorial conventions – most notably, he provides a realisation of the figured bass (i.e., he writes out an accompaniment whereas the original source only provides a bassline with numbers, indicating the chords that must be played) – it provides a readable and reasonably error-free version of the musical text. Such were the material factors that came into play as we navigated the transition from academic study to collaborative theatre practice.

From an acting perspective, the primary sources were less conflicting. The 1674 quarto of Shadwell's *The Tempest* provided the basis for all subsequent editions of the play for well over a century, so there were no variants in the dialogue portion of the script.[22] In preparing the script for our workshop and performances, Richard retained original spelling and

---

[20] Elizabeth Kenny describes her performance of Shadwell's *The Tempest* (2015) at the Globe in 'In Practice II: Adapting a Restoration Adaptation – *The Tempest, or the Enchanted Island*', in *Shakespeare, Music, and Performance*, ed. Bill Barclay and David Lindley (Cambridge: Cambridge University Press, 2017), 114–30. Her version featured an abridged version of Dryden–Davenant–Shadwell's text performed by two actors and a similar musical ensemble to the one we used in 2017 (four-part strings + continuo and SSATB singers), although she used children instead of adults for the devils.

[21] In 1674 Charles II gave permission for personnel from the Chapel Royal to sing in *The Tempest*, Lna LC 5/15, 3 (16 May 1674).

[22] Shadwell's 1674 version of *The Tempest*, which adapted Davenant and Dryden's 1670 version of Shakespeare's original play, was reprinted in 1676, 1690, 1692, 1695, 1701, 1710, 1720[?], 1733, 1735, and 1775.

punctuation throughout, because those elements might have implications for the playing style with respect to pronunciation, scansion, and pacing. The dialogue that prefaces the Masque of Devils and Masque of Neptune appears as prose in the original quarto, even though it was clearly written as pentameter blank verse. Richard corrected the typesetting error in our script, so that it was immediately clear to the actors that their characters spoke in blank verse.

Our company included four male actors, three of whom played Antonio, Alonzo, and Gonzalo in both masques and one of whom played Prospero, who in Shadwell's *The Tempest* presents the concluding Masque of Neptune to the assembled characters in the play. Because our acting company was small, and also because our main concern was the interaction between drama and music, we cut most of the lengthy scene that leads up to the masque. As a consequence, our performance of the Masque of Neptune omitted some characters meant to be watching the masque in silence: Miranda, Ferdinand, Dorinda, Hippolito, Ariel, Stephano, Trincalo, Mustacho, Ventoso, Caliban, and Sycorax. In the public workshop at the Wanamaker, we recruited a few audience members to play some of those parts during the Masque of Neptune to give a better sense of the scene's meta-theatrical nature.

We both felt that our script should retain the original stage directions and cues, which indicate musical flourishes, voices and music heard from within the substage area, and the appearance or disappearance of singing characters within the masques proper (e.g., devils, subterranean winds, Neptune, and other mythological figures). Only by using this original material in our workshop and performance could we fully explore the synthesis of sound, music, and dramatic acting in Restoration Shakespeare. Although we never sought to reconstruct a Restoration performance – moreover, we were cognizant that the stage directions printed in the 1674 quarto may not have reflected what actually happened in the original Dorset Garden production – we did seek to honour in our own theatre practice the distinctive dramaturgy of Restoration Shakespeare.

Still, there were limits to how much we could explore, because we had only a week for the workshops and performances, because the budget was tight, and because of the restrictions imposed by the Wanamaker itself. Thus, we chose not to engage with stage directions that involved onstage moveable scenery and machines, such as the spectacular moment in the Masque of Neptune when Neptune, Amphitrite, Oceanus, and Tethys suddenly 'appear in a chariot drawn with sea-horses', surrounded by sea-gods and sea-goddesses, Tritons and Nereides.[23] As we noted earlier, the Wanamaker was designed to suggest an indoor Jacobean theatre, not a Restoration playhouse. And yet despite the inevitable limitations, the Wanamaker's spatial affordances offered us a rich opportunity to stage Restoration Shakespeare.

Dorset Garden or The Wanamaker: Staging the Devils

In staging the Masque of Devils on the first day of our public workshop in the Sam Wanamaker Playhouse, we were immediately confronted by syncopated time. Indeed, how could it have been otherwise? On the one hand, Shadwell's play text and the music by Humfrey and Reggio suggested how the Masque of Devils may have been staged in the original 1674 production at Dorset Garden. On the other hand, our work was necessarily shaped by present-day concerns and contexts: Could the Wanamaker's intimate bare stage accommodate a scene written to be performed in a fully equipped proscenium theatre? Could scholars and artists deeply invested in historical knowledge find a way to utilise that knowledge in theatre practice without making historical authenticity their goal? Could the distinctive Restoration genre of dramatick opera be compelling and meaningful to a present-day audience? Such were the points of contact between past and present that defined and guided our collaborative work.

As noted earlier, the Masque of Devils is replete with cues for music and sound. The dialogue that precedes the masque is interrupted three times, first by '*A flourish of Musick*'.[24] This deceptively simple cue is dramatically significant, because the sound alerts Alonzo, Gonzalo, and Antonio to the invisible presence of supernatural beings. The three characters interpret the 'flourish' as ominous, an aural sign that they have been 'Shipwrack'd / On the dominions of some merry Devil'.[25] Indeed, they respond immediately to the unexpected sound in speech (they realise that unseen devils inhabit the island), in body (their fear erodes their physical strength), and in thought (the presence of devils signifies their own guilt in having forced Prospero into exile). In short, this one sound cue advances the drama and provides a rich acting challenge early in the scene.

---

[23] [Shadwell], *The Tempest*, 78.
[24] [Shadwell], *The Tempest*, 27.
[25] [Shadwell], *The Tempest*, 27. The devil is merry because he enjoys playing tricks on the castaways, not because his flourish is pleasing or jocular.

As if to make the point that performance reconstruction is impossible, there is no extant music for this flourish. But the absence of a historical source in this particular instance gave us the perfect opportunity to apply our practice-based research method, to create our own performance in a way that drew on historical knowledge but was not overly determined by that knowledge. Because we understood the music's dramatic function, we had a basis not just for experimenting with different sounds but for adjudicating and appraising them. Our task, then, was not to replicate the sound heard in 1674, but rather to create for ourselves a sound that fulfilled the dramatic imperative at this moment in the production. To accomplish that task, we rehearsed and reflected on four different sounds:

1) The instrumentalists first improvised in seventeenth century *concitato* style: that is, music with rapid repeated notes (often semiquavers) to represent anger and agitation.[26]
2) The musicians then played chords in a *concitato* style but in two different keys simultaneously, producing a highly dissonant effect that would probably not have been heard in the Restoration theatre.
3) One of the musicologists in the workshop suggested an instrumental arrangement of the devils' chorus ('In Hell with flames they shall reign') sung later in the scene. This corresponds to historical practice, as we know instrumental arrangements of vocal music were sometimes used in this way.
4) The musicians played dissonant harmonics on the strings and a tremolo on the continuo instruments, producing a distinctly eerie effect but in a way that was inconsistent with seventeenth-century musical practice.

The least popular choice – the straightforward *concitato* (option 1) – was the most historically correct one. But as we soon discovered, Restoration-period style (at least for this moment in *The Tempest*) did not satisfy a contemporary audience. Some audience members and some scholars liked the dissonance and agitation of the *concitato* played in two keys (option 2) and the musical foreshadowing of the devils' chorus (option 3). What appealed to them was not the historical correctness of the choice but rather its dramatic force, whether through affective intensity or anticipation of a later

---

[26] The composer Claudio Monteverdi first described *stile concitato* in the preface to his eighth book of madrigals (1638). Yet as Kate van Orden notes, elements of the style can be found in sixteenth-century compositions such as Clément Janequin's *La guerre* (1528). Van Orden, *Music, Discipline, and Arms in Early Modern France* (Chicago: University of Chicago Press, 2005), 26–7.

moment in the performance. Surprisingly, the musicians themselves and a majority of the musicologists responded most positively to the sound with the most tenuous relationship to historical practice (option 4). Despite its lack of historical fidelity, the dissonant harmonics of the strings and the tremolo played on the continuo instruments best conveyed the narrative twist and high emotional stakes of this moment in the scene.

As we rehearsed and responded to the various options, we learned to appraise them not as isolated musical passages but as forceful elements within the overall performance event. We've gone into some detail about a brief moment in the performance – the first flourish heard by Antonio, Alonzo, and Gonzalo lasted only a matter of seconds – to document as precisely as we can how our iterative research method worked in practice, as we moved cyclically from performance to interpretation and then to an intervention that led to a revised performance, at which point the cycle began again.

The Masque of Devils presented greater challenges than deciding how to play a musical flourish, mainly because the devils eventually do appear and command the stage.[27] Not surprisingly, our audience at the Wanamaker expected to be frightened by the devils – much as they might be frightened by creatures in a horror film – a presumption likewise shared by the singers who played the devils and the dark allegorical roles of Pride, Rapine, Fraud, and Murder.[28] As stage director, Richard felt that testing out this presumption was a good place to start in staging the Masque of Devils. To make their performance frightening, the singers chose menacing gestures as they crouched low with clawed hands, encircling and overpowering the terrified trio of Alonzo, Antonio, and Gonzalo. The singers and the actors did well in performing a scene where the diabolical suddenly appears to frighten the merely mortal. But as the theatre historians on the scholarly team and some audience members were quick to observe, the devils *looked* demonic but did not *sound* demonic. It was apparent to everyone involved that some of the music sung by the devils was quite jaunty, a perplexing incongruity for those who assumed (based on the conventions of popular horror films) that music for hellish creatures must always be dissonant and discordant.[29] Some

---

[27] As noted, children played some of the devils in the 1674 *Tempest*; but it remains unclear how Restoration audiences understood or reacted to their performances. Perhaps children playing devils was disturbing for the Dorset Garden audience, just as Damien, the boy Antichrist in *The Omen* (1976), terrified millions of movie-goers.

[28] 'Rapine' is plunder or pillage, the forced seizure of another's property.

[29] On the use of dances and major-key music for spiritually corrupt or evil characters, see Amanda Eubanks Winkler, *O Let Us Howle Some Heavy Note: Music for Witches, the Melancholic, and the Mad on the Seventeenth-Century English Stage* (Bloomington: Indiana University Press, 2006), 27–62.

scholars who initially preferred the historically informed flourish ended up wondering whether Restoration-era music could be meaningful to a modern theatre audience at all, given the radical disjunction between seventeenth-century musical conventions and twenty-first-century audience expectations. Complicating this interpretive process is the distinct possibility that some singers who played devils in 1674, the children of the Chapel Royal and even the adult Pietro Reggio, were not taken seriously by the Dorset Garden audience, even though the play text clearly indicates that the antic Masque of Devils succeeded in frightening its intended audience of Alonzo, Antonio, and Gonzalo. Yet again, performance history provides us not with a stable point of origin to which we might return but rather the occasion for inserting ourselves into a creative dialogue between past and present.

Divergence between the reactions of the fictive onstage audience and the actual theatre audience, whether contemporary or historical, is fully consistent with the scene's deliberate meta-theatricality: the actual audience watches dramatic characters watching a performance staged for them by yet other characters. In this sense, the actual audience are bystanders who witness a strangely musicalised incident of trauma directed at someone else. Indeed, the dramatic richness of the Masque of Devils may well turn precisely on this difference in responses: an audience today (and perhaps in the Restoration, too) can enjoy Alonzo, Antonio, and Gonzalo's fear of the devils emerging from the underworld. The scene's complexity of tone, utterly invisible on the printed page, was discoverable only through our iterative performance practice.

Filling the Gaps: Staging Neptune

As we noted earlier in this chapter, the prodigious scenic spectacle that characterised the original Masque of Neptune was an aspect of performance that we simply could not tackle in the Sam Wanamaker Playhouse, for both logistical and financial reasons. But there was another aspect of the masque – the genre's customary dances – that we were able to explore in our rehearsals and public workshops. The 1674 quarto of Shadwell's *The Tempest* tells us when the various dances occur in the Masque of Neptune and makes clear that singers and dancers are separate onstage groups (hence, the repeated stage direction 'Here the Dancers mingle with the Singers').[30] But because Giovanni Battista Draghi's original dance music does not survive, we do

---

[30] [Shadwell], *The Tempest*, 78, 80.

not know the duration of the dances, let alone the style, rhythm, and tempo of the accompanying music. In short, the historical record created a gap in the performance but then withheld guidance for how to fill it. Once again, the past invited the present into a syncopated time.

In our initial workshop planning we decided to use Tilmouth's reconstructed dance music for the Masque of Neptune to preserve the scene's original dramaturgical shape.[31] We never intended to fully choreograph these dances, given that our budget did not allow for a choreographer (let alone a team of dancers) and given that our schedule did not give us sufficient time to teach complicated dances to actors and singers. However, as the rehearsal process progressed, several members of our scholarly team were adamant that some kind of dance or stylised movement was needed in the Masque of Neptune. This feeling that something was missing in the staging arose not from any desire to reconstruct a Restoration performance but rather from informed critical observation, an attentiveness to what this moment in the performance required.

What the performance required was a sequence of synchronised gesture and movement that worked with the music to create dramatic meaning. It was not enough for the actors to act and the singers to sing. To add in the missing ingredient, Amanda (who has a background in dance) improvised some basic choreography for the masque's customary final dance. Because we did not have a separate troupe of dancers, we enlisted the singers and the actors playing Gonzalo, Antonio, and Alonzo to perform a simple round dance. Prospero presented the masque, and so it seemed odd for him to also participate in it.

We first choreographed the dance sequence in our closed rehearsals and then performed it before the workshop audience in the Wanamaker. One of the scholars suggested that we enhance the Masque of Neptune's inherent meta-theatricality – like the Masque of Devils, it was a performance within a performance – by recruiting audience members to play some of the other characters. In Shadwell's *The Tempest*, Prospero arranges the concluding masque as an apology for how roughly he has treated everyone on the island. We had no trouble finding volunteers to play Miranda, Ferdinand, Dorinda, and Hippolito. To accommodate the masque's

---

[31] Tilmouth sometimes reuses music from elsewhere in the score (i.e., part of Locke's 'Curtain Tune' for the Tryton's Dance I) and sometimes advises that the previous chorus should be repeated in an instrumental version for the dance, a typical Restoration practice. One of the members of the scholarly team, Silas Wollston, rightly pointed out the inappropriateness of some of Tilmouth's recycling choices (e.g., the reuse of the 'Curtain Tune') and did some editorial work 'on the fly' to replace these dances.

expanded audience, we placed a row of chairs on each side of the stage, a formal spatial arrangement that underlined the ceremony of the occasion. Additionally, we modified the choreography to include the new onstage audience. To suggest the 'mingling' between performers that the original stage directions indicate, we had everyone on the stage exit together while dancing. Again, our collective intent was not to recover an original staging – almost certainly our staging looked nothing like what happened in 1674 – but to explore the symbiosis between acting, singing, and dancing in Restoration Shakespeare. By having more actors on the stage – as, indeed, the scene required – we gained a stronger sense of how various modes of individual performance were held together by the masque's characteristically meta-theatrical frame.

Audience Responses

As should be evident from the preceding descriptions, we solicited oral responses as we blocked the two scenes in the Wanamaker and used audience and scholar feedback to shape the staging, a democratic approach that allowed us the flexibility to investigate multiple performance options. Another part of the process involved breakout sessions at the end of each day with the performers, scholarly team, and paying audience members. We also distributed an online survey, to which some participants responded. Several themes emerged: first, the tension between historical knowledge and practical performance; and second, the gap between past and present, how it might be bridged or, in some cases, reinforced through staging.

One recurring strand of commentary focused on our project's stance towards 'authenticity', a preoccupation undoubtedly shaped by the Globe and its association with original practices. One audience member commented that they liked our low-tech approach in the workshop, deeming it 'good' and 'glorious'. For this person, elaborate special effects 'muffle' the story onstage (in fact, the 1674 *Tempest* was a high-tech production, and using elaborate special effects would have been the more historically informed choice). Richard queried the desire for authenticity with his breakout group, explaining that we sought 'to honour the Restoration theatrical form, but not to resurrect it'. One audience member strongly disliked this, indicating that it was 'nice, but also a fudge'. The actor who played Alonzo had been involved with several original practices productions at the Globe and he remarked, 'I'm rowing back from positions of absolute right or wrong in my old age.' He was eager to play and experiment, and to explore what might emerge from 'seeing it [Restoration Shakespeare] as something in its own right'.

Another strand directly engaged with the relationship of past to present – the anxieties produced by syncopated time. One person commented upon the temporal juxtapositions that emerge when one replays something from the past, observing that 'the two centuries [the seventeenth and the twenty-first] are converging' in our project. One scholar noted that there was a three-way temporal tension – between Shakespeare's time, the Restoration, and modern London. Another wondered if our goal was to 'translate the aesthetic' or 'translate the audience'. Do we want to translate the Restoration aesthetic to make it palatable for modern audiences, or do we want to educate modern audiences enough that they will understand the Restoration aesthetic?

For some, this act of translation seemed impossible: one audience member noted that the Restoration-era music seemed to be of a very particular time and place and another commented that the music 'locks us into a specific time period'. For this reason, some wanted us to keep the Restoration spectacle and text, but 'change the music'. Why not pop music, if we were not doing an original practices production? Why not music that made the devils more recognisably evil for audiences today?

The musicians participating in the workshop protested loudly against this sentiment, and, indeed, this moment of conflict may again reveal disciplinary proclivities. Opera houses regularly stage works from the seventeenth through nineteenth centuries without modernising the music, transplanting them to whatever time period suits them, a recent example being David McVicar's postmodern production of Handel's eighteenth-century opera *Giulio Cesare* (Glyndebourne, 2005; Metropolitan Opera, 2013), set in a British colonial outpost with costuming from various periods and dance numbers of various styles, some nineteenth-century, some vaguely Celtic, and some Bollywood inflected. Very few musicians or opera directors would claim that Handel needs to be performed in an eighteenth-century setting for his music to make sense. Beyond the potential disciplinary divide, perhaps such responses have something to do with the canon. According to the logic of the canon, Handel's music, like Shakespeare's plays, is transcendent, and can be successfully transplanted to any era. Canonical works are timeless, but music by the little-known Pelham Humfrey or Pietro Reggio is not: it 'locks us into a specific time period'.

Others craved what we did not provide in a workshop setting at the Wanamaker – elaborate choreographies, scenic effects, and costuming. Several proposed ways of addressing the missing spectacle. One person wondered if projections might be used, as the Royal Shakespeare Company (RSC) did with its digital avatar Ariel, although such technology does not necessarily provide budgetary savings. Some believed elaborate costuming was needed to signal the identities of the mythological characters for a modern audience. Quite a few audience members discussed the importance of dance, although opinions differed. For some, Amanda's choreography in the Masque of Neptune was too historical given our 'stated goal' to make it 'exciting for a modern audience'. In truth Amanda's choreography had very little to do with seventeenth-century dance; regardless, the choreographies from Dorset Garden cannot be recovered as they were not written down. On the opposite end of the spectrum, one of the scholars felt that the dance was too modern and that we should have hired baroque dancers and a baroque dance specialist. Several people wanted a more stylised gestural language throughout the scene, a sentiment that was echoed by a few of the singers, because for them gestural stylisation was the equivalent of the formality in Humfrey's Restoration-era music. Our audience's desire for stylisation (both among the scholarly participants and the general audience) was also shaped by the notion that late-seventeenth-century acting was inherently artificial, although people at the time clearly did not find it so, as contemporary descriptions of Thomas Betterton's or Anne Bracegirdle's acting attest. It is only because David Garrick in the eighteenth century was thought to have inaugurated a new 'naturalistic' style that the previous acting style was retrospectively viewed in this way. As Richard has observed: 'the term "naturalistic" must always be put into context because each generation of theatre audiences has a different idea of what acting "naturally" means'.[32]

Conclusion

Staging scenes and songs from the Restoration *Tempest* in our workshop at the Sam Wanamaker Playhouse proved to us that 'syncopated time', far from being a purely theoretical conceit invoked only by scholars, really does exist in the rehearsal room. Our collaboration between scholars and performing artists was a concentrated effort to put the theatrical past and the theatrical present into contact: not to resurrect the past, but to let it make demands upon the present; to let the past tell us what was important in staging a Restoration version of *The Tempest*. How we then undertook that staging was, as theatre practice always is, conditioned by our own

---

[32] Richard Schoch, 'How One Actor Forever Changed the Way We See Shakespeare', *British Council Voices Magazine*, 19 April 2016, www.britishcouncil.org/voices-magazine/how-one-actor-forever-changed-way-we-see-shakespeare.

previous experience, by the affordances of the space in which we worked, by the pressures of time, and the restraints of budgets. As we learned in the workshop, those conditions were not distractions from our pursuit of a hypothetical or ideal performance. Indeed, our work affirmed no such teleology. Rather, those conditions were the specific and inevitable context in which our creative and intellectual processes would unfold, conditions that were as unique to us as were the conditions that defined and delimited the work of the Duke's Company when it first performed Shadwell's version of *The Tempest* at Dorset Garden in 1674.

The symbiosis of music, dance, and drama in the Restoration *Tempest*, a symbiosis broadly characteristic of the most inventive and most popular Restoration versions of Shakespeare, was for us an invitation to be attentive in our theatre practice. We strove to explore how seventeenth-century stage conventions could be put 'in play' when scholars and artists work side by side to create contemporary performances of a historical performance genre. In so doing, we were mindful of our responsibility to use theatre practice to understand in an experiential and embodied way the intermedial nature of Restoration Shakespeare in a holistic performance event. To reflect our collaborative work, as we have done in this chapter, we have used words such as 'attentive' and 'responsibility'. This implies an ethical dimension to our attempt to inhabit the syncopated time of performing Restoration Shakespeare today. The ethical demand of our contemporary practice-led research was neither to fetishise the theatrical past nor to disregard it, but rather to place it alongside the present, and thereby come to know each through the other.

Bibliography

An act against vagrants, and wandring, idle, dissolute persons. At the Parliament begun at Westminster the 17th day of September, an. Dom. 1656. London: Hen. Hills and John Field, 1657; Wing E972.
Allsopp, Niall. *Poetry and Sovereignty in the English Revolution*. Oxford: Oxford University Press, 2020.
The Ariels Songs in the Play call'd the Tempest. London, [1675].
Ashbee, Andrew, ed. *Records of English Court Music*. Volume 1. Snodland: Andrew Ashbee, 1986.
Austin, Hailey J. '"If She Be Worthy": Performance of Female Masculinity and Toxic Geek Masculinity in Jason Aaron's Thor: The Goddess of Thunder'. In *Superheroes and Masculinity: Unmasking the Gender Performance of Heroism*, ed. Sean Parson and J. L. Schatz, 29–46. Lanham, MD: Lexington Books, 2019.
Bailey, Candace. 'The Challenge of Domesticity in Men's Manuscripts in Restoration England'. In *Beyond Boundaries: Rethinking Music Circulation in Early Modern England*, ed. Linda Phyllis Austern, Candace Bailey, and Amanda Eubanks Winkler, 114–26. Bloomington and Indianapolis: Indiana University Press, 2017.
Benedetti, Jean. *David Garrick and the Birth of Modern Theatre*. London: Methuen, 2001.
Blake, Ann. 'Children and Suffering in Shakespeare's Plays'. *The Yearbook of English Studies*, 23 (1993): 293–304.
Boyle, Roger. *The Dramatic Works of Roger Boyle, Earl of Orrery*, ed. William Smith Clark II. 2 volumes. Cambridge, MA: Harvard University Press, 1937.
Bradley, Lynne. *Adapting King Lear for the Stage*. London: Routledge, 2016.
Burden, Michael. 'Shakespeare and Opera'. In *Eighteenth-Century Shakespeare*, ed. Peter Sabor and Fiona Ritchie, 204–24. Cambridge: Cambridge University Press, 2012.
Burgoyne, John. *The Lord of the Manor*. London: Evans, 1781.
Burnaby, William. *Love Betray'd; Or, The Agreable Disapointment*. London: Printed for D. Brown … F. Coggan … W. Davis … and G. Strahan, 1703.
Burnim, Kalman A. *David Garrick, Director*. Pittsburgh, PA: University of Pittsburgh Press, 1961.

Burrow, Colin. *Epic Romance from Homer to Milton*. Oxford: Clarendon Press, 1993.
Butler, Martin. *Theatre and Crisis, 1632–1642*. Cambridge: Cambridge University Press, 1984.
Canfield, J. Douglas. *Heroes and States: On the Ideology of Restoration Tragedy*. Lexington: University Press of Kentucky, 2000.
Carson, Christie and Farah Karim-Cooper, eds. *Shakespeare's Globe: A Theatrical Experiment*. Cambridge: Cambridge University Press, 2008.
Chambers, E. K. *William Shakespeare: A Study of Facts and Problems*. 2 volumes. Oxford: Clarendon Press, 1930.
Chan, Mary. 'Drolls, Drolleries and Mid-Seventeenth-Century Dramatic Music in England'. *Royal Musical Association Research Chronicle*, 15 (1979): 117–73.
Chan, Mary. 'John Hilton's Manuscript British Library Add. MS 11608'. *Music & Letters*, 60.4 (1979): 440–9.
Charteris, Richard. *An Annotated Catalogue of the Music Manuscripts in the Folger Shakespeare Library, Washington, D.C.* New York: Pendragon Press, 2005.
Chua, Brandon. *Ravishment of Reason: Governance and the Heroic Idioms of the Late Stuart Stage, 1660–1690*. Lanham, MD: Bucknell University Press, 2014.
Cibber, Colley. *An Apology for the Life of Mr. Colley Cibber, Comedian ...*, 2nd ed. London: Printed by John Watts for the Author, 1740.
Clare, Janet, ed. *Drama of the English Republic, 1640–1660*. Manchester: Manchester University Press, 2002.
Clark, Sandra, ed. *Shakespeare Made Fit*. London: Everyman, 1997.
Crystal, Ben and David Crystal. *Shakespeare's Words: A Glossary and Language Companion*. London: Penguin, 2004.
Cunningham, Vanessa. *Shakespeare and Garrick*. Cambridge: Cambridge University Press, 2008.
Cutts, John P. 'Robert Johnson: King's Musician in His Majesty's Public Entertainment'. *Music & Letters*, 36.2 (1955): 110–25.
Cutts, John P. 'Seventeenth-Century Songs and Lyrics in Edinburgh University Library Music MS DC.1.69'. *Musica Disciplina*, 13 (1959): 169–94.
Davenant, William. *Gondibert*, ed. David F. Gladish. Oxford: Clarendon Press, 1971.
Davenant, William. 'Macbeth: A Tragedy'. In *Five Restoration Adaptations of Shakespeare*, ed. Christopher Spencer, 33–107. Urbana: University of Illinois Press, 1965.
[Davenant, William]. *A Proposition for the Advancement of Moralitie, by a New Way of Entertainment of the People*. London, 1654 [/3].
Davenant, William. *The Works of Sr William D'avenant*. London: Printed by T. N. for Henry Herringman, 1673.
Davies, Thomas. *Dramatic Miscellanies, Consisting of Critical Observations on Several Plays of Shakespeare*. London: Davies, 1783.
De Marinis, Marco and Marie Pecorari. 'New Theatrology and Performance Studies: Starting Points towards a Dialogue'. *The Drama Review*, 55.4 (2011): 64–74.

Depledge, Emma. *Shakespeare's Rise to Cultural Prominence: Politics, Print and Alteration*. Cambridge: Cambridge University Press, 2018.
Dessen, Alan. '"Original Practices" at the Globe'. In *Shakespeare's Globe: A Theatrical Experiment*, ed. Christie Carson and Farah Karim-Cooper, 45–54. Cambridge: Cambridge University Press, 2008.
Donington, Robert. 'James Talbot's Manuscript'. *The Galpin Society Journal*, 3 (1950): 27–45.
Doyle, A. I. 'Publication by Members of the Religious Orders'. In *Book Production and Publishing in Britain, 1375–1475*, ed. Jeremy Griffiths and Derek Pearsall, 109–23. Cambridge: Cambridge University Press, 1989.
Downes, John. *Roscius Anglicanus, or an Historical Review of the Stage*. London: Printed and sold by H. Playford, 1708.
Downes, John. *Roscius Anglicanus*, ed. Judith Milhous and Robert D. Hume. London: The Society for Theatre Research, 1987.
Drouin, Jennifer. 'Cross-Dressing, Drag, and Passing: Slippages in Shakespearean Comedy'. In *Shakespeare Re-Dressed: Cross-Gender Casting in Contemporary Performance*, ed. James C. Bulman, 23–57. Madison, NJ: Fairleigh Dickinson University Press, 2008.
Dryden, John. *The Works of John Dryden*, ed. H. T. Swedenberg Jr. et al. 20 volumes. Berkeley and Los Angeles: University of California, 1956–2002.
Duckles, Vincent. 'The "Curious" Art of John Wilson (1595–1674): An Introduction to his Songs and Lute Music'. *Journal of the American Musicological Society*, 7.2 (1954): 93–112.
Duffin, Ross W. 'Catching the Burthen: A New Round of Shakespearean Musical Hunting'. *Studies in Music from the University of Western Ontario*, 19–20 (2000): 1–15.
Duffin, Ross W. *Shakespeare's Songbook*. New York and London: W. W. Norton & Company, 2004.
Dyson, Peter. 'Changes in Dramatic Perspective: From Shakespeare's *Macbeth* to Davenant's'. *Shakespeare Quarterly* 30.3 (1979): 402–7.
Edmond, Mary. *Rare Sir William Davenant: Poet Laureate, Playwright, Civil War General, Restoration Theatre Manager*. Manchester: Manchester University Press, 1987.
England's Memorable Accidents, From the 19th of Decemb. to the 26th of the same, 1642. London: for Stephen Bowtell, 1642; Thomason/E.244[26].
Estill, Laura. *Dramatic Extracts in Seventeenth-Century English Manuscripts: Watching, Reading, Changing Plays*. Newark: University of Delaware Press, 2015.
Eubanks Winkler, Amanda. 'The Intermedial Dramaturgy of Dramatick Opera: Understanding Genre through Performance'. *Restoration: Studies in English Literary Culture, 1660–1700*, 42.2 (2018): 13–38.
Eubanks Winkler, Amanda. '"Let's Have a Dance": Staging Shakespeare in Restoration London'. In *The Oxford Handbook of Shakespeare and Music*, ed. Christopher R. Wilson and Mervyn Cooke, 387–408. Oxford: Oxford University Press, 2022.

Eubanks Winkler, Amanda. *Music, Dance, and Drama in Early Modern English Schools*. Cambridge: Cambridge University Press, 2020.

Eubanks Winkler, Amanda. *O Let Us Howle Some Heavy Note: Music for Witches, the Melancholic, and the Mad on the Seventeenth-Century English Stage*. Bloomington: Indiana University Press, 2006.

Eubanks Winkler, Amanda. 'Opera in England'. In *The Cambridge Companion to Seventeenth-Century Opera*, ed. Jacqueline Waeber, 224–47. Cambridge: Cambridge University Press, 2022.

Eubanks Winkler, Amanda. 'Sexless Spirits? Gender Ideology and Dryden's Musical Magic'. *The Musical Quarterly* 93.2 (2010): 297–328.

Eubanks Winkler, Amanda. 'A Thousand Voices: Performing Ariel'. In *A Feminist Companion to Shakespeare*, 2nd ed., ed. Dympna Callaghan, 520–38. Chichester: Wiley Blackwell, 2016.

Eubanks Winkler, Amanda, ed. *Music for Macbeth*. Middleton, WI: A-R Editions, 2004.

Eubanks Winkler, Amanda and Richard Schoch. *Shakespeare in the Theatre: Sir William Davenant and the Duke's Company*. London: Arden Bloomsbury, 2021.

Firth, C. H. and R. S. Rait, eds. *Acts and Ordinances of the Interregnum, 1642–1660*. 3 volumes. Ontario: Tannritchie Publishing, 2005.

Fiske, Roger. *English Theatre Music in the Eighteenth Century*. London: Oxford University Press, 1973.

Fiske, Roger. 'The *Macbeth* Music'. *Music and Letters*, 45.2 (1964): 114–25.

Fitzmaurice, James, ed. *Sociable Letters: Margaret Cavendish*. Ontario: Broadview Press, 2004.

Ford, Robert. 'The Filmer Manuscripts: A Handlist'. *Notes*, 34.4 (1978): 814–25.

Ford, Robert. 'Osborn MS 515: A Guardbook of Restoration Instrumental Music'. *Fontes Artis Musicae*, 30.3 (1983): 174–84.

Forde, Thomas. *Virtus Rediviva; Or, A Panegyrick On the Late K. Charls the I. Second Monarch of Great Britain*. London: Printed by R. and W. Leybourn, for William Grantham, 1660.

Freehafer, John. 'Brome, Suckling, and Davenant's Theatre Project of 1639'. *Texas Studies in Language and Literature*, 10 (1968): 367–83.

Freeman, Jane. 'Beyond Bombast: David Garrick's Performances of Benedick and King Lear'. *Restoration and 18th Century Theatre Research*, 14.2 (1999): 1–21.

Freeman, Lisa A. *Character's Theater: Genre and Identity on the Eighteenth-Century English Stage*. Philadelphia: University of Pennsylvania Press, 2002.

Fretz, Claude. '"marvellous and surprizing conduct": The "Masque of Devils" and Dramatic Genre in Thomas Shadwell's *The Tempest*'. *Restoration: Studies in English Literary Culture, 1660–1700*, 43.2 (Fall 2019): 3–28.

Fretz, Claude. 'Performing Restoration Shakespeare "Then" and "Now": A Case Study of Davenant's *Macbeth*'. *Concentric: Literary and Cultural Studies*, 48.1 (March 2022): 27–56.

Friedman-Rommell, Beth H. 'Breaking the Code: Toward a Reception Theory of Theatrical Cross-Dressing in Eighteenth-Century London'. *Theatre Journal*, 47.4 (1995): 459–79.

Furnivall, F. J., ed. *A New Variorum of Shakespeare*. Volume 9. Philadelphia: J.B. Lippincott Co., 1892.

Garrick, David. *The Private Correspondence of David Garrick …*, ed. James Boaden. Volume 1. London: Colburn and Bentley, 1831.

Greenfield, Anne. 'D'Avenant's Lady Macduff: Ideal Feminism and Subversive Politics'. *Restoration*, 37.1 (Spring 2013): 39–60.

Greeting, Thomas. *The Pleasant Companion*. London: Printed for John Playford, 1673.

Harris, Arthur John. 'Garrick, Colman, and King Lear: A Reconsideration'. *Shakespeare Quarterly*, 22.1 (1971): 57–66.

Haynes, Bruce. *The End of Early Music*. Oxford: Oxford University Press, 2007.

Herissone, Rebecca. 'Daniel Henstridge and the Aural Transmission of Music in Restoration England'. In *Beyond Boundaries*, ed. Linda Austern, Candace Bailey, and Amanda Eubanks Winkler, 165–86. Bloomington and Indianapolis: Indiana University Press, 2017.

Herissone, Rebecca. *Musical Creativity in Restoration England*. Cambridge and New York: Cambridge University Press, 2013.

Higgott, Gordon. 'Reassessing the Drawings for the Inigo Jones Theatre: A Restoration Project by John Webb?' The Chamber of Demonstrations: Reconstructing the Jacobean Indoor Playhouse. www.bristol.ac.uk/drama/jacobean/research4.html.

Hill, John. *The Actor: A Treatise on the Art of Playing*. London: Griffiths, 1750.

Hilton, John. *Catch that Catch can*. London: W. Godbid for J. Playford, 1667; Wing H2039.

Hobbes, Thomas. *The Clarendon Edition of the Works of Thomas Hobbes*, vol. 4: *Leviathan: The English and Latin Texts (i)*, ed. Noel Malcolm. Oxford: Clarendon Press, 2012.

Holland, Peter. *The Ornament of Action: Text and Performance in Restoration Comedy*. Cambridge: Cambridge University Press, 1979.

Holman, Peter. 'Commentary, Item 95'. In *Fine Printed and Manuscript Music*. London: Sotheby's, 1999.

Holman, Peter. *Four and Twenty Fiddlers*. Oxford: Clarendon Press, 1993.

Holman, Peter. 'Introduction'. In *Restoration Theatre Airs*, ed. Peter Holman and Andrew Woolley. Musica Britannica, forthcoming.

Home, Henry, Lord Kames. *Elements of Criticism*, ed. Peter Jones. Volume 2. Indianapolis: Liberty Fund, 2005.

Hotson, Leslie. *The Commonwealth and Restoration Stage*. Cambridge, MA: Harvard University Press, 1928.

Hotson, Leslie. *The Commonwealth and Restoration Stage*. New York: Russell & Russell, 1962.

Houck, Stacey. 'John Playford and the English Musical Market'. In *'Noyses, sounds and sweet aires': Music in Early Modern England*, ed. Jessie Ann Owens, 48–61. Washington, DC: The Folger Shakespeare Library, 2006.

Howard, Alan. 'A Midcentury Musical Friendship: Silas Taylor and Matthew Locke'. In *Beyond Boundaries: Rethinking Music Circulation in Early Modern England*, ed. Linda Austern, Candace Bailey, and Amanda Eubanks Winkler, 127–49. Bloomington and Indianapolis: Indiana University Press, 2017.

Howard, Jean. 'Crossdressing, the Theatre, and Gender Struggle in Early Modern England'. *Shakespeare Quarterly*, 39.4 (1988): 418–40.

Howe, Elizabeth. *The First English Actresses: Women and Drama, 1660–1700*. Cambridge: Cambridge University Press, 1992.

Hughes, Derek. 'Heroic Drama and Tragicomedy'. In *A Companion to Restoration Drama*, ed. Susan J. Owen, 195–210. Oxford: Blackwell, 2008.

Hume, Robert D. 'The Dorset Garden Theatre: A Review of Facts and Problems'. *Theatre Notebook*, 33.2 (1979): 4–17.

Ingler, William. *Certaine informations from severall parts of the kingdome, 30 October–6 November 1643*. London: for Henry Overton, 1643–1644; Thomason/E.75[3].

Iwanisziw, Susan B. 'The Shameful Allure of Sycorax and Wowski: Dramatic Precursors of Sartje, the Hottentot Venus'. *Restoration and 18th Century Theatre Research*, 16.2 (2001): 3–10.

Jacob, James R. and Timothy Raylor. 'Opera and Obedience: Thomas Hobbes and *A Proposition for Advancement of Moralitie* by Sir William Davenant'. *The Seventeenth Century*, 6.2 (1991): 205–50.

Johnston, Freya. 'Samuel Johnson'. In *Great Shakespeareans: Dryden, Pope, Johnson, Malone*, ed. Claude Rawson, 115–59. London: Continuum, 2010.

Jorgens, Elise Bickford, ed. *Edinburgh University Library Manuscript Ms, Dc. 169. English Song 1600–1675*. Volume 8. New York and London: Garland Publishing, 1987.

Jose, Nicholas. *Ideas of the Restoration in English Literature, 1660–71*. London: Macmillan, 1984.

Keenan, Timothy. *Restoration Staging, 1660–74*. Abingdon: Routledge, 2017.

Kenny, Elizabeth. 'In Practice II: Adapting a Restoration Adaptation – *The Tempest, or the Enchanted Island*'. In *Shakespeare, Music, and Performance*, ed. Bill Barclay and David Lindley, 114–30. Cambridge: Cambridge University Press, 2017.

Kernodle, George R. 'Style, Stylization, and Styles of Acting'. *Educational Theatre Journal*, 12.4 (1960): 251–61.

Kirkman, Francis. *The Wits, or, Sport upon Sport*. London: Printed for Henry Marsh, 1662; Wing W3218.

Kirwan, Peter. *Shakespeare in the Theatre: Cheek by Jowl*. London: Arden Shakespeare, 2019.

Kivy, Peter. *Authenticities: Philosophical Reflections on Musical Performance*. Ithaca, NY: Cornell University Press, 1995.

Kroll, Richard. 'Emblem and Empiricism in Davenant's *Macbeth*'. *English Literary History*, 57.3 (Winter 1990): 835–64.
Langhans, Edward A. *Eighteenth Century British and Irish Promptbooks: A Descriptive Bibliography*. New York: Greenwood Press, 1987.
Larson, Katherine R. *The Matter of Song in Early Modern England: Texts in and of the Air*. Oxford: Oxford University Press, 2019.
Latham, Robert and William Matthews, eds. *The Diary of Samuel Pepys: A New and Complete Transcription*. 11 volumes. Berkeley: University of California Press, 1971.
Law, Richard. 'The Heroic Ethos in John Dryden's Heroic Plays'. *Studies in English Literature 1500–1900*, 23.3 (1983): 389–98.
Leigh, Lori. *Shakespeare and the Embodied Heroine: Staging Female Characters in the Late Plays and Early Adaptations*. Basingstoke: Palgrave Macmillan, 2014.
L'Estrange, Roger. *A Memento Directed to all Those that Truly Reverence the Memory of King Charles the Martyr*. London: Printed for Henry Brome, 1662.
Lindenbaum, Peter. 'John Playford: Music and Politics in the Interregnum'. *Huntington Library Quarterly*, 64.1–2 (2001): 124–38.
Lindley, David. '"Sounds and Sweet Airs": Music in Shakespearean Performance History'. *Shakespeare Survey*, 64 (2011): 59–73.
Little, Patrick. 'Music at the Court of King Oliver'. *The Court Historian*, 12 (2007): 173–91.
Locke, Matthew. *Dramatic Music*, ed. Michael Tilmouth. Musica Britannica. Volume 51. London: Stainer and Bell, 1986.
Locke, Matthew. *The Rare Theatrical: Music for London Entertainment, 1660–1800*. Series A, Volume 4. London: Stainer and Bell, 1989.
Long, John H. *Shakespeare's Use of Music: The Final Comedies*. Gainesville: University of Florida Press, 1961.
Love, Harold. *Scribal Publication in Seventeenth-Century England*. Oxford: Clarendon Press, 1993.
McAfee, Helen, ed. *Pepys on the Restoration Stage*. New Haven, CT: Yale University Press, 1916.
McAuley, Gay. *Not Magic but Work: An Ethnographic Account of a Rehearsal Room Process*. Manchester: Manchester University Press, 2012.
[Magalotti, Lorenzo]. *Travels of Cosmo the Third, Grand Duke of Tuscany*. London: Printed for J. Mawman, 1821.
Maguire, Nancy Klein. *Regicide and Restoration: English Tragicomedy, 1660–1671*. Cambridge: Cambridge University Press, 1992.
Marotti, Arthur F. *Manuscript, Print and the English Renaissance Lyric*. Ithaca, NY, and London: Cornell University Press, 1995.
Marsden, Jean I. 'Improving Shakespeare: From the Restoration to Garrick'. In *The Cambridge Companion to Shakespeare on Stage*, ed. Stanley Wells and Sarah Stanton, 21–36. Cambridge: Cambridge University Press, 2002.
Mazer, Cary. 'Historicizing Spontaneity'. In *Shakespeare's Sense of Character*, ed. Yu Jin Ko and Michael Shurgot, 85–98. Burlington, VT: Ashgate, 2012.

Miller, Ted H. 'The Two Deaths of Lady Macduff: Antimetaphysics, Violence, and William Davenant's Restoration Revision of *Macbeth*'. *Political Theory*, 36.6 (2008): 856–82.
Moore, Robert E. 'The Music to *Macbeth*'. *Musical Quarterly*, 47.1 (1961): 22–40.
Muller, Frans and Julie Muller. 'Completing the Picture: The Importance of Reconstructing Early Opera'. *Early Music*, 33.4 (2005): 667–81.
Muller, Frans and Julie Muller. 'Purcell's *Dioclesian* on the Dorset Garden Stage'. In *Performing the Music of Henry Purcell*, ed. Michael Burden, 232–42. Oxford: Clarendon Press, 1996.
Murray, Barbara. *Restoration Shakespeare: Viewing the Voice*. Madison, NJ: Fairleigh Dickinson University Press, 2001.
Murray, Barbara. '"Strange Star": Same-Sex Love and William Burnaby's *Love Betray'd or The Agreeable Disapointment* (1703)'. *English Studies*, 93.2 (2012): 183–4.
O'Meara, Jennifer. 'What "The Bechdel Test" Doesn't Tell Us: Examining Women's Verbal and Vocal (Dis)empowerment in Cinema'. *Feminist Media Studies*, 16.6 (2016): 1120–3.
Oya, Reiko. *Representing Shakespearean Tragedy: Garrick, the Kembles, and Kean*. Cambridge: Cambridge University Press, 2011.
Payne, Deborah C. '"Damn you, Davenant!" The Perils and Possibilities of Restoration Shakespeare'. *Restoration and Eighteenth-Century Theatre Research*, 32.1 (Summer 2017): 21–40.
Payne, Deborah C. 'Reified Object or Emergent Professional? Retheorizing the Restoration Actress'. In *Cultural Readings of Restoration and Eighteenth-Century English Theater*, ed. J. Douglas Canfield and Deborah C. Payne, 13–38. Athens, GA: University of Georgia Press, 1995.
Pearson, Jacqueline. *The Prostituted Muse: Images of Women and Women Dramatists, 1642–1737*. New York: Harvester Wheatsheaf, 1988.
Pinto, David. *For ye Violls*. Richmond: Fretwork Editions, 1995.
Pisani, Michael V. *Music for the Melodramatic Theatre in Nineteenth-Century London and New York*. Iowa City: University of Iowa Press, 2014.
Plank, Steven E. '"And Now About the Cauldron Sing": Music and the Supernatural on the Restoration Stage'. *Early Music*, 28.3 (1990): 393–407.
Playford, John. *Apollo's Banquet*. London, 1669.
Playford, John. *The English dancing master: or, Plaine and easie rules for the dancing of country dances*. London: Thomas Harper, 1651; Thomason E.626[7].
Playford, John. *An Introduction to the Skill of Musick*. London: Printed by E. Jones, for Henry Playford, 1694.
Powell, Jocelyn. *Restoration Theatre Production*. London: Routledge & Kegan Paul, 1984.
Price, Curtis. *Music in the Restoration Theatre with a Catalogue of Instrumental Music in the Plays, 1665–1713*. Ann Arbor, MI: UMI Research Press, 1979.
Rackin, Phyllis. 'Shakespeare's Cross-Dressing Comedies'. In *A Companion to Shakespeare's Works: The Comedies*, ed. Richard Dutton and Jean E. Howard, 114–36. Malden, MA: Blackwell, 2003.

Raddadi, Mongi. *Davenant's Adaptations of Shakespeare*. Uppsala: Studia Anglistica Upsaliensis, 1979.
Radice, Mark A. 'Sites for Music in Purcell's Dorset Garden Theatre'. *The Musical Quarterly*, 81.3 (1997): 430–48.
Radice, Mark A. 'Theater Architecture at the Time of Purcell and Its Influence on His "Dramatick Operas"'. *The Musical Quarterly*, 74.1 (1990): 98–130.
Randall, Dale. *Winter Fruit: English Drama 1642–60*. Kentucky: University Press of Kentucky, 1995.
[Reggio, Pietro]. *Songs Set by Signior Pietro Reggio*. London, 1680.
Reimers, Sara. 'Rehearsal Notes: Davenant's *Macbeth* at the Folger Theatre', 6–18 August 2018. Unpublished field notes.
Reimers, Sara and Richard Schoch. 'Performing Restoration Shakespeare Today: Staging Davenant's *Macbeth*'. *Shakespeare Bulletin*, 37.4 (Winter 2019): 467–89.
Richmond, Robert, ed. '*Macbeth* By William Shakespeare, As Adapted and Amended by William Davenant'. Folger Shakespeare Theatre. 30 May 2018. Unpublished rehearsal script.
Ritchie, Leslie. *David Garrick and the Mediation of Celebrity*. Cambridge: Cambridge University Press, 2019.
Rosenthal, Laura J. 'Reading Masks: The Actress and the Spectatrix in Restoration Shakespeare'. In *Broken Boundaries: Women and Feminism in Restoration Drama*, ed. Katherine M. Quinsey, 201–18. Lexington: University Press of Kentucky, 1996.
Rylance, Mark. 'Playing the Globe: Artistic Policy and Practice'. In *Shakespeare's Globe Rebuilt*, ed. J. R. Mulryne and Margaret Shewring, 169–76. Cambridge: Cambridge University Press, 1997.
Rymer, Thomas. *Foedera*. London, 1735.
Sandys, William and Simon Andrew Forster. *The History of the Violin*. London: William Reeves Bookseller, 1864.
Scheil, Katherine West. *The Taste of the Town: Shakespearian Comedy and the Early Eighteenth-Century Theatre*. Lewisburg, PA: Bucknell University Press, 2003.
Schneider, Rebecca. *Performing Remains: Art and War in Times of Theatrical Reenactment*. Abingdon: Routledge, 2011.
Schille, Candy B. K. '"Man Hungry": Reconsidering Threats to Colonial and Patriarchal Order in Dryden and Davenant's *The Tempest*'. *Texas Studies in Literature and Language*, 48.4 (2006): 273–90.
Schoch, Richard. 'How One Actor Forever Changed the Way We See Shakespeare'. *British Council Voices Magazine*, 19 April 2016. www.britishcouncil.org/voices-magazine/how-one-actor-forever-changed-way-we-see-shakespeare.
Scouten, Arthur H. 'The Premiere of Davenant's Adaptation of *Macbeth*'. In *Shakespeare and the Dramatic Tradition: Essays in Honor of S. F. Johnson*, ed. W. R. Elton and William B. Long, 286–93. Cranbury, NJ: Associated University Presses, 1989.
Sedinger, Tracey. '"If Sight and Shape be True": The Epistemology of Crossdressing on the London Stage'. *Shakespeare Quarterly*, 48.1 (1997): 63–79.

Seng, Peter J. *The Vocal Songs in the Plays of Shakespeare*. Cambridge, MA: Harvard University Press, 1967.
[Shadwell, Thomas]. *The Tempest, Or the Enchanted Island*. London: Printed by T. N. for Henry Herringman, 1674.
Shakespeare, William. *Bell's Edition of Shakespeare's Plays*, ed. Francis Gentleman. London: Cornmarket, 1969.
Shakespeare, William. *King Lear*, ed. R. A. Foakes. London: Thomson Learning, 2006.
Shakespeare, William. *Macbeth*. Directed by Antoni Cimolino. Performed by Ian Lake, Krystin Pellerin, Michael Blake, Sarah Afful. Stratford Festival, 2016. www.digitaltheatreplus.com/education/collections/stratford-festival/macbeth.
Shakespeare, William. *Macbeth*. Directed by Gregory Doran. Performed by Antony Sher, Harriet Walter, Nigel Cooke, Diane Beck. Royal Shakespeare Company, 2001. www.digitaltheatreplus.com/education/collections/illuminations/macbeth-illuminations-rsc.
Shakespeare, William. *Macbeth*. Directed by Jatinder Verma. Performed by Robert Mountford, Shaheen Khan, Umar Pasha, Shalini Peiris. Tara Arts, 2015. www.digitaltheatreplus.com/education/collections/tara-arts/macbeth.
Shakespeare, William. *Macbeth*, ed. Sandra Clarke and Pamela Mason. London: Bloomsbury, 2015.
Shakespeare, William. *The Plays of William Shakespeare in Eight Volumes*, ed. Samuel Johnson. Volume 6. London: J. and R. Tonson, 1765.
Shapiro, Michael. *Gender in Play on the Shakespearean Stage: Boy Heroines and Female Pages*. Ann Arbor: University of Michigan Press, 1994.
Sharpe, Kevin. *Criticism and Compliment: The Politics of Literature in the England of Charles I*. Cambridge: Cambridge University Press, 1987.
Shebbeare, John. *Letters on the English Nation by Battista Angeloni, A Jesuit, Who Resided Many Years in London*. Volume 2. London, 1755.
Songs and Masques in the Tempest. London, 1674.
Sorbière, Samuel de. *Relation d'un voyage en Angleterre*. Paris, 1664.
Sorbière, Samuel de. *A Voyage to England*. London: Printed and Sold by J. Woodward, 1709.
Spencer, Christopher, ed. *Davenant's Macbeth from the Yale Manuscript: An Edition, with a Discussion of the Relation of Davenant's Text to Shakespeare's*. New Haven, CT: Yale University Press, 1961.
Spencer, Christopher, ed. *Five Restoration Adaptations of Shakespeare*. Urbana: University of Illinois Press, 1965.
Spencer, Hazelton. *Shakespeare Improved: The Restoration Versions in Quarto and on the Stage*. Cambridge, MA: Harvard University Press, 1927.
Spink, Ian, ed. *The Blackwell History of Music in Britain*, vol. 3: *The Seventeenth Century*. Oxford: Blackwell, 1992.
Sternfeld, Frederick W. 'Appendix II: Take, O Take Those Lips Away'. In *Measure for Measure*, ed. J. W. Lever. London: Methuen & Co., 1965.
Sternfeld, Frederick W. *Music in Shakespearean Tragedy*, 2nd ed. London: Routledge and Kegan Paul, 1967.

Stone, George Winchester, Jr. 'Garrick's Production of *King Lear*: A Study in the Temper of the Eighteenth-Century Mind'. *Studies in Philology*, 45.1 (1948): 89–103.

Taruskin, Richard. *Text and Act: Essays on Music and Performance*. Oxford: Oxford University Press, 1995.

[Tate, Nahum and David Garrick]. *The History of King Lear, A Tragedy: As it is now acted at the King's Theatres*. London: Hitch et al., 1756.

[Tate, Nahum and George Colman]. *The History of King Lear, As It Is Performed at The Theatre Royal in Covent Garden*. London: R. Baldwin and T. Becket, 1768.

Taylor, Gary. *Reinventing Shakespeare: A Cultural History from the Restoration to the Present*. New York: Weidenfeld & Nicholson, 1987.

Taylor, Gary and Andrew J. Sabol. 'Middleton, Music, and Dance'. In *Thomas Middleton and Early Modern Textual Culture: A Companion to the Collected Works*, ed. Gary Taylor and John Lavagnino, 119–81. Oxford: Clarendon Press, 2007.

Tosh, Will. *Playing Indoors: Staging Early Modern Drama in the Sam Wanamaker Playhouse*. London: Bloomsbury Arden Shakespeare, 2018.

A Transcript of the Registers of the Worshipful Company of Stationers, from 1640–1708, A.D. 3 volumes. London: privately printed, 1913.

Tuke, Samuel. *The Adventures of Five Hours*. London: Printed for Henry Herringman, 1663.

Van Lennep, William, Emmett L. Avery, Arthur H. Scouten, George Winchester Stone, Jr., and Charles Beecher Hogan, eds. *The London Stage, 1660–1800*. 5 parts in 11 volumes. Carbondale: Southern Illinois University Press, 1960–1968.

Van Orden, Kate. *Music, Discipline, and Arms in Early Modern France*. Chicago: University of Chicago Press, 2005.

Walkling, Andrew R. *English Dramatick Opera, 1661–1706*. Abingdon: Routledge, 2019.

Walkling, Andrew R. *Masque and Opera in England, 1656–1668*. Abingdon: Routledge, 2017.

Walls, Peter. *Music in the English Courtly Masque, 1604–1640*. Oxford: Clarendon Press, 1996.

Walter, Harriet. *Brutus and Other Heroines: Playing Shakespeare's Roles for Women*. London: Nick Hern Books, 2016.

Watkins, Stephen. 'The Protectorate Playhouse: William Davenant's Cockpit in the 1650s'. *Shakespeare Bulletin*, 37.1 (2019): 89–109.

Whitlock, Keith. 'John Playford's *The English Dancing Master* 1650/51 as Cultural Politics'. *Folk Music Journal*, 7.5 (1999): 548–78.

Wilders, John. *Macbeth: Shakespeare in Production*. Cambridge: Cambridge University Press, 2004.

Wilkes, Thomas. *A General View of the Stage*. London: Coote and Whetstone, 1759.

Wilkinson, Tate. 'Original Anecdotes Respecting the Stage, and the Actors of the Old School, with Remarks on Mr Murphy's "Life of Garrick"'. *Monthly Mirror*, 13 (February 1802): 122–4.

Wilson, John Harold. *All the King's Ladies: Actresses of the Restoration*. Chicago: University of Chicago Press, 1958.

Wilson, Michael I. *Nicholas Lanier: Master of the King's Musick*. London and New York: Routledge, 1994.

Winn, James A. 'Heroic Song: A Proposal for a Revised History of English Theatre and Opera, 1656–1711'. *Eighteenth-Century Studies*, 30.2 (Winter 1996/7): 113–37.

Winn, James A. *John Dryden and His World*. New Haven, CT: Yale University Press, 1987.

Winn, James A. *'When Beauty Fires the Blood': Love and the Arts in the Age of Dryden*. Ann Arbor: University of Michigan Press, 1992.

Wiseman, Susan. *Drama and Politics in the English Civil War*. Cambridge: Cambridge University Press, 1998.

Wollston, Silas. 'The Instrumentation of English Violin-Band Music'. PhD, The Open University, 2009.

Wollston, Silas. 'New Light on Purcell's Early Overtures'. *Early Music*, 37.4 (2009): 647–55.

Woods, Leigh. 'Crowns of Straw on Little Men: Garrick's New Heroes'. *Shakespeare Quarterly*, 32.1 (1981): 69–79.

Worthen, William B. *The Idea of the Actor: Drama and the Ethics of Performance*. Princeton, NJ: Princeton University Press, 1984.

Index

actor(s), 118, 122–4, 128–9, 131, 135, 139–40, 147, 149–50, 155–7
  Actor's Equity, xix, 146, 168
  actresses, 79, 83
  and blank verse, 189
  in Bedlam, 148
  bodies of, 14, 127
  in Burnaby's *Love Betray'd*, 83
  and Cibber, 124
  classical, 130
  and dance, 194
  in Davenant's *Macbeth*, xviii, xx, 13, 121
  in Davenant-Dryden-Shadwell's *Tempest*, 91, 188
  in the Duke's Company, 2, 122
  experimentation of, 125
  in Garrick's *King Lear*, 102, 108, 110
  and gender, 1, 4, 13, 79, 80, 82, 87, 89, 91, 92, 94, 96
  and gesture, 120, 125, 171
  and historical performance, 13
  in the King's Company, 2
  from Lazarus Theatre, 14
  modern, 136
  and musicians, 14, 25, 139, 146, 154, 183
  and performance, 195
  process of, 126–7
  in the Restoration, 132
  and Restoration acting style, 120
  and scholars, 120, 125, 164–6, 168–9, 170–2, 174, 176–9, 181
  in the seventeenth century, 130
  in Shadwell's *Tempest*, 189
  Shakespeare as, 2
  in Shakespeare's *Twelfth Night*, 82
  and singers, 192
  and spectator, 154
  and stereotypes, 177
  in Tasso's *Gerusalemme liberata*, 56
  in Tate's *King Lear*, 113
  and time, 195
  in the twenty-first century, 128, 130

actor-manager, 13, 97, 100, 102, 107, 109, 145
adaptation(s), 8, 32, 80, 97, 101, 150
  by Banister, 33
  by Burnaby, 80, 82, 83
  by Davenant, xviii, 3, 6, 38–40, 46, 55–60, 69, 78, 119, 132, 135, 163, 173
  by Davenant and Dryden, xix, 4, 7
  by Davenant-Dryden-Shadwell, 14
  by Dryden, 60, 97
  by Garrick, 102
  by Gildon, 135
  by Granville, 90
  by Lacey, 36
  by Middleton, 32
  by Phelps, 145
  by Shadwell, 109, 133, 182
  of Shakespeare, 4, 7–9, 12, 25, 28, 30, 31, 40, 54, 62, 79, 81–3, 86, 90–2, 95–7, 106, 112, 116, 133, 141, 142, 146, 159, 181, 182
  by Tate, 99, 116
  by Tate and Garrick, 98
Adventures of Five Hours, The (Tuke), 48
  Ernesto, 48
  Geraldo, 48
Afful, Sarah, 145
Afzal, John, 144
Arts and Humanities Research Council (AHRC), xix, xx, 9, 118, 132, 146, 181
As You Like It (Shakespeare), 80
  'Hunts up' / 'O sweet Oliver", 36
  'What shall he have that killed the deer?', 36
asylum. *see also* Bedlam Hospital
  Bedlam, xviii, 119, 120, 121, 127, 136, 163, 169
  Charenton, xviii

ballad(s), 16, 25, 26, 28, 29, 182
  'Bonny sweet Robin', 29
  'O Sweet Oliver', 29
  'Walsingham', 29
  anthologies of, 30
  broadside, 25, 29, 30

Index

ballad singer(s), 25, 28
Banister, John, 33, 34, 63, 73, 75, 76, 132, 133
Banqueting House, 5
Beaumont, Francis, 2
Bechdel, Alison, 147
    Bechdel Test, 147, 148
Beck, Diane, 143
Bedlam Hospital, xviii, 10, 120, 137, 139, 149, 150, 163, 169–71, 177, *see also* St. Mary Bethlehem Hospital
Bedlam Rep, xviii
Beeston's Boys, 1
Beeston, William, 1
Bell's Shakespeare, 99, 102, 105, 114
Benedetti, Jean, 102, 110, 111
Betterton, Thomas, 2, 4, 122, 123, 128, 134, 139, 180, 197
    Betterton's Company, 90
Bibliothèque Nationale, 187
Blackfriars Playhouse, 11, 184
Blake, Ann, 145
Bloody Brother (Fletcher-Jonson-Chapman-Massinger), 32, *see also* Rollo Duke of Normandy
Blow, John, 73
Boyce, William, 61
Boyle, Roger (Earl of Orrery), 40, 45–8, 54, 75
    Generall, The, 45, 46
    Henry the Fifth, 45, 54
    Tryphon. See *Tryphon* (Orrery)
Bracegirdle, Anne, 197
Bradley, Lynne, 111, 112
Bradshaw, John, 50
Bradshaw, Lucretia, 90
British Library, The, 97, 107
Bulwer, John, 171
    Chirologia, 120, 171–2
Burden, Michael, 7
Burden, Suzanne, 144
Burgoyne, John
    Lord of the Manor, 109
Burnaby, William, 80, 82–4, 90, 94
    Deceived, The, 82
    Love Betray'd. See *Love Betray'd* (Burnaby)
Burnim, Kalman, 104, 111, 112
Burrow, Colin, 43
Butelli, Louis, 13, 118, *119*, *128*, 140

Canfield, J. Douglas, 96
Cavendish, Margaret, 29, 95
Chan, Mary, 32
Chapel Royal, The, 73, 188, 193
Chapman, George, 32
    Bloody Brother. See *Bloody Brother* (Fletcher-Jonson-Massinger)

Charles I, 16, 41, 42, 72, 127
Charles II, 1, 2, 4, 5, 42, 46, 50, 54, 63, 72, 77, 127, 132, 133, 188
Chua, Brandon, 43
Cibber, Colley, 122, 123, 124, 180
    Apology for the Life of Mr. Colley Cibber, 123, 124, 180
Cibber, Theophilus, 91
Cimolino, Antoni, 145
Cisek, Tony, *119*, 127, *128*, *129*, 138, 148, *165*, 169
Clark, Sandra, 8
class, 80, 85, 88, 89, 96
Clifford, Richard, 135
Cockpit Theatre, the, 1, 39, 43
Coleman, Charles, 77
Colman, George, 100, 105–108, 114–16
    History of King Lear, The. See *History of King Lear, The* (Tate and Garrick)
    promptbook for *The History of King Lear*, 107
Comical Revenge, or Love in a Tub (Etherege), 78
concitato, 191
Conquest of Granada, The (Dryden), 45
Corneille, Pierre, 41
Covent Garden, 105, *106*, 109, 116
Cromwell, Oliver, 1, 41, 50
Cross, Richard, 99, 107
Cruelty of the Spaniards in Peru, The (Davenant), 1, 42
Cunningham, Vanessa, 99, 100, 103, 110
Cupid His Coronation (Jordan), 28
Cymbeline (Shakespeare), 80, 85

Davenant, Sir William, xvii, xviii, xix, xx, 1–4, 3, 1–7, 10–14, 28, 31, 33, 39–49, 52–61, 70, 78, 80–3, 90–2, 94–7, 118–50, 152, 153, 155, 157–9, 162–3, 164, 169, 172–4, 177, 179, 182, 184
    adaptions of Shakespeare, 3
    Cruelty of the Spaniards in Peru, The, 1, 42
    Gondibert An Heroick Poem, 44, 46, 49
    Hamlet. See *Hamlet* (Davenant)
    heroic idiom, 43, 47, 55
    'Heroick Representations', 1, 43
    History of Sir Frances Drake, The, 1
    language of, 13
    Law Against Lovers, The. See *Law against Lovers, The* (Davenant)
    Macbeth, 7, 10–13, 46, 48, 53, 54, 57, 78, 97, 118–21, 124–34, 136, 137, 139–43, 146, 148, 149, 150, 158, 163, 164,169, 172, 177, 179
    Proposition for Advancement of Moralitie, by a New Way of Entertainment of the People, A, 42
    Salmacida Spolia. See *Salmacida Spolia* (Davenant)

Siege of Rhodes, The, 1, 40, 42, 46, 184
Tempest, or The Enchanted Island, The. See *Tempest, or The Enchanted Island, The* (Davenant and Dryden)
Davies, Thomas, 102, 109
  Dramatic Miscellanies, 102
Davis, Mary ('Moll'), 4, 91
De Marinis, Marco, 164
de Sade, Marquis, xviii
de Sorbière, Samuel, 63
Depledge, Emma, 15
Dido and Aeneas (Purcell and Tate), xviii, 90, 133–7, 139, 140, 182
  Phoebus, 135
  Venus, 135
Diliberto, Brittany, *119*, *128*, 129, 138, *148*, *165*
disability
  lovesickness, 86
  mad, xvii
  madness, 104, 174
  spasms, xvii
  tic disorder, xvii, 171
divertissement, 4, 7
Dolle, William, *6*
Donnellan's Cheek, 145
Doran, Gregory, 144
Dorset Garden Theatre, The, 6, 7, 55, 59, 61, 62, 133, 137, 169, 183–90, 193, 197, 198
Downes, John, xviii, 6, 7, 61, 82
Draghi, Giovanni Battista, 193
Drake, Sir Francis, 59, 60
dramaturg, 130, 131, 146, 168
dramaturgy, 54, 142, 151, 153, 157, 183, 189
droll(s), 15, 27, 30
  drolleries, 27
  The Grave-makers, out of *Hamlet* Prince of Denmark. See Kirkman, Francis
  The merry conceited humors of Bottom the weaver, 30
Drury Lane, 1, 39, 97, 99, 106, 116
Dryden, John, xix, 4, 5, 7, 40–2, 53, 54, 56–8, 60, 80, 82, 83, 90–2, 94–6, 182
  Conquest of Granada, The, 41, see also *Conquest of Granada, The* (Dryden)
  Indian Emperour, The. See *Indian Emperour, The* (Dryden)
  King Arthur. See *King Arthur* (Dryden and Purcell); Purcell, Henry
  Tempest, or The Enchanted Island, The. See *Tempest, or The Enchanted Island, The* (Davenant and Dryden)
Dryden, John and Robert Howard
  Indian Queen, The. See *Indian Queen, The* (Howard and Dryden)
Duarti, Eleonora, 29

Duffin, Ross, 29
Duke of York's Company, the. See Duke's Company, the
Duke's Company, the, xviii, 2–7, 13, 45, 55, 56, 58, 62, 70, 75, 78, 122, 127, 128, 132, 182–6, 198
Dyson, Peter, 142

Eccles, John, 10, 61, 134, 137–8, 140, 152
Eisenstein, Robert, 11, 13, 126, 132
Empress of Morocco, The (Settle), *6*, 78
English Civil War, 1, 2
Etherege, George, 69, 75, 78
  Comical Revenge, or Love in a Tub, 78
  She would if she could, 78
Eubanks Winkler, Amanda, xix, 9, 10, 14, 132, 152, 166, 167
Evelyn, John, 56

Faithorne, William, *3*
Filmer, Edward, 34
  US-NH Misc. MS 170 Filmer 4, 34
Findlay, Polly, 145
Fletcher, John, 2, 32
  Bloody Brother. See *Bloody Brother* (Fletcher-Jonson-Massinger)
  Humorous Lieutenant, The. See *Humorous Lieutenant, The* (Fletcher)
Flynn, Graeme, 144
Folger Consort, xviii, 10, 13, 132, 134, 167
Folger Shakespeare Library, the, 9, 10, 13, 105, *106*, 118, *119*, 121, 124, 127–34, 136, *138*, 143, 145, 146, 147, *148*, 150, 154, 157, 159, 161, 163, 164, *165*, 166, 169, 170
Folger Theatre, the, xvii, xviii, xix, xx, 10, 11, 13, 14, 35, 118, *119*, 121, 124, *127*, 128–31, 133, 135, *137*, 142, 144–7, *148*, 149, 153, 156, 158, 160, 162–5, 168, 169
Forbes-Robertson, Johnston, 145
Ford, Robert, 74
Fordyce, George, 112
Freeman, Jane, 100, 108–10
Fretz, Claude, xix, 9
fridged. See fridging
fridging, 143–5
Friedman-Romell, Beth, 80, 91
Furnivall, F.J., 7, 8, 181

Garrick, David, 13, 97–116, 197
  adaptation of Shakespeare, 99
  History of King Lear, The. See *History of King Lear, The* (Tate and Garrick)
gender, 4, 80, 96, 161, 174, 175
  ambiguity of, 89, 96
  anxiety about, 85

Index

gender (cont.)
  and bravery, 83, 86
  breeches role, 4, 13, 80–3, 85, 86, 91, 92, 96
  cross-dressing, 79–84, 90–3, 95, 96
  drag, 88
  expression of, 79
  'firago', 85
  genderbending, 81, 89, 92
  identity of, 79, 87–91
  and sexuality, 90, 131
  issues of, 79
  misgendering, 84
  norms of, 88
  pronouns, 83
  transvestism, 81, 84
  transvestite, 81
  travesty role, 80, 91, 94, 96
  women, 79, 85
Genebach, Chris, 146, 147, 153
Generall, The (Orrery), 45, 46
genre(s), 7, 12, 13, 16, 27, 28, 40, 41, 47, 60, 179, 183
  comedy, 81, 139
  dramatic, 12
  dramatick opera, 7, 132, 134, 137, 139, 140, 190
  heroic opera, 13
  heroic play, 13, 46
  historical, 12, 141, 180, 198
  history, 4
  masque, 5, 6, 28, 42, 88, 90, 133, 135, 138, 188, 189, 190, 193, 194, 195
  tragedy, xix, 4, 6, 7, 60, 70, 81, 100, 109, 112, 114–17, 139, 171, 173
  tragicomedy, 4
Gentleman, Francis, 103, 114
Gerusalemme liberata (Tasso), 55
gesture(s), xvii, xx, 34, 54, 70, 110, 116, 120, 121, 124, 125, 126, 171, 172, 192, 194
Gildon, Charles, 31, 90, 133, 134, 135, 139
Giulio Cesare (Handel), 196
Globe Theatre, the, 185, *see also* Shakespeare's Globe, London
Gondibert (Davenant), 43–7, 49
  Preface, 46, 55, 56
Granville, George (1st Baron Lansdowne)
  Jew of Venice, The. See *Jew of Venice* (Granville)
Great Fire of London, 10, 120, 163
Greenfield, Anne, 142, 154, 156, 160, 161
Greenhill, John, 3
Gwynn, Nell, 4

Hale, Mariah, *119*, *127*, *128*, *129*, *138*, *148*, *165*
Hamlet (Davenant)
  Ophelia, 4
Hamlet (Shakespeare), 2, 30, 81
  'Bonny sweet Robin', 30

Hamlet, 108, 123, 124
  'Walsingham', 30
Handel, George Friederic, 196
  Giulio Cesare, 196
Harriman-Smith, James, 13
Harris, Arthur John, 100
Harris, Henry, 139
Harwood, Ralph, 99, 107
Heard, Rob, 147
Henrietta Maria, 42
Henry IV (Shakespeare), 2
Henry VIII (Shakespeare), 2, 25, 78
Henry the Fifth (Orrery), 45, 54
  Prince Hal, 54
Henstridge, Daniel, 187
Hill, John, 113, 114, 117
  Actor, The, 113, 115
Hilton, John, 27, 30, 32, 35–6
  Catch That Catch Can, 30, 35, 36, 37
  GB-Lbl Add. 11608, 27
  US-Ws v.a.409, 36, 37
  Us-Ws v.a.409, f. 17r, *37*
History of King Lear, The (Tate and Garrick), 5, 13, 97, 98, 99, 100–103, *104*, *106*, 109–11, 114–16
  Albany, 102, 103, 114
  Cordelia, 97, 101, 109, 115
  Cornwall, 115
  Edgar, 97, 108, 110, 112–15
  Edmund, 100, 107, 115
  'Five fathom and half, poor Tom', 108
  Gloucester, 97, 107, 108, 110, 115
  Goneril, 100, 101–103, 112, 114
  Kent, 108, 115
  Lear, 97, 100–16
History of Sir Francis Drake, The (Davenant), 1, 42, 59
Hobbes, Thomas, 46, 47, 49, 50, 53, 56
  Leviathan, 49
Holland, Peter, 8
Home, Henry (Lord Kames), 115, 117
  Elements of Criticism, 116
Horace, 84
  'To Gabinius', 84
Hotson, Leslie, 24
Howard, Edward, 46, 47
  Usurper, The, 46, *see also Usurper, The* (Howard)
Howard, Robert, 45, 53, 54, 56–8
Humfrey, Pelham, 73, 133, 187, 190, 196, 197
Humorous Lieutenant, The (Fletcher), 56

Indian Emperour, The (Dryden), 45
Indian Queen, The (Howard and Dryden), 45, 53, 56, 57, 59, 60
  Hecate, 57
  Ismeron, 57, 58

Montezuma, 53
Zempoalla, 53, 57, 58
Indian Queen, The (Purcell), 34
Inman, Ben, 188
instrumental music. *See* Locke, Matthew
Interregnum, 1, 12, 15, 16, 24, 25, 27–37, 42, 59, 95
Ireton, Henry, 50
Irving, Henry, 145
Iwanisziw, Susan, 96

Jacobi, Sir Derek, 135
James, Paula, 147
Jenkins, John, 76, 77
Jew of Venice, The (Granville), 90
    Antonio, 90
    Bassanio, 90
    Gratiano, 90
    Peleus, 90
    Portia, 90
    Shylock, 90
    Thetis, 90
Johnson, Robert, 33, 34, 70
    'Full fathom five', 33
    and part songs, 33
    and solo songs, 33
    'Where the bee sucks', 33
Johnson, Samuel, 115
Jones, Inigo, 5, 42
Jonson, Ben, 2, 28, 32, 70
    Masque of Queens, 70
Jordan, Thomas, 28
    Cupid His Coronation, 28

Kean, Charles, 145
Kemble, John Philip, 145
Kenny, Elizabeth, 188
Killigrew, Thomas, 2, 40, 45, 56, 60, 81
King Arthur (Dryden and Purcell), 134, 182
King's Company, the, 2, 6, 56, 58, 132
King Lear (Shakespeare), 2, 30, 98, 99, 100, 113, 114
    Cordelia, 5, 114
    Edmund, 114
    Lear, 5
    music in, 110
    Oswald, 110
King's Men, the, 2, 31, 184
King's Theatre, the, 2
Kirkman, Francis, 30
    Wits, or, Sport upon sport, The, 30
Kirwan, Peter, 145

Lacy, James, 97
Laishley, Christopher, 147
Lang, Franciscus, xx
    Dissertatio de actione scenica, xx
Langhans, Edward, 99, 100, 107

Lanier, Nicholas, 24, 42
    Hero and Leander, 24
Law against Lovers, The (Davenant), 3, 4, 31, 40, 134
Law, Richard, 46
Lawes, Henry, 25, 42
Lawes, William, 76, 77
Lazarus Theatre (London), 14
Ledwidge, Sarah, 12, 146
Leigh, Lori, 92, 95, 96
leitmotif, 138
L'Estrange, Roger
    Memento Directed to all Those that Truly Reverence the Memory of King Charles the Martyr, A, 48
Leveridge, Richard, 61, 134, 137
Lincoln's Inn Fields, 4, 39, 40, 43, 45, 46, 55, 56, 62, 75, 83, 90, 121, 134, 136, 184
Lisle's Tennis Court, 62
Locke, Matthew, 13, 24, 25, 61–3, 70–8, 132–4, 136, 137, 182, 194, *see also Macbeth*; *Tempest, or the Enchanted Island, The*; *Psyche* (Locke)
    Act Tune, 69
    'Black spirits and white', 59
    'Broken Consort', 77
    'Come away, Hecate', 59
    'Curtain Tune', 69, 62, 69–71, 74, 194
    The English Opera, or, the Vocal Musick in Psyche, 74
    'Fantastick, The', 70, *71*, 72, 73, 75
    GB-Lbl Add. MS 17108, 24
    instrumental music by, 63, 73, 78
    'Let's have a dance', 61, 70, 152–4
    Musick's Delight on the Cithern, 62
    'Opera Tune by Mr Lock, The', 77
    'Rare Theatrical' manuscript, 63, 69, 70, 72, 73, 75–8, 133, 134
    Sarabrand, 74
    theatre ayres, 62, 63, 69
    theatre music by, 62, 63, 69, 77, 78
    US-NH Filmer MS 7, 63, 73, 74, 78
    US-NYp Drexel MS 3849, 63
    US-NYp Drexel MS 3976, 63, *71*
    US-NYp Drexel MS 5061, 63, 73, 76, 78
    'The Witches Dance', 62
Loftis, John, 57
Louis XIV, 62, 132
Love and Honour (Davenant), 44, 78
Love Betray'd (Burnaby), 80–2, 87, 89, 90, 91, 94, 96
    Cesario, 83–90, 94
    Drances, 83, 85
    Dromia, 83
    Emilia, 83, 86
    Laura, 83–7
    Moreno, 83–9

Love Betray'd (Burnaby) (cont.)
  Rodoregue, 83, 86
  Rosalind, 84
  Sebastian, 84–90
  Sir Andrew, 85
  Taquilet, 83, 85, 86
  Villaretta, 83–90
  Viola, 83–5, 87, 89
  Viola/Cesario, 85
Love, Harold, 27
Lowe, Edward, 34, 186
  GB-Ob Mus, d. 238, 34
Lully, Jean-Baptiste, 133

Macbeth (Davenant), xvii–xix, 4–5, 6–7, 10–14, 38–41, 46–60, 118–20, 62, 75, 78, 97, 119, 120, 121–2, 124–5, 127, *128*, *129*, 128–31, *138*, 143, 145–7, *148*, 149, 150, 158, 163, 164, *165*, 169, 171–2, 174, 176, 177, 179
  'Black spirits and white', 138, 139
  Banquo, 49, 50, 52, 170
  Duncan, 6, 10, 13, 39, 47, 49, 50, 52, 118, *119*, 120, 127, 138, 140, 145, 152, 153, 163, 170, 173
  female roles in, 172
  Fleance, 129, *148*
  Hecate, 129
  'Hecate! Oh, come away', 137, 138
  King Duncan, xviii
  Lady Macbeth, xvii, xviii, xix, 4, 11, 14, 48, 49, 51–3, 118, 119, 129, 142, 144, 146–51, 161–4, *165*, 168, 170, 172–5, 177
  Lady Macduff, 4, 6, 14, 38, 39, 47, 51, 53, 129, 137, 138, 142, 143, 144, 145, 146, 147, *148*, 149, 150, 151, 152, 154, 155, 156, 157, 158, 159, 160, 161, 162, 172
  'Let's have a dance', 137, 138
  Macbeth, 38, 47–54, 118, 119, 121, 129, 138, 144, 146, 147, 151, 154, 156, 158, 159, 172, 173, 174, 177
  Macduff, 6, 38, 39, 47, 50–4, 138, 145, 146, 147, 152, 154–9
  Malcolm, 50, 51, 54
  music in, 61–2, 71, 72, 134, 136–43
  Seyton, 51, 52, 158, 159
  'Speak, sister, speak', 137, 138, 152–4
  staging of, 132–4
Macbeth (Shakespeare), 2, 25, 57, 58, 118, 142, 144, 146, 147, 152, 159
  Duncan, 118
  Lady Macduff, 142–4, 150
  Macbeth, 57, 58, 143, 144
  Macduff, 143, 144
  Ross, 144
  Young Macduff, 144
Macready, William, 145

Maguire, Nancy Klein, 46, 47
manuscript(s), 16, 26, 27, 29, 32, 34
  instrumental music. *See* Locke, Matthew
  of Shakespeare songs, 12
  sources of music in the plays, 15, 186, 187
  sources of plays, 185
Marat, Jean-Paul, xviii
Marotti, Arthur F., 26
Marsden, Jean, 103, 104
Masque of Queens. See Jonson, Ben
Massinger, Philip, 32
  Bloody Brother. See Bloody Brother (Fletcher-Jonson-Massinger)
McVicar, David, 196
Measure for Measure (Davenant), 33
  'Take, o take those lips away', 31
Measure for Measure (Middleton), 32
Measure for Measure (Shadwell), 31
Measure for Measure (Shakespeare), 2, 3, 31, 135
  'Take, o take those lips away', 30, 31
Measure for Measure, Or Beauty the Best Advocate (Gildon), 90, 133–5, 139
  'Black spirits and white', 137
  'Take, o take those lips away', 31
  Angelo, 136, 139
  Isabella, 136
Merchant of Venice, The (Shakespeare), 30, 80, 90
Merry Wives of Windsor, The (Shakespeare), 2, 80
  'Come live with me and be my love', 30
Middleton, Thomas, 32
  Witch, The, 137
Midsummer Night's Dream, A (Shakespeare), 2, 3, 135
Milhous, Judith, 8
Modha, Deven, 143
Montgomery, Rachael, *119*, *137*
Much Ado About Nothing (Shakespeare), 2, 3, 31, 133
  Beatrice, 4
  Isabella, 4
Murray, Barbara, 8, 84, 89, 180
music
  act tune, 13
  curtain tune(s), 13, 70, 132, 133, 137
  dance, 132
  entr'acte, 132
  in the Baroque period, 177
  in the Restoration, 12
  instrumental, 132
  overture, 132
Mustapha (Orrery), 45

Nau, Etienne, 72
Noël, Emily, *119*, 138, 139
Norris, Kate Eastwood, xvii, 11, 14, *128*, 129, 146, *165*

Odell, G.C.D., 8
Old Jewry Music Society, 27, 35
opera, 1, 196
Osherow, Michele, 130
Othello (Shakespeare), 2, 30, 81
Oya, Reiko, 99, 100, 112

Pack, George, 90
palimpsest, 100
Peakes, Ian Merrill, 125, *128*, *129*, 146
Peakes, Karen, 129, 146, *148*, 153
Peakes, Owen, 129, *148*
Pecorari, Marie, 164
Peiris, Shalini, 144
Pepys, Samuel, xviii, 2, 4, 6, 7, 24, 56, 60–2, 75, 78, 82, 91, 92, 121, 122, 184
  Diary, 124
performance(s), 5, 6, 8–16, 24–9, 32–5, 37, 39, 41, 61–3, 80–2, 92, 96, 99, 101–4, 108, 110–13, 116, 120–5, 130, 144, 146–9, 152, 154, 156, 157, 159–61, 163, 164, 166, 169, 172, 175, 176, 178–82, 185–9, 191–5, 198
  abstract, 32
  of actors, 125
  anglophone, 143
  in Bedlam, 120, 127
  of Betterton, 122
  collection of, 97
  in concert, 135
  contemporary, 11, 13, 167, 170, 185
  of *Dido and Aeneas*, 135
  early modern, 11, 185
  feminist, 143
  feminist potential in contemporary, 147
  historians of, 180
  historical, 11–14, 140, 141, 179, 180, 183, 198
  history of, 40, 145, 150, 180, 186, 1
  holistic, 198
  of gender, 92, 94
  Italianate, 33
  of Lady Macduff, 142
  multimedia, 7
  music and theatre, 13
  music in, 132
  operatic, 7
  practices of, 14, 164, 180, 193
  private, 1, 30, 31, 187
  public, 12, 15
  in the Restoration, 10, 15, 30, 35, 97, 120, 136
  of sexuality, 96
  of song repertoire, 26
  space of, 184
  spaces of, 14
  on stage, 141, 142
  studies of, 12
  styles of, 184
  theatrical, 1, 183
  tradition of, 35
  in the twenty-first century, 134, 143, 170
  twenty-first century performance of, 152
  vehicles for, 9
performer(s), 80
Performing Restoration Shakespeare, xix, xx, 9, 11, 13, 118, 132, 146, 147, 164, 165, 166, 167, 176, 178, 181, 183, 198
Phelps, Samuel, 145
Playford, John, 28, 30, 32, 35, 36
  Apollo's Banquet, 62, 70, 75
  English Dancing Master, 28, 35
  GB-Ge MSS Euing R.d.58–61, 35
  GB-Lbl Add. MS 11608, 25, 32, 33
  'Long Cold Nights', 138
  Music's Recreation on the Viol, 35
  treasury of musick, The, 31
  US-Ws v.a.411, 27, 35
  'Witches Dance', 70
Playhouse to be Let (Davenant), 59, 60
poetry
  dramatic, 14
Posner, Aaron, 129, 145, 146
Powell, Jocelyn, 92
print
  sources of music, 15
  sources of plays, 185
print(s), 16, 26, 27, 35
promptbook, 99, 100, 101, 103–105, 110, 111
  British Library, The, 100, 103
  Drury Lane, 99, 110, 114
  of Colman, 105, 107, 108
prompter, xviii, 6, 7, 61, 99, 103
Psyche (Locke), 74, 182
Purcell, Henry, xviii, 75, 133–4, 136, 137
  'From silent shades', 137, 139
  Abdelazar or the Moor's Revenge, 134
  Bess of Bedlam, 136
  Dido and Aeneas. See Dido and Aeneas (Purcell and Tate)
  Dioclesian, 134
  Fairy Queen, The, 134
  Funeral March for Queen Mary, 137, 138
  King Arthur. See King Arthur (Dryden and Purcell); Dryden, John

questionaire
  acting and scholarship, 176–9

race, 80, 96
Rackin, Phyllis, 80
Randall, Dale, 16
Reggio, Pietro, 187, 188, 193, 196

218   Index

rehearsal studies, 146
Reimers, Sara, 14
Restoration
  acting in the, 120, 121, 124–8, 171
  adaptations in the. *See* adaptations(s)
  audiences in the, 3, 192
  comedy, 70
  drama in the, 81, 113, 115–7
  dramatick opera in the, 139
  dramatists in the, 5
  era of the, 12
  era of theatre, 5
  instrumental musical practice in the, 194
  moveable scenery in the, xx
  music in plays of the, 110
  music in the, 34, 135, 136, 195
  performance in the, 90
  period of, 36
  playhouses in, 9
  public stage, 6
  royalists at the, 48
  settings of music, 182
  Shakespeare adaptation in. *See* adaptation
  Shakespeare in the, xviii, xx, 2, 4, 7–14, 97–101, 103, 109, 111, 112, 116, 118, 131, 134, 139–41, 167, 179–81, 183–5, 188–90, 195, 198
  stage in, 5
  stagings of *Macbeth*, 62
  Sycorax performance in the, 91
  tastes in theatre, 5
  theatre artists of the, 5
  theatre in the, 4, 5, 12, 46, 59, 60, 81, 118, 120, 121, 127, *129*, 131–3, 135, 139, 163, 164, 168–71, 177, 182, 183, 184, 190, 191, 196, 197, 198
  versions of, 14
  writers in, 114
Richard III (Shakespeare), 69
Richmond, Robert, xviii, 10, 11, *119*, 126, *128*, *129*, 130, 136, *138*, 146, 149, *165*, 169, 170
Ritchie, Fiona, 13
Rollo Duke of Normandy (Fletcher-Jonson-Chapman-Massinger), 32, *see also Bloody Brother* (Fletcher-Jonson-Chapman-Massinger)
Romeo and Juliet (Shakespeare), 2
  Juliet, 4
Rosenthal, Laura, 95
Royal Shakespeare Company, 144
Rutland House, 1, 28, 39, 42, 43, 184
Ryan, Lacey, 113
Rylance, Mark, 185

Salisbury Court Theatre, 1
Salmacida Spolia (Davenant), 42

Sam Wanamaker Playhouse, xix, xx, 9, 10–11, 14, 181, 183–5, 189, 190, 192–5, 197
Saunderson, Mary, 4
Sauny the Scot or The Taming of the Shrew (Lacey)
  'It was the friar', 36
Scheil, Katherine West, 83, 90
Schille, Candy, 93
Schneider, Rebecca, 180
Schoch, Richard, xix, 9, 14, 118, 134, 136, 166, 167, 171, 178
Settle, Elkanah, 78
  Empress of Morocco. *See Empress of Morocco, The* (Settle)
sexuality, 54, 83, 89, 90, 92–6, 145, *see also* gender
  double entendres, 94
  female, 95
  heteronormative, 94
  heteronormativity, 89
  heterosexual, 95
  homoerotic, 83, 95
  and gender, 131
Shadwell, Thomas, 7, 90, 91, 109, 133, 182, 186
  Tempest, or The Enchanted Island, The. See Tempest, or The Enchanted Island, The (Davenant-Dryden-Shadwell)
Shakespeare, William, xvii, xviii, 2, 5, 15, 16, 27, 33, 50, 57, 79–85, 111–13, 115, 116, 118, 145, 166, 172, 173, 174, 182, 184
  adaptations of, 80, *see also* adaptation(s)
  As You Like It. See As You Like It (Shakespeare)
  authorship of, 32
  blank verse of, 39
  company of, 5
  Hamlet. See Hamlet (Shakespeare)
  Henry IV. See Henry IV (Shakespeare)
  Henry VIII. See Henry VIII (Shakespeare)
  King Lear. See King Lear (Shakespeare)
  Macbeth. See Macbeth (Shakespeare)
  Merchant of Venice, The. See Merchant of Venice, The (Shakespeare)
  Othello. See Othello (Shakespeare)
  plays of, xx, 2, 3, 5, 12, 13
  reception history of, 16
  in the Restoration, 16, 24, 25, 28, 35, 37, 80, 90, 96
  Richard III, 69
  song(s) in the plays of, 12, 15, 16, 25, 27–32, 36, 37
  studies of, 10, 11, 181
  Tempest, The. See Tempest, The (Shakespeare)
  Twelfth Night. See Twelfth Night (Shakespeare)

Two Gentleman of Verona, The. See Two
  Gentleman of Verona, The (Shakespeare)
Winter's Tale. See Winter's Tale, The
  (Shakespeare)
  works of, 5, 15, 79, 81, 82, 84
Shakespeare's First Folio, 163
Shakespeare's Globe, London, xix, 9, 11, 181, 184,
  185, 195
Shakespearean canon, 29, 80
Shamiso, Miranda, 147
Shanson, Esther, 147
She would if she could (Etherege), 75, 78
Shebbeare, John, 102
Siege of Rhodes, The (Davenant), 1, 28, 39–43,
  45–7, 50–1, 54–5, 184
  Alphonso, 45, 50–2, 59
  Ianthe, 59
  Solyman, 51
  Villerius, 51
Simone, Gail, 143
singer(s), 139, 140
Smith, Robert, 73, 74
  Act Tunes in *The Tempest*, 74
song(s), 25, 27, 30–2, 132
  anthologies of, 30
  dramatic, 15
  in the plays of Shakespeare, 88
  in Shakespeare plays, 32
  transmission of, 27
St. Mary Bethlehem Hospital. *See* Bedlam Hospital
Stein, Gertrude, 180
Stone, George Winchester, 100
Stratford Festival, 145
Stuart monarchy, 5, 46
Summers, Montagu, 8
syncopated time, 180, 183, 185, 190, 194, 196, 197, 198

Taming of the Shrew, The (Shakespeare), 80
  'The friar and the nun', 36
Tara Arts, 144
Tasso, Torquato, 56
  Gerusalemme liberata, 55
Tate, Nahum, xviii, 5, 98, 99, 100, 112–15
  Dido and Aeneas. See Dido and Aeneas
    (Purcell and Tate)
  History of King Lear, The. See History of King
    Lear, The (Tate and Garrick)
  King Lear. See History of King Lear, The (Tate
    and Garrick)
Taylor, Gary, 16
Teller, Raymond Joseph, 129, 145, 146
Tempest, or The Enchanted Island, The (Banister), 33
Tempest, or The Enchanted Island, The (Davenant
  and Dryden), xix, 4, 5, 10, 60, 83, 90, 91,
  133, 182

Ariel, 4, 34, 93, 94, 182
Caliban, 4, 91–3, 182
Dorinda, 4, 91–5
Ferdinand, 93, 94
Hippolito, 5, 82, 91–6
Milcha, 4, 94
Miranda, 4, 83, 91–4
Mustacho, 93
Prospero, 93
Stephano, 93
Sycorax, 4, 82, 91, 93, 94, 96
Trincalo, 91, 93, 94
Ventoso, 93
Tempest, or The Enchanted Island, The
  (Davenant-Dryden-Shadwell), 4, 5, 7, 8,
  9, 12, 14, 25, 33, 62, 63, 69, 70, 73, 109, 133,
  137, 141, 181, 182, 183, 185, 186, 187, 188, 191,
  195, 197, 198
  'Arise ye subterranean winds', 187
  'Go thy way', 9, 10, 182
  'Echo Duet', 139
  Alonzo, 182, 189, 190, 192, 193, 195
  Amphitrite, 189
  Antonio, 182, 189, 190, 192, 193
  Ariel, 186, 189, 196
  Caliban, 189
  concitato, 191
  Dorinda, 189, 194
  Ferdinand, 139, 182, 189, 194
  GB-Bc Acc. No. 57316, 34
  Gonzalo, 182, 189, 190, 192, 193
  Hippolito, 189, 194
  Locke's music in, 78
  Masque of Devils, 9, 133, 182, 183, 184, 187–94
  Masque of Neptune, 9, 133, 182, 183, 187, 188,
    189, 193, 194, 19
  Miranda, 189, 194
  Mustacho, 189
  Neptune, 189
  Nereides, 190
  Oceanus, 189
  Prospero, 189, 190, 194
  Stephano, 189
  Sycorax, 189
  Tethys, 189
  Trincalo, 189
  Tritons, 190
  Ventoso, 189
Tempest, The (Shakespeare), 33, 35, 81, 181, 182,
  see also Davenant, Sir William; Dryden,
  John; Shadwell, Thomas; Shakespeare,
  William
  'Full fathom five', 30, 31
  Miranda, 5
  'Where the bee sucks', 30, 31

Theatre Royal, the, 40, 45, 56, 97, *106*
theatre studies, 164
Tilmouth, Michael, 188, 194
time, 16, 69, 70, 160, 174, 178, 179, 188, 194, 198,
    see also syncopated time
Tiramani, Jenny, 185
Tosh, Will, 11, 181
Tryphon (Orrery), 45, 48
Tuke, Samuel, 48
    Adventures of Five Hours, The. See *Adventures of Five Hours, The* (Tuke)
Twelfth Night (Shakespeare), 2, 80, 81–3, 85, 88, 94, 96
    Antonio, 83
    Cesario, 82–5, 88, 89
    Feste, 88
    Malvolio, 83
    Olivia, 83
    Orsino, 83, 88, 89
    Sebastian, 83
    Sir Andrew Aguecheek, 83
    Sir Toby, 83
    Viola, 82–5, 88, 89
Two Gentlemen of Verona, The (Shakespeare), 80

United Company, the, 2
Usurper, The (Howard), 45

van Kampen, Claire, 185
Verma, Jatinder, 144
Virgil, 55

Walkling, Andrew, 56, 60
Walter, Harriet, 79, 144
    Brutus and Other Heroines, 79
Watermeier, Ethan, *119*, *138*

Watkins, Stephen, 12, 13
Webb, John, 5, 184
Weiss, Peter
    Marat/Sade, 10, 120, 149
Weldon, John, 31, 182
Wilkes, Thomas, 107
    General View of the Stage, 104
Wilkinson, Tate, 111
Wilson, John, 37, 25–7, 30–6, 80–1
    Cheerfull ayres, 26, 33–5
    GB-Eu Dc.1.69, 26, 34, 35
    GB-Ob Mus.d.238, 35
    music in *the Tempest*, 37
    songs in *the Tempest*, 34, 35
    songs in *The Tempest*, 33
    'Take, o take', 32
    US-NYp Drexel 4041, 34
    'Where the bee sucks', 30, 31, 33–5
Winn, James A., 40, 57
Winter's Tale, The (Shakespeare), 35
    'Jog on', 36
witches
    in Davenant's *Macbeth*, xviii, 7, 55, 60–2, 70, 142, 152–4, 170, 177
    incantations of, 58
    in Jonson's *Masque of Queens*, 70
    music in Macbeth, 138–40
    prophecies of, 49
    in Purcell's *Dido and Aeneas*, 140
    in Shakespeare's *Macbeth*, 57
    singing, xviii, 10
    speeches of, 58
    in Tasso's *Gerusalemme liberata*, 55, 56
Witmore, Michael, 118, 125
Wollston, Silas, 13, 134, 194
women, 4, *see also* gender
Woods, Leigh, 108, 109

For EU product safety concerns, contact us at Calle de José Abascal, 56–1°,
28003 Madrid, Spain or eugpsr@cambridge.org.

www.ingramcontent.com/pod-product-compliance
Ingram Content Group UK Ltd.
Pitfield, Milton Keynes, MK11 3LW, UK
UKHW022321251025
464339UK00023B/1515